JERUSALEM

ALBION AND JESUS

WILLIAM BLAKE

Jerusalem

———————

A SIMPLIFIED VERSION
PREPARED AND EDITED
WITH COMMENTARY AND NOTES
BY
WILLIAM R. HUGHES

BARNES & NOBLE, INC.
NEW YORK

PRINTED IN GREAT BRITAIN

The prophet-voice of William Blake
Still on our inner hearing falls—
'England, awake! awake! awake!
Jerusalem thy sister calls!'

What the pencil? what the art?
Dare draft the heavenly city's plan?
His, who beheld each tiniest part—
Jerusalem in every man!

I a sleeper, thou a seer,
Speak in fire! I weep to hear!
William Blake, God bless thee!
William Blake, God bless thee!

Lighten mine eyes, lest I sleep the sleep
of death.
Psalm XIII. v. 3.

FOREWORD

It was Dr Greville MacDonald, son of the poet and novelist George MacDonald, who, fifty years ago, first brought me into the company of William Blake. Both he and his father wrote symbolical fairy tales which showed many signs of Blake's influence. Greville MacDonald prepared lantern slides of Blake's pictures, and used them to introduce the poet and artist to audiences of working folk. An amplified version of one of these lectures was published by Fifield in 1908 under the title of *The Sanity of William Blake*, and is still well worth reading.

At the time the amount of criticism and interpretation of Blake was quite small in comparison with all that has since appeared. Dr MacDonald was eager to defend Blake against various misunderstandings of his character and his teachings, and to reveal him as the sanest of visionaries, as a messenger of eternity to the children of time, one whose message is perennially pertinent.

I found then, as I have found so often since, and as multitudes of others have found, that to keep company with William Blake was a sort of purifying intoxication; that to read his poems and study his pictures was to be touched by an 'energy which is eternal delight'. For me, no other English poet has been able to do this so excitingly and so deeply. Like other stimulants, this one also should perhaps be taken not too often or in too large a dose. Perhaps it was well that the strong wine was stored in strange bottles, difficult to uncork.

At first I was satisfied to read what seemed simplest to understand—the *Songs of Innocence and Experience*, and the stimulating paradoxes of *The Marriage of Heaven and Hell*. But behind the singing and the innocence one could feel the urgent drive of a fiery energy—typified by the flames in the pictures—and the call of a daunting yet attractive visionary philosophy hidden within the mysterious recesses of the so-called 'prophetic' books.

And so from time to time I made a venture into '*Vala*', or a little exploration of *Jerusalem*. But the symbolism was so obscure, the queerly-named characters so unknown and so Protean, the transitions so abrupt, that I soon felt lost in a tangling jungle of ideas and images, and inclined to be angry with the poet for his wilfulness and lack of self-criticism.

But I always came back, sometimes with a quick attraction, sometimes after a long interval, during which the leaven of Blake had no doubt been working in my sub-consciousness. Each fresh reading brought me a little farther into the richness of the forest, and I met some of its inhabitants again, not as strange wild creatures, but as incipient friends and companions. Thus, making one exploration after another, and helped by some guidance from others who had shared Blake's experiences more closely, I gradually became more at home in this new world, able to walk about in it, if still with labour, yet with increasing delight. At length I began to suspect that it was indeed no strange country, but our true homeland, and that my life hitherto had been spent mostly in foreign parts.

It is a common experience for a reader to sit down to one of Blake's longer 'prophetic' books, and either to give up the attempt in laughter, or in despair, or else to complete the task with a feeling of baffled resentment. Commentaries and interpretations may be consulted, which throw light on some of the mysteries, but leave many others as dark as ever. No reader, I think, will profess to have understood every passage, and some may remain so cryptic as to be nearly valueless to us. Yet we find so much that is revealing, suggestive, or wildly stimulating, that we long to introduce the books to as many of our friends as possible.

To provide a first introduction to Blake's final prophecy, which he named *Jerusalem*, is the purpose of this little book. I hope it may help its readers to become acquainted with Blake's outlook, with his language, and with the leading characters in his Myth of Man, so that they may the more easily enter some of those spiritual regions of human life which we visit so seldom, and in which William was so much at home.

WILLIAM R. HUGHES

CONTENTS

A Personal Introduction to the Author of 'Jerusalem'

Instead of trying to present my own mental picture of William Blake now, more than two hundred years after his birth, I will give the moving description written by his friend Samuel Palmer, one of the little band of younger artists who gathered around Blake in his last years, acknowledging him as master and inspirer.

'Blake, once known, could never be forgotten. In him you saw at once the Maker, the Inventor; one of the few in any age; a fitting companion for Dante. He was energy itself, and shed around him a kindling influence, an atmosphere of life, full of the ideal. To walk with him in the country was to perceive the soul of beauty through the forms of matter; and the high, gloomy buildings between which, from his study window, a glimpse was caught of the Thames and the Surrey shore, assumed a kind of grandeur from the man dwelling near them. Those may laugh at this who never knew such a one as Blake; but of him it is the simple truth.

'He was a man without a mask; his aim single, his path straightforwards, and his wants few; so he was free, noble and happy. His voice and manner were quiet, yet all awake with intellect. Above the tricks of littleness, or the least taint of affectation, with a natural dignity which few would have dared to affront, he was gentle and affectionate, loving to be with little children and to talk about them. "That is Heaven", he said to a friend, leading him to the window, and pointing to a group of them at play.

'Declining, like Socrates, whom in many respects he resembled, the common objects of ambition, and pitying the scuffle to obtain them, he thought that no one could be truly great who had not humbled himself "even as a little child". This was a subject which he loved to dwell upon and to illustrate.

'His eye was the finest I ever saw; brilliant, but not roving; clear and intent, yet susceptible; it flashed with genius, or melted in tenderness. It could also be terrible. Cunning and falsehood quailed under it, but it was never busy with them. It pierced them, and turned away.

'Nor was his mouth less expressive; the lips flexible, and quivering with feeling. I can yet recall it when, on one occasion, dwelling upon the exquisite beauty of the parable of the Prodigal, he began to repeat a part of it; but at the words, "When he was yet a great way off, his father saw him", he could go no further; his voice faltered, and he was in tears.

'Such was Blake, as I remember him. He was one of the few to be met with in our passage through life who are not, in some way or other, "double-minded" and inconsistent with themselves; one of the very few who cannot be depressed by neglect, and to whose name rank and station could add no lustre. Moving apart, in a sphere above the attraction of worldly honours, he did not accept greatness, but confer it. He ennobled poverty, and by his conversation and the influence of his genius made two small rooms in Fountain Court more attractive than the threshold of princes.'

As a footnote to this tribute we may add the witness of another of the young painters of Blake's circle, John Linnell: 'He was more like the ancient patterns of virtue than I ever expected to see in this world. He feared nothing so much as being rich, lest he should lose his spiritual riches.'

This is the William Blake who offers to share some of his spiritual riches with us, through the medium of his testament in *Jerusalem*. It was written with pains and difficulty, and it can be read only with pains and difficulty; but, coming from such a man, we approach it with expectant excitement.

2

How 'Jerusalem' was
conceived and produced

Most people know that Blake never issued any of his books through the ordinary medium of the printing press, though some friends did print his early verses. The only use he made of this method was to issue an annotated catalogue of the pictures shown in the only 'one man exhibition' which he ever attempted. The show was unsuccessful; but the catalogue remains with us as a valuable legacy. It is partly a very polemical defence of himself as an artist, but also a revelation of his visionary outlook, and of many of his leading ideas, often expressed in brief and memorable sentences. This direct address to the public was written at the same time as Blake was at work on the *Jerusalem*, and gives us much help towards the understanding of the poem, particularly in his descriptions of the picture of the Canterbury Pilgrims and another of the Ancient Britons.

This printed catalogue was supplemented by equally revealing and valuable notes preserved in the so-called 'Rossetti Manuscript'. They include an elaborate description of an elaborate wall picture of the Last Judgment, which has unfortunately not been preserved, for it would clearly have been a great pictorial commentary on much of *Jerusalem*. A smaller version, however, is still available for our study.

These two sources, in which Blake comments at length on his own work, should be read again and again by all who wish to enter the Holy City and are not content merely to catch distant glimpses of its gates and towers.

For his poems and prophecies Blake demanded a finer means of presentation than was possible with printer's types and black ink. He invented a method by which he sought to convey his visions by picture and poem in combination. He was a man gifted as seer, poet, designer and painter, was a skilled engraver by profession, and one who brought unending, detailed hard work to the service of his enthusiasm and insight. He believed that he had been sent into time from eternity with a special work to do, an opening of the eyes of his fellows, and he held to this faith firmly, even through the dark times when vision failed, and he must humbly kneel down with his faithful wife and pray for its return.

He resolved that what he wrote, being for the benefit of future generations, if despised by his own, should be so produced that each page should be a work of art, executed to the very best of his skill and ability. He therefore produced, printed and coloured his own books, all with his own hands. For each separate page he purchased a copper plate, making this a first charge upon his very slender income, and on the plate, using some acid-resisting medium, he wrote his verse in a plain neat hand. Often the verse occupied only a part of the plate, the rest of it being reserved for an outlined illustrative drawing. The details of his special method are still not certainly known; he believed it was revealed to him by the spirit of a beloved brother who had died young. Its result was that after the plate had been bitten by acid the writing and its accompanying design stood up like a stereotype. And yet the writing was not 'looking-glass writing' as it would have been if he had written it in the ordinary way. An impression of the plate was then made on good paper, usually in coloured ink, and finally the illustrations and decorated margins were carefully hand-painted in water-colour. Even when a page had no illustration its whole area was coloured in varying shades. The designs were often differently coloured in different copies, so that the little volumes made of such pages, stitched together in boards by Mrs Blake, were each a unique work of art.

Among the earlier books published in this fashion the most successful and famous are the *Songs of Innocence* (1789, when Blake was thirty-two years old), the *Marriage of Heaven and Hell* (1790) and the *Songs of Experience* (1794). The two little books of songs 'showing the contrary states of the human soul' were usually bound together, making one of the loveliest and most significant of the productions of man. The *Marriage of Heaven and Hell* is a lively, paradoxical collection of challenges to conventional and repressive forms of religion and morality made in the name of youth, energy and prophecy.

The years of Blake's early manhood were those of the French Revolution and the achievement of independence by the American colonies. Like many other young Englishmen he found it bliss to be alive in such a dawn. He felt the ferment working within himself, and was one of the few who openly wore the Cap of Liberty in the streets of London. He wrote poems on both events, linking the historical happenings with his own characteristically mythical interpretation of their spiritual meaning.

In the years 1793 to 1795 he also wrote and illustrated the first six of his 'prophetic' books, as he himself named them. This set of small books is often labelled the 'Lambeth books', because he resided in Lambeth during these years. They deal chiefly with the main characters of his imaginative world—

14

Urizen, the false God of sterile reasoning, repressive morality and dead religion, who has been ruling in so many forms throughout human history; Los, the embodiment of creative energy and prophecy in mankind; and Orc, son of Los, the flaming spirit of revolt, the deliverer who will save the world by the overthrow of kings, priests and oppressors. The poems include obscure creation stories, telling how these Great Ones came themselves into being, and how they created their own worlds. Each book describes some episode in the super-temporal story, but it is not at all clear how they can be fitted together. We might perhaps compare Blake during this period with Shelley, two young poets sharing the illusion of so many revolutionaries, that to dethrone tyrants was almost the only thing necessary for bringing in the age of gold.

Blake himself was evidently not satisfied with his achievement in these works. During the next few years he laboured at the task of writing a more inclusive epic history of mankind, which should combine all his visions in one vast comprehensive picture. He was immensely busy with his other laborious daily work, though the income which it brought him was sometimes hardly enough for daily bread. But he could not cease from his mental and spiritual struggle to set down his own insights and assurances in such a form that others could experience them also. The material grew under his hands, but still he could not master it and order it. His own ideas were changing. The course of events in France had brought disillusionment. Some of the former characters on his spiritual stage began to drop out, or change their parts; new characters began to appear. He wrote and re-wrote, and finally made a fair copy of the whole of the work, in the form of *A Dream of Nine Nights*, with many preparatory sketches for illustrations. For its title he hesitated between *Vala* and *The Four Zoas*. This long manuscript still survives. It is a great work, containing many beauties and many profundities, but also much re-writing, obscurity and inextricable confusion. Blake was evidently still baffled and dissatisfied, for he put it aside and never began to engrave it. He was going through a long period in which inner conflict was often severe, and the first freshness of his inspiration often seemed to have disappeared.

Then in 1800 came a change which meant a lifting of the clouds and a renewal of the joys of vision. Blake was introduced by the sculptor Flaxman to William Hayley, a versifier who delighted to patronize poets. Hayley arranged for Blake and his wife to move to a cottage near his own home, at Felpham, close to Bognor on the Sussex coast. This change to easier conditions of life, and into a lovely countryside by the sea, brought correspondingly lovely inner experiences. Blake felt in touch with Heaven again. He resumed work on *Vala*, but finding its bulk and form unsatisfactory, began two new prophetic poems, using for each a good deal of his accumulated material. One was *Milton*, and the other *Jerusalem*. With the Milton we are not here concerned, but must recommend its reading, not only because many of its passages illustrate others in *Jerusalem*, but for its own sake. It is written rather more simply than *Jerusalem*, though not so wide in its scope.

The close of Blake's stay in Sussex was disturbed by two things. One was the attempt of Hayley to induce him to give up the work which he knew to be his spiritual vocation, and to make a living by painting miniatures and engraving book illustrations. The other was the bringing of a charge of treason against Blake by a soldier whom he had forcibly turned out of his garden. The case was tried at Chichester in 1804, and Blake was triumphantly acquitted. But he had been in real danger, and he experienced the whole episode as something having a deep allegorical meaning. Satan had struck at him outwardly as well as inwardly, and had been defeated.

Back in London in 1804 Blake experienced a sudden renewal of his visual imagination. He wrote to Hayley 'I am really drunk with intellectual vision whenever I take a pencil or graver into my hand, even as I used to be in my youth'. It was after this date that his greatest pictorial work was to be done, and it was in this same year that he began the designing and engraving of the plates for *Jerusalem*. The book has the date 1804 on its title page, but much labour, spread over years, was still necessary before all the pages were completed, and Blake still had doubts about what should be included, and made tentative rearrangements of the plates, in an attempt to order the rich, diverse material. Finally the engraving was finished and the plates arranged in four books of twenty-five pages each. Some impressions in black ink were made and some pages experimentally coloured. This was apparently about the year 1818. But to produce a complete work demanded yet the long and delicate task of colouring the hundred pages in rainbow water-colours. Blake completed one such copy, not before 1820, with the intention of selling it. No purchaser was found, and no second copy completed. In 1827, the year of his death, Blake wrote to his friend Cumberland, 'The last work I produced is a poem entitled *Jerusalem, the Emanation of the Giant Albion*, but find that to print it will cost my time the amount of twenty guineas. One I have finished, but it is not likely I shall find a customer for it.'

Blake died, singing songs of joy and triumph on his deathbed. But the work in which he had tried to express himself and his message most fully survived complete in a single copy, which had been seen by only a few of his friends, and probably but little understood by any of them. Was his confidence, that it had been published in Heaven and was bound to find its way into men's hearts, to prove but the self-deception of a dreamer?

No! After many years of neglect and misunderstanding the power and beauty of Blake's work began to receive a steadily growing recognition, at first in small circles, and today by an almost general acclaim. Scholars and poets all over the world have been studying the text of *Jerusalem*, reading its meaning ever more clearly. But it is one thing to read the printed text on a white page, and quite another thing to take in the words from the middle of Blake's glowing coloured pages. One copy could not go round very far, but now this experience is open to far more readers, for in 1951 the William Blake Trust published an exact reproduction of the coloured book, carefully and lovingly made by special processes, which needed over two years for their completion. This naturally makes the book too expensive for the ordinary pocket, but I urge all readers to spend some hours with a copy, in a public library or elsewhere. *Jerusalem* without its jewels is a fine enough city, but not fully glorious.

3

On the Chief Difficulties met with in reading 'Jerusalem'

Here is a short passage from page thirty-four of the poem.

'Is this the Female Will, O ye lovely Daughters of Albion, To
Converse concerning Weight and Distance in the Wilds of
Newton and Locke?'

So Los spoke standing on Mam-Tor looking over Europe
and Asia.
The Graves thunder beneath his feet from Ireland to Japan.
Reuben slept in Bashan like one dead in the valley,
Cut off from Albion's mountains & from all the Earth's
summits,
Between Succoth and Zaretan beside the Stone of Bohan,
While the Daughters of Albion divided Luvah into three
Bodies.'

Understandest thou what thou readest? This extract illustrates
a number of the formidable difficulties that face every reader
and which have frightened so many away. Blake was not much
concerned to make his meaning plain to everybody. In a lively
letter to a Rev. Dr Trusler, a matter-of-fact divine who had
written a book called *The way to be Rich and Respectable*, Blake
wrote, 'That which can be made explicit to the idiot is not
worth my care. The wisest of the ancients considered what is not
too explicit as the fittest for instruction, because it rouses the
faculties to act. I name Moses, Solomon, Esop, Homer, Plato
. . . What is it sets Homer, Virgil and Milton in so high a rank
of art? Why is the Bible more entertaining and instructive than
any other book? Is it not because they are addressed to the
imagination, which is spiritual sensation, and but mediately to
the understanding and reason?'

While we may be ready to accept Blake's challenge to our
powers, we often feel that it is too severe for us, and wish that he
had allowed himself more criticism, whether from his own
soberer self or from his friends.

Neglecting some minor obstacles, such as doubtful punctuation and specialized use of individual words, let us make a list of the reader's major difficulties.

(1) A general lack of structure and continuity, shown in abrupt breaks and changes of scene, discursiveness and repetitions. This lack of clear form was due not only to the nature of the subject-matter, but also to Blake's absorption in his immediate vision and his reliance on the method by which it came to him. He tells us that he often wrote twenty or thirty lines without labour or sense of time, as if at the immediate dictation of some spirit. As his ideas changed or developed he seemed unwilling to jettison or adjust the older visions as the new ones arrived, although his manuscripts show that he often made changes of substance or of order. Another reason for the discontinuities lay in the intractable nature of copper plates. Once engraved, no alterations were possible, beyond erasures, and Blake must have often been in doubt whether to sacrifice a plate, or to preserve it even if it did not fit well with its neighbours, or contained something which he would have preferred to alter.

The existence of this lack of logical or narrative order, and the fact that Blake himself seemed uncertain how to arrange some of his pages, makes me feel less guilty in altering the order of just a few passages in the accompanying shortened version of the poem. I have not altered any of Blake's words, though I have added punctuation.

(2) Our unfamiliarity with the imaginative regions in which Blake sets his scenes, with his strange characters and their quaint names, and with many of his favourite symbols. This difficulty becomes progressively less the more often and the more widely we read Blake's poems; he does most of his own explaining, but in an incidental and scattered way. The beginner needs a good deal of help in getting over the first hurdles, and I have tried to give some of this help in the following pages.

(3) Our unfamiliarity with some of the sources which provided Blake with ideas or characters—including the Bible, of which he made such constant use. I have omitted some of the more remote references. I think, for example, that no modern reader is likely to catch the allusions, in the passage quoted above, to 'between Succoth and Zaretan' (a reference to 'clay ground' see I Kings vii. 46), or to 'the stone of Bohan' (see Joshua xv. 6).

(4) Blake's attempts to work out numerical and geographical correspondences in detail. These often seem to have very little value, and I have omitted many.

(5) Our own rational, prosaic, unimaginative minds, which demand limitations which Blake was trying to transcend. He wrote with 'the whole man', and must be read with 'the whole man', and not with the brain alone.

4

How Blake beheld Things

Blake was never tired of insisting that just as all men possessed physical senses, so also they possessed spiritual senses, however little they might use them. All men had faculties of vision, of imagination, of creation, of exploring interior, eternal worlds, of encountering Divinity. Man's sight was fourfold. The physical eye saw the material world; the mental eye saw order, abstraction and symbol; the passionate eye saw loves and jealousies and wars; but the spiritual eye saw, through all veils of matter or of symbol, the everlasting realities—God, the universal Father, and all the Sons of God, shouting for joy as they performed His will. Blake too shouted with joy when, in moments of illumination, he attained to a fullness of vision, in which he saw four worlds at once, but knew that only one was eternal. The other three were built of mingled shadow and faith, constructions of imperfect vision, destined to disappear, however apparently real and solid in the experience of those whose eyes were not yet opened and healed by the touch of the divine mercy. Blake knew that we all commonly lived in these twilight worlds, and that his appointed task was

'to open the immortal Eyes
Of man inwards, into the worlds of Thought, into Eternity
Ever expanding in the Bosom of God—the Human Imagination.'

He had been entrusted with a mighty visual imagination as well as with a poetic ability in the use of words, and both must be dedicated unreservedly to this great task. And so he laboured year after year to write *Jerusalem* for us.

Man, says William Blake, is an inhabitant of four worlds, apt to migrate from one to another as his thoughts, desires and insights change. In his temporal life he finds himself fallen into the lowest of these worlds, and his eternal task is to climb upwards, refusing to settle in the more shadowy worlds, because his birthright citizenship is in Heaven, his highest world, in which his pilgrimage is to end. Time will be finished when he enters its gates.

The commonest names which Blake gives to his four worlds are, in ascending order, Ulro, Generation, Beulah and Eden. Ulro is the lowest form of human existence. Divine Providence has set a limit to man's fall; if he could go lower, says Blake, it would be into nothingness, or 'non-Entity'. Ulro is the state of ultimate error, in which men believe that nothing is real except what can be perceived by the bodily senses and can be measured or weighed, and that man's life consists in sensual and selfish enjoyment and a multitude of possessions. His vision is 'single' (though not in the Biblical sense), and so shrunken and false that the result of his living in accordance with it is that he makes his own Hell upon earth.

The world of 'Generation' (also called vegetated, sexual, or created) is that of our daily, normal, unenlightened experience, the biological and social life of earthly aims and activities, of mingled warfare and co-operation. It seems to us a very real world, and yet there is a restless urgency within each one of us which refuses to be satisfied with it, and warns us that we shall have to leave it as naked as we came into it, and that our abiding home is elsewhere.

Our third realm of experience Blake names 'Beulah'. It is entered when we are enjoying beauty or sympathy, when we have forgotten our selfish aims and meet our fellows in friendship or when we experience the inner union of a true marriage. (By derivation Beulah means marriage: see Isaiah lxii. 4.) It is a state of rest from the struggles and doubts of life, in which we receive intimations of immortality, inspirations, glimpses of eternity, being the country where, as Bunyan says, 'the

21

Shining Ones commonly walk, because it is upon the borders of Heaven'. Beulah is a lovely land, given to us in mercy, but it has a dream-like quality. It is like the quiet night, lit by the moon's reflected light and not by the full blaze of sunlight.

Lastly, there is man's supreme possible experience, his highest vision, the final victory of his active imaginative life, the state in which his sense of a separated existence falls away, and he realizes his eternal union with God and with his fellows. This state is named 'Eden' by Blake, because it means man's return to his pure and primal image, the guilt-free humanity which can converse with its Maker in the Garden. It is a state rarely reached by man on earth. Those who have been in Eden are the prophets, seers and saviours of our history. They report to us their full vision of the same real world, each in his own particular form and language. Because of his own inner experience in decisive moments of illumination, Blake found himself at home in this company. He lived much with the Biblical seers, with Isaiah, Ezekiel, the author of Job, and the visionary of Patmos, and with later writers who tried to put their visions of eternity into pictures and words—Plato, Dante, Boehme, Theresa, Milton were among his special friends. He studied their works and delighted to illustrate them with his pencil and his graver. But his own experience had to be told in his own individual manner. In drawing for us the picture of *Jerusalem* he was also drawing a picture of himself.

HOW BLAKE LOOKED AT MAN

When we use our faculty of eternal or imaginative vision to look at mankind, says Blake, we behold at the same time a great multitude and a single individual. We may focus our attention on one, but the other is always in the background of the picture. Humanity, as a general concept, has no meaning unless we think of an innumerable host of its 'minute particulars', individual men and women, crowding space and time, each with his own special features and unique personal destiny, yet all formed in the common image of the divine 'human form' or essence. And on the other hand we cannot look on an individual man aright unless we see him united to all his fellows within one living whole, and know that in a very real sense he is in them and they in him. We see humanity as One Man, and every man as humanity individualized. The eye of fallen man sees every neighbour as a separate being, a stranger, a potential enemy. The eye of risen man sees every neighbour as a sharer in one life, as a brother to be taken into his own heart.

We must therefore remember, in reading Blake, that when he sets out a myth or an allegory it always can, and must, be read in two ways at once—as a tale in the history of mankind, and as an exploration of individual souls, including those of the writer and the reader. Since every man is man-in-humanity, to trace the course of the psychological life of an individual is also to get a glimpse of the age-long development of our race.

THE FOURFOLD NATURE OF MAN

We must remember that Blake lived long before the beginning of any full study, or comprehension, of the sub-conscious element in the human soul. He had therefore no ready-made language in which to report what he found within the dark caverns of personality. He was a pioneer in such explorations, and it has been pointed out many times that his prophetic books contain much that can be translated into the terms used by a modern psychologist, perhaps by Jung especially. But Blake's findings are not put into a systematic argumentative form; they are given to us in his own vivid and suggestive combination of picture and poem.

Within every man, said Blake, one finds four fundamental elements, powers, faculties or faces, each a potential servant of the whole man, but each also capable of warping his life, if the balance between them is upset. And correspondingly, if one uses the eye of the spirit to see humanity as One Man, we see with him, in him, four great elemental Beings, Powers or Potentates, existent from eternity. Blake held that all spiritual vision would see the same fourfoldness, and so equated his four with the four great cherubinic figures seen by Ezekiel in his vision of the supreme reality, and the four mighty creatures whom the Patmos John saw standing round the Throne of God. And therefore he named them 'The Four Zoas', or Living Creatures, incidentally making an English singular word from a Greek plural, probably with intent more than because of a limited knowledge of the Greek language.

The names which Blake gave to the Four Zoas are Urizen,

Luvah, Tharmas and Urthona (or Los, when incarnated). In general Urizen may be taken to represent man's power of abstract reasoning; this is closely associated with unimaginative, egoistic and materialistic outlooks. Luvah represents the emotions and affections. (We may note here that Blake's names seem often to be adopted quite casually, or derived from unknown associations; but in this case it seems likely that Urizen contains the root sound of 'reason', and Luvah that of 'love'); Tharmas is a less prominent and more shadowy figure; he seems to stand for the bodily senses and their associated instincts. Urthona (or Los) stands for man's powers of intuition, vision and creativeness, what we call commonly the spiritual side of his nature.

When these four energies of a man keep to their proper functions, working under the direction of the essential and divine humanity, then the man is on the march to Eden, to the inclusive unity of the family of God. But in the history of a man, and of humanity, there occur endless wars, failures and sufferings, because the Zoas have not been kept in their rightful places. When any one of them leaves his station and seeks to take the place of another, man falls into confusion and sin. Blake worked hard in an attempt to give a connected history of such successive falls, and in *Vala*, or *The Four Zoas*, sought to tell how each Zoa in turn tried to usurp the throne of another in man, and of all the terrors and disasters that ensued. But clarity in such an epic story proved impossible to achieve; man's experience is too confused a field of battle to admit of ordered description. By the time that Blake came to bring *Jerusalem* into its final shape his team of the Four Zoas had retired from the front of the stage, in favour of a simpler presentation of the inward drama of man's existence. For a full reading of Blake it is necessary to become familiar with the whole range of correspondences by which he could speak of the Four Zoas in terms of the four geographical quarters, four senses, four elements, and so forth. But for our first simplified reading of *Jerusalem* this is not of prime importance.

THE DEMON AND THE ANGEL IN MAN

In place of the Four Living Creatures, who sometimes had appeared almost as independent Gods determining the course of cosmic evolution, Blake now lays more emphasis on the guidance and planning of history by Divine Providence. And he fell back on a more usual way of picturing man, as a twofold rather than a fourfold being. Yet Blake remains original, and is not content to speak of matter and spirit, flesh and spirit, or body and soul. He says that there is in every man a 'Spectre' and an 'Emanation'. It is necessary for us to become familiar with the conceptions named by these key words.

If a man uses his critical reason to analyse and classify his sensual and mental experiences, without seeing them in an eternal setting and harmony; if he asserts his sovereign separateness from other men, and seeks for power and possessions; if he believes that goodness consists in obedience to a set of negative, constricting moral laws; if he judges, condemns and punishes his fellow-sinners in a spirit of self-righteousness; then he has become a fully-developed 'Spectre', a figure of horror, also known as 'Selfhood'. To him the world appears full of hostile fellow-spectres; and his imagined God, made in his own image, is seen as a Great Spectre and Punisher. In the illustrations to his books Blake pictures the Spectre as a beaked, bat-winged creature of darkness. All men, says Blake, know the experience of being in their Spectre's power, and long to be free from it. Our chief business in life is to learn to achieve this, by means of 'self-annihilation', the opening of our spiritual eyes and the seeking of forgiveness by forgiving. This means the discovery of our real, eternal life, for the Spectre, after all, is but a Ghost, an unreal construction, one of those things which are destined to be destroyed because they are essentially meaningless, self-contradictory, destructible.

Deeper within man is a very different element, his power of intuition and vision, by which he sees the infinite in all things, and especially in his fellow-men, with whom he is called to share an eternal life of mutual forgiveness and co-operation. This element, uniting man with God and with all other men, Blake pictures as a lovely and glorious female spirit, over against the stark ugliness of the male Spectre. He names her man's 'Emanation', a measure of the divine image and love in him which emanates from God to him, and from him to his fellows. It is his indestructible possession, the assurance of his part in the great unity of the spiritual world.

One who is in the grip of his Spectre has, as it were, banished his Emanation. He has refused to look on her, or even to believe in her existence. Yet without her he is a lost man. Her return is his salvation—and his freedom.

When he looked at mankind as one whole Blake saw the myriad little blind and cruel Spectres of individual men combining to form a writhing 'polypus' of diseased life—the Great Spectre, the God of this World, known also as Satan, as Antichrist, and also labelled by Blake 'The Covering Cherub', a curious term, used as a figure for sinful Tyre in Ezekiel xxviii. 16.

On the other hand he saw the glorious whole of all the individual Emanations uniting mankind with 'fibres of love'. This inclusive Great Emanation he named 'Jerusalem', the spirit of the City of God and of redeemed humanity, seen in vision as a lovely winged female form, clothed in brightness and glory.

5

What is 'Jerusalem' all about?

Let us now take a general look at the subject-matter of this great illuminated myth and see what Blake is trying to do. Its full title is *Jerusalem, the Emanation of the Giant Albion*. For the 'Giant Albion' he might well have said more simply 'Man'. The poem is an attempt to tell the story of the fall and redemption of Man in the widest possible context. But Blake—'English Blake', as he called himself—was not satisfied to use the name of Adam. He accepted, whether literally or not we cannot be quite sure, a theory propounded by unscientific historians of his day, that Britain, or Albion of the white cliffs, was the seat of a primitive religion and culture, that of 'the Druids', from which all other religions and cultures were later derived. So Blake pictured the heroic, gigantic form of *Albion* as living in innocence on our own green hills, and conversing with the Eternal in this Eden, until he fell, as Adam fell. The depth of the fall was shown historically by the fact that the Druids took to the blasphemy of human sacrifices, and now became the type and source of all false religions. We are all included in the being and the fate of the titan Albion, for all have sinned and dimmed their original

26

image of glory. Blake had a strong sense of place and of geography (too strong, at times!) and just as Jerusalem could be seen either as a woman or as a city, so could Albion be seen either as a man or as a map—the giant with one foot at the North Foreland and the other at Land's End.

The book is also the detailed story of the fall, the internal divisions and disasters, and the final redemption, of every individual man, and in particular, of course, this story as experienced by Blake himself. It is his personal testament, his adventure tale of voyages into his own personality, and yours and mine, as well as his sketch of the long history of his own land, of all societies, of the whole cosmic history. We must learn to read in fourfold, often in many-fold fashion, as we journey with William Blake from Innocence, through Experience, to Forgiveness.

The theme of the whole poem is announced in its first two lines:

Of the sleep of Ulro and of the passage through
Eternal Death and of the awakening to Eternal Life.

While the course of the history of a man, or of mankind, through the delusions and disasters of the error-state of 'Ulro' is being pursued, the eternal or spiritual real being of the man is not dead but sleeping. His essential form can never be destroyed. But all the interim activities of the state of error will in the end show themselves for what they are—unreal and dangerous, and will be outgrown and abandoned. We shall awake at last, come together and set out on a new and eternal way of life.

And what is the process through which Albion, and each one of us, will be redeemed? It is through the self-giving lives and labours of all who have caught a glimpse of the Divine love and reality, and through the persistent mutual forgiveness of all the blows and offences we have given one another. On the cosmic, mythical scale this saving activity is pictured as the ceaseless creative, forging labours of the great figure of Los, the eternal prophet and builder. It is Los who has been at work in all the long succession of seers, poets, artists and saints who have been faithful to the divine vision, and have been crying Awake! Awake! through all the six thousand years which Blake accepted as the time-span of our human history. In another

27

aspect Los is seen as Time itself, a creative agency and the bearer of mercy to mankind. Blake himself worked as a son of Los. In the climax of the poem the figure of Los merges into that of Jesus, the ultimate revelation of the man who sacrifices himself for enemies as well as for friends, the awakener, the saviour, who taught men that to live is to forgive, and to enter into one another's bosoms, made one in the divine humanity.

Another leading figure in Blake's huge myth is named Vala. She also is a lovely female figure, but only as it were the shadow of Jerusalem. In the days of innocence they worked and played together like sisters; but in the experience of fallen man Vala becomes temptress and seducer, claiming man's sole worship, and denying the very existence of the exiled Jerusalem. Vala appears as a being clothed in all the beauty of the material world; she is, in this aspect, our 'Mother Nature'. She personifies also a corresponding materialistic 'natural' religion and morality. Her deceit lies in persuading man to deny vision and spirit and to accept the illusions of materialism and of a selfish morality. She weaves a deceptively attractive 'veil' (as her name implies) of these appearances in order to catch the souls of men. Blake equates her with a string of Biblical figures—Mystery, Babylon the Great, and so forth, especially when she appears in her temporal manifestations of 'Rahab' and 'Tirzah', who teach men the false religion of an imagined jealous, cruel and punitive Deity. To yield to their persuasions is to have one's senses and intuitions limited, bound down to earth, cut off from eternity, to be prepared to take part in tortures and in wars. We may remark here that the poem *To Tirzah* was evidently a later addition to the *Songs of Experience*, and is hard to understand unless we know how Blake had come to use the name of this false claimant to the title of being our Mother.

A prominent set of figures in the epic are the Sons and Daughters of Albion. During the spiritual sleep of their father they carry on a restless life, in the mind of man or in history, with confused activities of self-assertion, pride, jealousy, cruelty, and a general war against imagination. We may think of them both as the various thoughts and passions contending within the soul of a fallen man, or as individual types of fallen human beings.

The Sons partake of the nature of the Spectre, relying upon abstract philosophies, encouraging enmities, denying the values for which Los and Jerusalem stand. After the pattern of the twelve tribes of Israel Blake names twelve representative Sons of Albion, but does not attempt to characterize them all in detail. The roll of their names is very strange to us, awakening no known associations—Hand, Hyle, Coban, Gwantok, Peachey, Brereton, Slayd, Hutton, Skofield, Kox, Kotope and Bowen! Some of the mystery of this choice disappears when we learn that two of the names are those of the soldiers who accused Blake of High Treason, and others those of the magistrates who tried him. This illustrates how he took some of his types directly from his own experiences, and how little he cared about using labels that would convey their own meaning. Enough that the sons of fallen man should be recognized for what they are— accusers, judges and punishers of one another. When he found a set of twelve characters too difficult to manage together, Blake uses the figures of the first two, Hand and Hyle, as representing all their brethren. (Hyle, by the way, should be pronounced as two syllables. Its origin is probably the Greek word ὕλη, matter, but there may also be a punning reference to friend Hayley, who had tried to tempt Blake away from his imaginative work.) Blake never states how or where he picked up the names with which he christened his characters.

The Daughters of Albion are also twelve in number, as we might expect, and they also are often represented by their two leading figures, Gwendolen and Cambel. The names of the twelve are those of characters in the legendary history of ancient Britain; one may read of them in chronicles such as that of Geoffrey of Monmouth. They partake of the nature of Vala, lovely, but dangerous in their unredeemed activities. One must think of them, in general, as personifying the emotional falsities that have sway among mankind, while the Sons typify the more intellectual errors. The Daughters, so long as pity and forgiveness are asleep with Albion, torture themselves, their brethren and their father, with the hates, jealousies and cruelties of selfish loves and a punitive religion.

6

Blake's Religious Conceptions

To assist in making the reading of *Jerusalem* somewhat easier we must try first to understand some more of Blake's general and guiding conceptions. Let us begin with the way in which he thought of God. What we may know of the nature of God, he said, is revealed to us by the highest qualities which we can see in a man, and in humanity. The practice of 'honouring His gifts in other men, each according to his genius, and loving the greatest men best' was in itself a worship of God. The most sublime human character, enlarged to inclusiveness and pervasiveness, would give us the best conception of God, the 'God-Man', known to us in the first place through the Divine Humanity which is the eternal essence of every man's being. To think of God merely as impersonal Light or Power was to Blake a form of heathenism.

> 'God appears and God is Light
> To those poor souls who dwell in night;
> But does a human form display
> To those who dwell in realms of Day.'

The nature of 'God, our Father dear', is known to us by the continuous outflowing of those same qualities which we intuitively recognize as the most lovely and significant ones in 'Man, his child and care'—the preserving and creative powers of 'Mercy, Pity, Peace and Love'. To picture God as a remote, stern Judge and Punisher, needing victims to satisfy His demand for justice, is blasphemy and 'sin against the Holy Ghost'.

Blake did not stay content, in his final reverence, with the idea of God as an Almighty Loving Father, enthroned in a Heaven. Not only was the Divine Being immanent in some measure in all mankind, but in its own depths could be found the Many as well as the One, able to create other worlds than ours. And so Blake would speak of a Divine Family or of a Council of the Eternals, as better representing our utmost outreach of imagination towards the ultimate reality than the conception of an absolute and undifferentiated One. The Glory of God, like the lesser glory of man, was the radiant unity of an interpenetrating company of Beings.

As we might expect, Blake was concerned through all his life with the figure of Jesus. During his earlier days, those of rebellious assertion of freedom from outdone beliefs and imposed negative rules of morality, he tended to see Jesus also as rebel and freedom-bringing heretic. He closed *The Marriage of Heaven and Hell* with a lively dialogue between an imaginative 'devil' and a conventional 'angel', in which the devil claims honour for Jesus Christ, not because he was God's special incarnation, sent to give sanction to the ten commandments (as the angel maintained), but because he was the greatest of men, whose virtue was shown by his breaking of the commandments; one who was 'all virtue, and acted from impulse, not from rules'. This picture of Jesus Blake sought to enlarge later on, in the striking poem called *The Everlasting Gospel*, which he kept long upon the stocks but never finished. This gives a tremendous impression of the spiritual energy and insight which drove Jesus along His way and vitalized His words and deeds into the miraculous. But it may be that the poem was never completed or engraved because Blake, as he clearly showed in his later work, came to regard his picture of Jesus the impulsive, imaginative rebel and denouncer, as being insufficient and incomplete. He had now come to a recognition of Jesus as the destined Lord and Saviour of the human race. Not only did Jesus incorporate the 'Divine Humanity' and its imaginative energy in the most complete form ever known upon our earth, being thus the supreme representative of essential human nature, but Blake now saw His appearance in our world as a central event in history, long prepared for by an over-ruling Providence, and destined to redeem and elevate into a state of joyful unity the whole human race. That spiritual energy of imaginative love in every man, always creative and uniting him inwardly with all his fellows, which Blake had at first labelled as his 'Poetic Genius', and later as his 'Imagination', 'Human Form', or 'Divine Vision' became finally recognized as the 'I in you' of which Jesus had spoken to His disciples and followers. Even when man had fallen into the depths of materialism and self-will, this pattern of his true manhood still remained visible within him to the eye of faith.

'The Divine Vision still was seen,
Still was the Human Form divine;
Weeping, in weak and mortal clay,
O Jesus, still the form was Thine.'

One may in fact say that *Jerusalem* was written as a gospel, to tell of the cosmic saving work of Jesus, the image of God within the limits and history of humanity. At the start of the poem Blake tells us that it was written under the inspiration of the spirit of Jesus 'spreading His beams of love and dictating words'. We notice also that whereas *The Four Zoas* or *Vala*, bears as motto, in Greek, the passage from Ephesians which speaks of wrestling against principalities, powers and the rulers of darkness, the motto at the head of the first page of *Jerusalem*, also in Greek, is 'Jesus only'. The accompanying design shows a heavenly spirit, perhaps Jerusalem herself, pointing out these words to the human souls she is guiding aloft.

For Blake the central message of Jesus, exemplified in His life as well as taught in His parables, was that of the forgiveness of sins. Other teachers and seers may have given ethical teaching comparable with his ('If morality was Christianity', Blake said, 'Socrates was the Saviour'), but no one else had demanded that we should love our enemies and forgive the faults of a brother to seventy times seven. In the practice of this eternal forgiveness lay the secret of that 'perfect' way of life to which Jesus called us all.

But how can we, why should we, forgive all the hardened scoundrels, proud oppressors and sly cheaters whom we may meet in our daily courses? If they were indeed what they think they are, little competing selves, struggling to gain advantage in their brief passage through a world of equally selfish rivals, then the role of a forgiver would seem a hopeless one. But the case is not so, says Blake. These men are in fact immortal, imaginative spirits who have not yet discovered their true nature and destiny. They have been placed on earth in order to learn to love and be loved, but have become entangled and blinded in nets of false conceptions and false desires. Each is living in some 'State' of error and consequent disaster. Yet deep within his being lies hidden the Divine human Form, which makes him a member of the family of Jesus, and this, the immortal part of man, has not consented to the error and the sin. Our business is the same as that which Jesus exemplified, to speak to this hidden man of the heart, awaking him to activity by the display of truth and sympathy and love. Then the man may recognize the ugliness and falsity of the 'State' through which he has been travelling, and move forward out of it. Blake saw all history, whether of a man or of a nation, as a progress through a series of typical 'States' towards the final freedom of Jesus and Jerusalem. We must expose and condemn the false 'State', but pity, forgive and aid the man who is its prisoner, until he himself sees its evil and casts it off for ever. 'States', says Blake, are followed by their own punishment; we do not need to add ours. They have no place in eternity.

> 'Judge then of thy Own Self; thy Eternal Lineaments explore,
> What is Eternal and what Changeable and what annihilable.
> The Imagination is not a State: it is the Human Existence
>   itself.'

One who lives by Imagination is *ipso facto* a forgiver, a merciful man, a lover and pitier of all his sick and sinning brothers.

7

Blake and his own Times

We have seen that, like all true poetry, Blake's work can be read on many different levels at once and in different contexts. Some commentators have sought, often with a somewhat perverse ingenuity, to relate his visions very closely to the events of his personal life, and in particular to his experience of married life, until they would almost have us take Albion and Jerusalem as little more than disguises for the figures of William and Catherine Blake. Of course there is an element of truth in this; Blake was interpreting his own inner struggles and experiences, but in a setting of eternity. Yet he was doing much more than this. His poems take the widest of cosmic and psychological sweeps, but his eyes were turned outward as well as inward, and he had clear insight into the ways of the world around him. All his work, while it is a voyaging into the depths of the individual soul, may also be read as one long, indignant, forceful protest against the evils and cruelties of his own day. He saw church, state, and society as the blinded victims of 'spectral' misconceptions and selfish Pharisaic aims. In him we hear again the voice of an ancient Jewish prophet denouncing the sins of king, priest and idolatrous people. His early association with a circle of talkers and thinkers working for political freedom was succeeded by a withdrawal into the more creative atmosphere of a tiny dwelling in London, in which a lonely man spent long hours bent over his note-book, drawing-board or copper plate. His poems continually break out into passages of direct, volcanic denunciation of the blindness of contemporary philosophers, the coldness and hypocrisy of contemporary churches, and the cruelty of contemporary industrialists. He believed that what he thus wrote in solitude was of first importance for the 'eternal salvation' of each reader, and he had a strong assurance that, if he could keep faithful to his vision, labouring to translate it into words and designs, it would speak directly to the 'humanity' in others, and have more powerful effect in the world than any direct political action could produce. He went through dark times, and was often resentful when the public despised or neglected his works. But he always resumed his eternal business. Time has already justified his faith, and his influence is still growing today, awaking and inspiring multitudes of readers.

8

Blake's own Introduction to 'Jerusalem'

Blake struggled for long, without any real final success, to arrange the pages of *Jerusalem* consecutively into four equal chapters of twenty-five plates each. To this end he inserted new plates and tried changes of order, without attaining any clear narrative or logical succession; one feels that the visions might almost equally well have been set in some other sequence. This fourfold division, however, gave him the opportunity to engrave four introductory plates, addressed directly to his readers. They contain clear statements of his outlook and purpose, written in

34

vigorous prose, supplemented by less clear poems, in traditional metre, which epitomize some of the main contents of the work they introduce.

The preface to the first chapter is addressed 'To the Public' and those of the remaining three chapters are headed respectively 'To the Jews', 'To the Deists', and 'To the Christians'. They do not seem to be very closely or clearly linked with the contents of their following chapters, and we may take them together as Blake's general introduction to his poem, addressed in turn to different classes of readers. I propose to give first the bulk of the prose introductions, and to follow with the associated lyrical poems, with some elucidation of difficulties they present to new readers.

At the top of the last introductory plate (To the Christians) stands a verse, with an accompanying sketch, which may be taken as Blake's personal invitation to each reader to come with him, at the cost of continuous effort, on man's essential inward spiritual journey. The verse runs:

> I give you the end of a golden string,
> Only wind it into a ball,
> It will lead you in at Heaven's gate
> Built in Jerusalem's wall.

The accompanying drawing, stretched across the top of the page, shows a little child standing beneath the white cliffs of Albion, which form also the outer wall of Jerusalem. The child holds the end of a golden string, which runs across the page and out of its top left-hand corner, towards the distant, unseen gate of Heaven. To wind the string into a ball, to read this book with the open eye of innocence, will lead the child into the arms of Jesus, the reader into the courts of Heaven.

This was a great claim to make. But Blake, having himself explored the long and dangerous Pilgrim's Way, could not refuse the part of Greatheart and guide, which the divine voice bid him to undertake. His firm sense of mission, of being an interpreter of the message of Jesus, is made, immediately and clearly, in his introductory page, addressed 'To the Public', but it is accompanied by a humble confession of his personal unworthiness.

The page has a number of deletions, especially in the first paragraph, in which he says 'I hope the reader will be with me wholly One in Jesus our Lord, to whom the Ancients look'd and saw his day afar off, with trembling and amazement'.

And then he goes straight on, 'The Spirit of Jesus is continual forgiveness of Sin: he who waits to be righteous before he enters into the Saviour's kingdom, the Divine Body, will never enter there. I am perhaps the most sinful of men: I pretend not to holiness; yet I pretend to love, to see, to converse with daily, as man to man, and the more to have an interest in the Friend of Sinners.'

And then this humble man makes his stupendous claim in a brief verse—that he is writing this book as the bearer of a direct message from the Eternal Spirit, from the God

'Who in mysterious Sinai's awful cave
To Man the wond'rous art of writing gave;
Again he speaks in thunder and in fire,
Thunder of Thought, and flames of fierce desire.
Even from the depths of Hell his voice I hear
Within the unfathom'd caverns of my Ear.
Therefore I print; nor vain my types shall be:
Heaven, Earth, and Hell henceforth shall live in harmony.'

In writing this last line Blake no doubt had in mind his earlier attempt to interpret the nature and history of Man which he had made in his *Marriage of Heaven and Hell*. Now, with added experience and deeper insight, he sets out to rewrite his prophetic message in more majestic and inclusive form.

The introduction to the second chapter of *Jerusalem*, addressed 'To the Jews', may be passed over rapidly. It sets out Blake's acceptance of a patriotic theory of some antiquaries of his day (also referred to in Milton's *Areopagitica*) that Britain was the original seat of pure and true religion, that of the early Druids, described by Blake as identical with the religion of Jesus. Other religions and philosophies, as found all over the earth, were corrupt derivations from this. Thus Blake could think and write of the Biblical patriarchs as druids, and believe that some of the original druidical teaching was preserved in the Kabbalah, especially when it told of the archetypal man, Adam Kadmon, who 'contain'd in his mighty limbs all things in Heaven and Earth'. He identified this Giant Man with his Albion, calling him 'parent of the Druids', in whose fall or sleep the whole world fell into disaster, and Satan and Adam came upon the

36

scene. At the opening of the introduction Blake writes in great excitement, as though he had just made a discovery, of his conviction that there is historical truth in his chosen title, that *Jerusalem*, with all the wealth of Jewish religion and history hidden in that name, was in actual fact something which had emanated from the prior existence and religion of our own 'Giant Albion'. He quotes two key-lines from his own poem, as summarizing the glorious past, and the present sickness, of the Man and of the Country.

'All things begin and End in Albion's Ancient Druid Rocky Shore.'

'But now the Starry Heavens are fled from the mighty limbs of Albion.'

This introduction to Chapter Two ends with a condensed assertion that the Jewish religion had been debased through the acceptance of the practices of cruel sacrifices and of war, though a line of prophets had always foretold that the Lamb, the Saviour, the Divine Human, would be born from among the seed of Abraham. The Return of Israel would be to 'mental' sacrifice and war, in place of the physical. 'Take up the Cross, O Israel, and follow Jesus!'

The introduction to Chapter Three is addressed 'To the Deists'. It is a wonderfully vigorous and comprehensive, if not always quite fair, outburst against the type of philosophy and religion which Blake found encompassing him in his own time. 'Deists', to him, were typified by Rousseau, Voltaire, Gibbon and Hume. They were those who believed that man was born good, and needed to be saved from all visionaries, enthusiasts and religious irrationalists, in order that his natural virtues might grow and blossom. There was no need of a revelation or a Saviour; man could find God by the use of his own reason and by seeking his own natural ends. They held, in Blake's language, that man was already righteous 'in his Vegetated Spectre', that is, as a self-seeking rational materialist. All this, to William Blake, was anathema; it was the worship of Satan, the self-contradictory 'Natural Religion', which must lead to persecutions and wars.

The introduction, which I give here in full, can be read without much difficulty. We note how Blake illustrates in it his doctrine of 'States', by saying that the Deist is in 'the State named Rahab'; and how he ends by re-stating his own definition of the core of religion, 'The Glory of Christianity is to conquer by Forgiveness'.

'He never can be a Friend to the Human Race who is the Preacher of Natural Morality or Natural Religion; he is a flatterer who means to betray, to perpetuate Tyrant Pride & the Laws of that Babylon which, he foresees, shall shortly be destroyed with the Spiritual and not the Natural Sword. He is in the State named Rahab; which State must be put off before he can be the Friend of Man.

'You, O Deists, profess yourselves the Enemies of Christianity; and you are so: you are also the Enemies of the Human Race & of Universal Nature. Man is born a Spectre or Satan, & is altogether an Evil, & requires a New Selfhood continually, & must continually be changed into his direct Contrary. But your Greek Philosophy (which is a remnant of Druidism) teaches that Man is Righteous in his Vegetated Spectre, an Opinion of fatal & accursed consequence to Man, as the Ancients saw plainly by Revelation, to the entire abrogation of Experimental Theory: and many believed what they saw, and Prophesied of Jesus.

'Man must & will have Some Religion: if he has not the Religion of Jesus, he will have the Religion of Satan, & will erect the Synagogue of Satan, calling the Prince of this World, God, and destroying all who do not worship Satan under the Name of God. Will any one say: "Where are those who worship Satan under the name of God?" Where are they? Listen! Every Religion that Preaches Vengeance for Sin is the Religion of the Enemy and Avenger, and not of the Forgiver of Sin; and their God is Satan, named by the Divine Name. Your Religion, O Deists, Deism, is the worship of the God of this World by the means of what you call Natural Religion and Natural Philosophy, and of Natural Morality or Self-Righteousness, the Selfish Virtues of the Natural Heart. This was the Religion of the Pharisees who murder'd Jesus. Deism is the same & ends in the same.

'Voltaire, Rousseau, Gibbon, Hume charge the Spiritually Religious with Hypocrisy; but how a Monk, or a Methodist either, can be a Hypocrite, I cannot Conceive. We are Men

38

of like passions with others, & pretend not to be holier than others; therefore, when a Religious Man falls into Sin, he ought not to be called a Hypocrite; this title is more properly to be given to a Player who falls into Sin, whose profession is Virtue & Morality, & the making Men Self-Righteous. Foote, in calling Whitefield Hypocrite, was himself one; for Whitefield pretended not to be holier than others, but confessed his Sins before all the World. Voltaire! Rousseau! You cannot escape my charge that you are Pharisees & Hypocrites; for you are constantly talking of the Virtues of the Human Heart and particularly of your own, that you may accuse others, & especially the Religious, whose errors you, by this display of pretended Virtue, chiefly design to expose. Rousseau thought Men Good by Nature: he found them Evil & found no friend. Friendship cannot exist without Forgiveness of Sins continually. The Book written by Rousseau, call'd his Confessions, is an apology & Cloke for his sin, & not a confession.

'But you also charge the poor Monks & Religious with being the causes of War, while you acquit & flatter the Alexanders & Caesars, the Lewis's & Fredericks, who alone are its causes & its actors. But the Religion of Jesus, Forgiveness of Sin, can never be the cause of a War, nor of a single Martyrdom. Those who Martyr others, or who cause War, are Deists, but never can be Forgivers of Sin. The Glory of Christianity is To Conquer by Forgiveness. All the Destruction, therefore, in Christian Europe has arisen from Deism, which is Natural Religion.'

The introduction to Chapter Four is addressed 'To the Christians'. The prose part of it is one of Blake's most vigorous statements and appeals, calling on everyone who professed and called himself Christian to awake to vision and turn his whole activities into that way of seeing and living that would restore Jerusalem to Albion. It reminds us of the introduction to his *Milton*, which cries 'Rouze up, O Young Men of the New Age', follows on with the universally known lines beginning 'And did those feet in Ancient Times', and ends with the quotation 'Would to God that all the Lord's People were Prophets!'

The present appeal, which here follows in full, is pure Blake. It is easy as well as stirring to read, but one note is perhaps necessary. One should be warned to read the words Intellectual,

Mental, and Science, not as referring merely to brainwork and reasoning, but as describing the knowledge and activity of the man of full vision, the awakened man, who sees into Eternity. It is spiritual science of which he is speaking.

'We are told to abstain from fleshly desires that we may lose no time from the Work of the Lord. Every moment lost is a moment that cannot be redeemed; every pleasure that intermingles with the duty of our station is a folly unredeemable, & is planted like the seed of a wild flower among our wheat. All the tortures of repentance are tortures of self-reproach on account of our leaving the Divine Harvest to the Enemy, the struggles of intanglement with incoherent roots.

'I know of no other Christianity and of no other Gospel than the liberty both of body & mind to exercise the Divine Arts of Imagination—Imagination, the real and eternal World of which this Vegetable Universe is but a faint shadow, & in which we shall live in our Eternal and Imaginative Bodies, when these Vegetable Mortal Bodies are no more. The Apostles knew of no other Gospel. What were all their spiritual gifts? What is the Divine Spirit? Is the Holy Ghost any other than an Intellectual Fountain? What is the Harvest of the Gospel & its Labours? What is that Talent which it is a curse to hide? What are the Treasures of Heaven which we are to lay up for ourselves? Are they any other than Mental Studies & Performances? What are all the Gifts of the Gospels? Are they not all Mental Gifts? Is God a Spirit who must be worshipped in Spirit & in Truth, and are not the Gifts of the Spirit Everything to Man? O ye Religious, discountenance every one among you who shall pretend to despise Art and Science! I call upon you in the name of Jesus! What is the Life of Man but Art and Science. Is it Meat and Drink? Is not the Body more than Raiment? What is Mortality but the things relating to the Body which Dies? What is Immortality but the things relating to the Spirit which Lives Eternally? What is the Joy of Heaven but Improvement in the things of the Spirit? What are the Pains of Hell but Ignorance, Bodily Lust, Idleness & devastation of the things of the Spirit? Answer this to yourselves, & expel from among you those who pretend to despise the labours of Art &

Science, which alone are the labours of the Gospel. Is not this plain & manifest to the thought? Can you think at all, & not pronounce heartily: That to Labour in Knowledge is to Build up Jerusalem, and to Despise Knowledge is to Despise Jerusalem & her Builders? And remember, He who despises & mocks a Mental Gift in another, calling it pride & selfishness & sin, mocks Jesus, the giver of every Mental Gift, which always appear to the ignorance-loving Hypocrite as Sins: but that which is a Sin in the sight of cruel Man is not so in the sight of our kind God. Let every Christian, as much as in him lies, engage himself openly & publicly before all the World in some Mental pursuit for the Building up of Jerusalem.'

We will turn now to the poems which Blake has imbedded in these chapter introductions. It is plain that he was trying in these to put in condensed and more lyrical form some of the main things which he wished to say in the epic itself. It is worth while therefore to try to understand them as clearly as we can, and I shall make some annotations to this end. They become clearer when read again after we have become familiar with the main body of the work.

The first and longest of these poems is inserted in the address to the Jews. It is both a comment on the theme of Britain as the seat of primitive innocence and pure religion, and also a summary of the whole story to be unfolded in *Jerusalem*. Here it is.

> The fields from Islington to Marybone,
> To Primrose Hill and Saint John's Wood,
>   Were builded over with pillars of gold;
> And there Jerusalem's pillars stood.
>
> Her Little-ones ran on the fields,
> The Lamb of God among them seen,
>   And fair Jerusalem, his Bride,
> Among the little meadows green.
>
> Pancrass & Kentish-town repose
> Among her golden pillars high,
>   Among her golden arches which
> Shine upon the starry sky.

The Jew's-harp-house & the Green Man,
The Ponds where Boys to bathe delight,
   The fields of Cows by Willans' farm,
Shine in Jerusalem's pleasant sight.

She walks upon our meadows green;
The Lamb of God walks by her side;
   And every English Child is seen,
Children of Jesus & his Bride,

Forgiving trespasses and sins
Lest Babylon, with cruel Og,
   With Moral & Self-righteous Law,
Should crucify in Satan's Synagogue.

What are those golden Builders doing
Near mournful ever-weeping Paddington,
   Standing above that mighty Ruin
Where Satan the first victory won;

Where Albion slept beneath the fatal Tree,
And the Druids' golden Knife
   Rioted in human gore,
In Offerings of Human Life?

They groan'd aloud on London Stone,
They groan'd aloud on Tyburn's Brook;
   Albion gave his deadly groan,
And all the Atlantic Mountains shook.

Albion's Spectre from his Loins,
Tore forth in all the pomp of War;
   Satan his name; in flames of fire
He stretched his Druid Pillars far.

Jerusalem fell from Lambeth's Vale,
Down thro' Poplar & Old Bow,
   Thro' Malden & across the Sea
In War & howling, death & woe.

The Rhine was red with human blood;
The Danube roll'd a purple tide;
   On the Euphrates Satan stood,
And over Asia stretched his pride.

42

He wither'd up sweet Zion's Hill
From every Nation of the Earth;
   He wither'd up Jerusalem's Gates,
And in a dark Land gave her birth.

He wither'd up the Human Form
By laws of sacrifice for sin,
   Till it became a Mortal Worm,
But O! translucent all within.

The Divine Vision still was seen,
Still was the Human Form Divine;
   Weeping, in weak & mortal clay,
O Jesus, still the Form was thine!

And thine the Human Face, & thine
The Human Hands & Feet & Breath,
   Entering thro' the Gates of Birth,
And passing thro' the Gates of Death.

And O thou Lamb of God, whom I
Slew in my dark self-righteous pride,
   Art thou return'd to Albion's Land,
And is Jerusalem thy Bride?

Come to my arms, & never more
Depart, but dwell for ever here;
   Create my Spirit to thy Love;
Subdue my Spectre to thy Fear.

Spectre of Albion! warlike Fiend!
In clouds of blood & ruin roll'd,
   I here reclaim thee as my own,
My Selfhood! Satan arm'd in gold!

Is this thy soft Family-Love,
Thy cruel Patriarchal pride,
   Planting thy Family alone,
Destroying all the World beside?

A man's worst enemies are those
Of his own house & family;
   And he who makes his law a curse
By his own law shall surely die.

In my Exchanges every Land
Shall walk; & mine in every Land
Mutual shall build Jerusalem
Both heart in heart & hand in hand.

If the reader will now look back to the sketch I have already
given of the main story of *Jerusalem* (p. 26) he will see that
these verses cover the same ground, in a more condensed,
allusive and lyrical way. The first seven verses give a picture of
the golden age of innocence and harmony, when the Lamb of
God and His religion ruled in every heart in ancient times in
Albion, and the glorious city of Jerusalem was built upon the
Thames. Characteristically Blake concentrates his gaze on the
children, and equally characteristically he sees them running
over the very meadows where he played with his young
companions in the days of his own innocence. All the places
mentioned were within walking distance of his own home.
Willans' farm was on ground now known as Regent's Park. As
was his custom Blake combines in one statement the universal,
the historical, and the individual experience.

In the sixth stanza the note of fear and foreboding enters,
with the first mention of Satan. In the next verse the poet leaps
ahead in time and, still looking out from his early home, westward, sees the 'golden Builders'—Los and all his friends who are
faithful to vision, once more building a Jerusalem on a site
covered by monstrous ruins. But before any such restoration can
be made the whole fierce history of Satan's reign in human
hearts, and all across the globe, has to be transacted, as the
next seven stanzas tell. Blake's local, Biblical and geographical symbols crowd on one another's heels as usual, borne
on the torrent of his indignation and sorrow. Anyone
familiar with Blake's work can move along easily with the
flow, but new readers need to be helped to catch all the
allusions.

'Babylon' is the figure taken from the Apocalypse, of the
jewelled whore 'Mystery, Babylon the Great', Satan's colleague,
identified by Blake with the goddess of this world, the sensual
that veils the spiritual. Og, the heathen king of Bashan, he
often uses as one of many symbols of the rule of blind, punishing
power. 'Satan's Synagogue' stands for any court or assembly
that applies hard 'Moral and Self-Righteous Law', and the

word 'crucifying' of course points to the Jewish Sanhedrin that condemned Jesus, as a supreme example of such courts.

And this whole fall from innocence into cruelty began, says Blake, in our homeland. It was when the Druids listened to the whisper of Satan and failed to resist the temptation to use their golden knives, not to cut mistletoe from the oak, but to slay a human sacrifice. He hears the groans of the victims, slaughtered on the traditional sacred London Stone, and of the succeeding vast succession of such victims, stretching down to his own day, who had been sacrificed by cruel laws 'on Tyburn's brook'. Tyburn, the execution place, in the district of Paddington (which must ever mourn the connection), lay where the Marble Arch now stands, and was flanked by an open stream which ran down towards the Thames. Here took place the fearful festivals of public executions, some of which were probably seen by Blake in his youth, for it was but a short walk from his dwelling.

The triumph of the devil's doctrines meant that the human race, the Giant Albion, had fallen into a deathlike sleep, so far as his essential divine Humanity, his 'Human Form', was concerned. His Spectre, Selfhood, or Satan, had broken loose and taken charge, and in Albion's fall the whole creation was shaken. And his Emanation, his Jerusalem, his power of vision, love and forgiveness, his very soul, he had thus banished from him. Her flight from Albion and his land is described as leaving Lambeth, the spiritual centre of London (where Blake had also written his first prophecies), and travelling away from the Western light, over the eastern suburbs of London, over Essex and across the sea, to be hidden in some dark refuge until the day of Albion's regeneration should bring her back.

The rule of Satan meant the rule of war. His proud figure was seen stalking over the European battlefields on Rhine and Danube, as it had earlier over the Asian battlefields on the Euphrates.

Acceptance of the Satanic outlook also meant that man lost the use of his sense of the divine and infinite in all things, and sank to a depth in which he saw a grain of sand as simply a grain of sand, and saw himself as simply a biological creature—a 'mortal worm'. His real, indestructible 'Human Form' of Love remained invisible to the bodily eye and to a heart that was seeking to punish all his fellows for their sins.

But all was not lost. Throughout history there were always

individuals who kept the divine vision, and at length it was revealed that the unclouded Human Form Divine could be seen in Jesus, entering by the Gate of Birth to take upon Himself all the restrictions of our 'mortal clay'.

Then comes the awakening, the repentance. Blake speaks in his own name as well as in that of Albion, welcoming the Lamb of God back to his own heart and to Albion's land. The Spectre is subdued and recalled, to be given its own ordered place in the new life, with all its powers of will and personality now put at the service of humanity and forgiveness. And with the Spectre, Jerusalem comes back, welcomed as a bride.

Two stanzas now come in, somewhat awkwardly, to point out that the Spectre had sinned not only in personal self-assertion, but also by exclusive pride in family or nation. All these were causes of war, and a tyrant who enforced merciless laws to punish others would assuredly fall a victim to them himself at last.

In a final quatrain Albion prophesies that the primal state of peace within, and between, nations, will now be restored again. The Spirit of Jesus rules in England, and London, the seat of Albion, becomes the great Exchange Centre of the world, not for gold and goods, but for mutual giving and goodwill, as it had been in the golden days of innocence, when

'In the Exchanges of London every Nation walk'd
And London walk'd in every Nation, mutual in love and
    harmony',
for

'All things begin and end in Albion's Ancient Druid Rocky
    Shore'.

After reading through the whole poem of *Jerusalem* the reader should turn back to these verses, and he will see how closely they recapitulate the theme and the story of the work.

The second introductory poem is attached to the prose address to the Deists, and follows close on the sentence about the glory of Christianity being to conquer by forgiveness. It is an adapted form of a longer poem which Blake called *The Grey Monk*, in which he dramatizes the teaching that suffering and forgiveness are the only finally effective weapons available to man, and suggests that the symbolic Grey Monk was one

46

with Jesus in his use of them. The whole of the longer poem
should be read, for it contains such fine condensed stanzas as
this:

> The hand of Vengeance sought the bed
> To which the purple tyrant fled;
> The iron hand crush'd the tyrant's head—
> And became a tyrant in his stead.

Here then are the verses in which Blake drove home his attack
on the 'Deists' as the originators of martyrdoms and wars.
They require no annotation, though we must remember that
Blake wrote 'intellectual' where we should write 'spiritual'.

> I saw a Monk of Charlemaine
> Arise before my sight;
> I talk'd with the Grey Monk as we stood
> In beams of infernal light.

> Gibbon arose with a lash of steel,
> And Voltaire with a wracking wheel;
> The Schools, in clouds of learning roll'd,
> Arose with war in iron and gold.

> 'Thou lazy Monk!' they sound afar,
> 'In vain condemning glorious War;
> And in your Cell you shall ever dwell:
> Rise, War, & bind him in his Cell!'

> The blood red ran from the Grey Monk's side,
> His hands and feet were wounded wide,
> His body bent, his arms and knees
> Like to the roots of ancient trees.

> When Satan first the black bow bent
> And the Moral Law from the Gospel rent,
> He forg'd the Law into a Sword,
> And spill'd the blood of Mercy's Lord.

> Titus! Constantine! Charlemaine!
> O Voltaire! Rousseau! Gibbon! Vain
> Your Grecian mocks and Roman Sword
> Against this image of his Lord!

47

For a Tear is an Intellectual thing;
And a Sigh is the Sword of an Angel King;
And the bitter groan of a Martyr's woe
Is an Arrow from the Almightie's Bow.

The last of the introductory poems, which is written in blank verse, with a brief rhymed invocation to conclude it, is appended to the prose appeal to Christians. It is in effect a variation and enlargement of the preceding poem's theme, the contrast between the 'Natural Religion' of the unimaginative, scientific, rational 'Deist', looked upon as successor to the Pharisees, and the loving, freeing, forgiving Gospel of Jesus. The former knows nothing of the 'Human Form Divine', but looks on man as a little flesh-built creature, a 'root a fathom long', whose restricted senses see sun and moon, not as majestic miracles, but just as spheres of matter travelling through space. This blind Pharisaic religion involves the whole world in fear and wars by setting up its system of punishment, tyranny and wrath. Blake seems to be describing how he saw all this revealed in an actual vision seen amid the Sussex hills, at Felpham, where he began to write *Jerusalem*. The terrible and fatal delusion of the false religion appears to him as a great devouring Wheel of Fire, threatening to destroy man and the whole creation. The voice of the spirit tells him to prophesy against it, in the name of the religion of self-denial and forgiveness which Jesus had preached.

I stood among my valleys of the south,
And saw a flame of fire, even as a Wheel
Of Fire surrounding all the heavens: it went
From west to east against the current of
Creation, and devour'd all things in its loud
Fury & thundering course round heaven & earth.
By it the Sun was roll'd into an orb;
By it the Moon faded into a globe
Travelling through the night; for from its dire
And restless fury Man himself shrunk up
Into a little root a fathom long.
And I asked a Watcher & a Holy-One
Its Name: he answer'd: 'It is the Wheel of Religion'.
I wept & said: 'Is this the law of Jesus,
This terrible devouring sword turning every way?'

48

He answer'd: 'Jesus died because he strove
Against the current of this Wheel: its Name
Is Caiaphas, the dark Preacher of Death,
Of sin, of sorrow & of punishment,
Opposing Nature. It is Natural Religion.
But Jesus is the bright Preacher of Life,
Creating Nature from this fiery Law
By self-denial & forgiveness of Sin.
Go, therefore, cast out devils in Christ's name!
Heal thou the sick of spiritual disease!
Pity the evil; for thou art not sent
To smite with terror and with punishments
Those that are sick, like to the Pharisees,
Crucifying, & encompassing sea & land
For proselytes to tyranny & wrath.
But to the Publicans & Harlots go!
Teach them True Happiness, but let no curse
Go forth out of thy mouth to blight their peace.
For Hell is open'd to Heaven; thine eyes behold
The dungeons burst, & the prisoners set free.'

But Blake ends his prefaces to *Jerusalem*, not with the foregoing
lines but, remembering perhaps the similar and more famous
invocation at the beginning of his *Milton*, with an appeal to his
fellow-countrymen to share his own conviction that the re-
building of Jerusalem, the return of Albion's golden age, was
surely coming in our own day, if others would only rise and
share in his own prophetic work.

England! awake! awake! awake!
  Jerusalem thy Sister calls!
Why wilt thou sleep the sleep of death,
  And close her from thy ancient walls?

Thy hills & valleys felt her feet
  Gently upon their bosoms move:
Thy gates beheld sweet Zion's ways;
  Then was a time of joy and love.

And now the time returns again:
  Our souls exult, & London's towers
Recieve the Lamb of God to dwell
  In England's green & pleasant bowers.

Such was William Blake's own introduction to the work on which he laboured so long and so intensely. We are already well within his mind and, I hope, already sharing some of his own conviction and enthusiasm, as we now start to read the poem itself. It will be a stern but a rewarding exercise. The shortened form which I now present may be regarded by those who know their Blake well as an iconoclastic outrage; I must beg their patience and forgiveness. I have of course not altered any of Blake's words, but I have made very many cuts, some-times indicated by broken lines, without using the disturbing device of rows of dots. In omitting lines which I do not myself understand, and also many of the passages crowded and confused with Biblical and topographical references, I have no doubt sometimes left out what others have found valuable or beautiful. The reader can always return finally to the whole poem, and I hope that my attempt to help him by notes and comments will form a simple approach to further understanding and study. I would here remind him also to try to include the study of a fully coloured copy, and to seek illumination also by reading Blake's other writings of his later period, particularly the poem *Milton*.

The titlings of the sections into which this version of *Jerusalem* is divided are my own, and not Blake's.

Jesus Only
J.E.R.U.S.A.L.E.M.

Albion rejects the call of the Divine Humanity and Chaos is come again

Of the Sleep of Ulro and of the passage through
Eternal Death and of the awaking to Eternal Life.

    This theme calls me in sleep night after night, & ev'ry
      morn
Awakes me at sun-rise; then I see the Saviour over me
Spreading his beams of love & dictating the words of this
      mild song:
    'Awake! awake! O sleeper in the land of shadows, wake!
      expand!
I am in you and you in me, mutual in love divine,
Fibres of love from man to man thro' Albion's pleasant land!
Return, Albion, return!
Thy brothers call thee; and thy fathers and thy sons,
Thy nurses and thy mothers, thy sisters and thy daughters
Weep at thy soul's disease, and the Divine Vision is darken'd.
Thy Emanation that was wont to play before thy face,
Beaming forth with her daughters into the Divine bosom,—
Where hast thou hidden thy Emanation, lovely Jerusalem,
From the vision and fruition of the Holy-one?
I am not a God afar off: I am a brother and friend;
Within your bosoms I reside, and you reside in me.
Lo! we are One, forgiving all Evil, not seeking recompense;
Ye are my members, O ye sleepers of Beulah, land of shades!'

    But the perturbèd Man away turns down the valleys dark:
'Phantom of the over-heated brain! shadow of immortality!
Seeking to keep my soul a victim to thy Love, which binds
Man, the enemy of man, into deceitful friendships,
Jerusalem is not! her daughters are indefinite.

By demonstration man alone can live, and not by faith.
My mountains are my own, and I will keep them to myself:
The Malvern and the Cheviot, the Wolds, Plinlimmon &
    Snowdon
Are mine. Here will I build my Laws of Moral Virtue.
Humanity shall be no more, but war & princedom & Victory!'

So spoke Albion in jealous fears, hiding his Emanation
Upon the Thames and Medway, rivers of Beulah, dissembling
His jealousy before the throne divine, darkening, cold.

The banks of the Thames are clouded! the ancient porches
    of Albion are
Darken'd! they are drawn through unbounded space,
    scatter'd upon
The Void in incoherent despair. Cambridge & Oxford &
    London
Are driven among the starry wheels, rent away and dissipated
In Chasms and Abysses of sorrow, enlarg'd without dimen-
    sion, terrible.
Albion's mountains run with blood: the cries of war & of
    tumult
Resound into the unbounded night; every Human perfection
Of mountain & river & city are small & wither'd &
    darken'd.
Cam is a little stream! Ely is almost swallow'd up!
Wales and Scotland shrink themselves to the west and to the
    north,
Mourning for fear of the warriors.
Jerusalem is scatter'd abroad like a cloud of smoke thro'
    non-entity.
Trembling I sit day and night. My friends are astonish'd
    at me,
Yet they forgive my wanderings. I rest not from my great task
To open the Eternal Worlds, to open the immortal Eyes
Of Man inwards into the worlds of Thought, into Eternity
Ever expanding in the Bosom of God, the Human Imagina-
    tion.
O Saviour! pour upon me thy Spirit of meekness & love!
Annihilate the Selfhood in me! Be thou all my life!
Guide thou my hand, which trembles exceedingly upon the
    rock of ages,

While I write
Of the terrible sons & daughters of Albion and their Genera-
tions.
I behold them, and their rushing fires overwhelm my Soul
In London's darkness, and my tears fall day and night.

The Starry Wheels revolv'd heavily over the Furnaces,
Drawing Jerusalem in anguish of maternal love
Eastward, a pillar of a cloud,
Out from the Furnaces of Los above the head of Los,
A pillar of smoke writhing afar, outstretch'd among the
Starry Wheels
Which revolve heavily in the mighty Void above the
Furnaces.

O what avail the loves & tears of Beulah's lovely daughters?
They hold the Immortal Form in gentle bands & tender
tears.
But all within is open'd into the deeps of
A dark and unknown night, indefinite, unmeasurable, with-
out end,
Abstract Philosophy warring in enmity against Imagination,
(Which is the Divine Body of the Lord Jesus, blessed for
ever).
And there Jerusalem wanders with Vala upon the moun-
tains,
Lamenting for her children, for the sons & daughters of
Albion.

II

The Temptation of Los and his contentions with his Spectre

Los heard her lamentations in the deeps afar! his tears fall
Incessant before the Furnaces, and his Emanation divided in
pain
Eastward towards the Starry Wheels. But Westward, a black
Horror,
His Spectre, driv'n by the Starry Wheels of Albion's sons,
black and
Opake, divided from his back: he labours and he mourns.

For as his Emanation divided, his Spectre also divided
In terror of those starry wheels. And the Spectre stood over
Los
Howling in pain, a black'ning Shadow, black'ning dark and
opake,
Cursing the terrible Los, bitterly cursing him for his friend-
ship
To Albion, suggesting murderous thoughts against Albion.
Los rag'd and stamp'd the earth in his might & terrible
wrath.
He stood and stamp'd the earth: then he threw down his
hammer in rage &
In fury: then he sat down and wept, terrified! Then arose
And chaunted his song, labouring with the tongs and hammer.
But still the Spectre divided, and still his pain increas'd.
In pain the Spectre divided, in pain of hunger and thirst,
To devour Los's Human Perfection. But when he saw that
Los
Was living, panting like a frighted wolf and howling
He stood over the Immortal, in the solitude and darkness
Upon the dark'ning Thames, across the whole Island west-
ward,
A horrible Shadow of Death among the Furnaces, beneath
The pillar of folding smoke. And he sought by other means
To lure Los, by tears, by arguments of science, & by terrors,
Terrors in every Nerve, by spasms and extended pains;
While Los answer'd unterrified to the opake blackening
Fiend.
And thus the Spectre spoke: 'Wilt thou still go on to destruc-
tion?
Till thy life is all taken away by this deceitful Friendship?
He drinks thee up like water; like wine he pours thee
Into his tuns; thy Daughters are trodden in his vintage;
He makes thy Sons the trampling of his bulls; they are plow'd
And harrow'd for his profit. Lo! thy stolen Emanation
Is his garden of pleasure! All the Spectres of his Sons mock
thee.
Look how they scorn thy once admirèd palaces, now in ruins
Because of Albion, because of deceit and friendship!'
Los answer'd: 'Altho' I know not this, I know far worse
than this.

54

I know that Albion hath divided me, and that thou, O my
    Spectre,
Hast just cause to be irritated. But look stedfastly upon me;
Comfort thyself in my strength. The time will arrive
When all Albion's injuries shall cease, and when we shall
Embrace him, tenfold bright, rising from his tomb in im-
    mortality.
They have divided themselves by Wrath, they must be united
    by
Pity. Let us therefore take example & warning, O my
    Spectre.
O that I could abstain from wrath! O that the Lamb
Of God would look upon me and pity me in my fury,
In anguish of regeneration, in terrors of self-annihilation!
Pity must join together those whom wrath has torn in sunder,
And the Religion of Generation, which was meant for the
    destruction
Of Jerusalem, become her covering till the time of the End.
O holy Generation, Image of regeneration!
O point of mutual forgiveness between Enemies!
Birthplace of the Lamb of God incomprehensible!
The Dead despise & scorn thee, & cast thee out as accursèd,
Seeing the Lamb of God in thy gardens & thy palaces,
Where they desire to place the Abomination of Desolation.
  O Spectre,
I know thy deceit and thy revenges, and unless thou desist
I will certainly create an eternal Hell for thee. Listen!
Be attentive! Be obedient! Lo! the Furnaces are ready to
    receive thee.
I will break thee into shivers & melt thee in the furnaces of
    death;
I will cast thee into forms of abhorrence & torment if thou
Desist not from thine own will & obey not my stern com-
    mand.
I am clos'd up from my children; my Emanation is dividing,
And thou, my Spectre, art divided against me. But mark,
I will compel thee to assist me in my terrible labours, to beat
These hypocritic Selfhoods on the Anvils of bitter Death.
I am inspired: I act not for myself: for Albion's sake
I now am what I am, a horror and an astonishment,
Shudd'ring the heavens to look upon me.'

55

While Los spoke, the terrible Spectre fell shudd'ring before
him,
Watching his time, with glowing eyes, to leap upon his prey.
Los open'd the Furnaces. In fear the Spectre saw the tortures
of the Victims,
He saw now from the outside what he before saw & felt from
within.
He saw that Los was the sole uncontroll'd Lord of the
Furnaces.
Groaning he kneel'd before Los's iron-shod feet on London
Stone.
Hung'ring & thirsting for Los's life, yet pretending obedience,
While Los pursu'd his speech in threat'nings loud & fierce:
'Thou art my Pride & Self-righteousness. I have found
thee out.
Thou art reveal'd before me in all thy magnitude & power.
Thy Uncircumcised pretences to Chastity must be cut in
sunder.
Thy holy wrath & deep deceit cannot avail against me.
For I am one of the living: dare not to mock my inspired fury.
If thou wast cast forth from my life, if I was dead upon the
mountains,
Thou mightiest be pitied & loved; but now I am living!
Unless
Thou abstain ravening I will create an eternal Hell for thee.
Take thou this Hammer & in patience heave the thundering
Bellows.
Take thou these Tongs; strike thou alternate with me; labour
obedient.
  Hand has absorbed all his Brethren in his might;
All the infant Loves and Graces were lost, for the mighty
Hand
Condens'd his Emanations into hard opake substances,
And his infant thoughts and desires into cold dark cliffs of
death.
His hammer of gold he siez'd and his anvil of adamant.
He siez'd the bars of condensed thoughts, to forge them
Into the sword of war, into the bow and arrow,
Into the thundering cannon and into the murdering gun.
I saw the limbs form'd for exercise contemn'd, & the beauty of
Eternity look'd upon as deformity, & loveliness as a dry tree.

I saw disease forming a Body of Death around the Lamb
Of God, to destroy Jerusalem & devour the body of Albion,
By war and stratagem to win the labour of the husbandman;
Awkwardness arm'd in steel, Folly in a helmet of gold,
Weakness with horns and talons, ignorance with a rav'ning
     beak;
Every Emanative joy forbidden as a Crime,
And the Emanations buried alive in the earth with pomp of
     religion;
Inspiration deny'd; Genius forbidden by laws of punishment.
I saw terrified. I took the sighs & tears & bitter groans;
I lifted them into my Furnaces, to form the spiritual sword
That lays open the hidden heart. I drew forth the pang
Of sorrow red hot; I work'd it on my resolute anvil:
I heated it in the flames nine times.
Loud roar my Furnaces and loud my hammer is heard:
I labour day and night. I behold the soft affections
Condense beneath my hammer into forms of cruelty.
But still I labour in hope, tho' still my tears flow down,
That he who will not defend Truth may be compell'd to
     defend
A Lie, that he may be snared and caught and snared and
     taken,
That Enthusiasm and Life may not cease. Arise, Spectre,
     arise!'
   Thus they contended among the Furnaces with groans and
     tears.
Groaning the Spectre heav'd the bellows, obeying Los's
     frowns,
Till the Spaces of Erin were perfected in the furnaces
Of affliction: and Los drew them forth, compelling the harsh
     Spectre
Into the Furnaces
Till he should bring the Sons & Daughters of Jerusalem to be
The Sons & Daughters of Los, that he might protect them
     from
Albion's dread Spectres. Storming, loud, thunderous &
     mighty
The Bellows & the Hammers move compell'd by Los's hand.
   His Spectre divides, and Los in fury compells it to divide,
To labour in the fire, in the water, in the earth, in the air,

To follow the Daughters of Albion as the hound follows the
  scent
Of the wild inhabitant of the forest, to drive them from his
  own,
To make a way for the Children of Los to come from the
  Furnaces.
  But Los himself against Albion's Sons his fury bends, for he
Dare not approach the Daughters openly, lest he be con-
  sumed
In the fire of their beauty and perfection & be Vegetated
  beneath
Their Looms, in a Generation of death, and resurrection to
  forgetfulness.
  For Los said: 'Tho' my Spectre is divided, as I am a
  Living Man
I must compell him to obey me wholly, that Enitharmon may
  not
Be lost, & lest he should devour Enitharmon. Ah me!
Piteous image of my soft desires and loves, O Enitharmon!
I will compell my Spectre to obey. I will restore to thee thy
  children.
No one bruises or starves himself to make himself fit for
  labour.
  Tormented with fierce desire for these beauties of Albion,
They would never love my power if they did not seek to
  destroy
Enitharmon. Vala would never have sought and loved Albion
If she had not sought to destroy Jerusalem. Such is that false
And Generating Love, a pretence of love to destroy love,
Cruel hipocrisy, unlike the lovely delusions of Beulah,
And cruel forms unlike the merciful forms of Beulah's Night.
  They know not why they love, nor wherefore they sicken
  & die,
Calling that Holy Love which is Envy, Revenge & Cruelty,
Which separated the stars from the mountains, the mountains
  from Man,
And left Man a little grovelling Root, outside of Himself.
  Negations are not Contraries. Contraries mutually exist,
But Negations Exist not. Exceptions & Objections & Un-
  beliefs
Exist not, nor shall they ever be Organized for ever & ever.

If thou separate from me, thou art a Negation, a meer
Reasoning & Derogation from me, an Objecting & cruel
    Spite
And Malice & Envy. Nor shall that which is above
Ever descend into thee, but thou shalt be a Non-Entity for
    ever.
And if any enter into thee, thou shalt be an Unquenchable
    Fire,
And he shall be a never dying Worm, mutually tormented by
Those that thou tormentest, a Hell & Despair for ever &
    ever.'
  So Los in secret with himself communed, & Enitharmon
    heard
In her darkness, & was comforted. Yet still she divided away
In gnawing pain from Los's bosom in the deadly Night,
And the Spectrous Darkness from his back divided, in
    temptations
And in grinding agonies, in threats, stiflings & direful
    strugglings.

III

Los conquers the Spectre

This is the manner of the Sons of Albion in their strength:
They take the two Contraries, which are called Qualities,
    with which
Every Substance is clothed; they name them Good & Evil.
From them they make an Abstract, which is a negation
Not only of the Substance from which it is derived,
A murderer of its own Body, but also a murderer
Of every Divine Member. It is the Reasoning Power,
An Abstract objecting power that Negatives every thing.
This is the Spectre of Man, the Holy Reasoning Power,
And in its Holiness is closed the Abomination of Desolation.
  Therefore Los stands in London, building Golgonooza,
Compelling his Spectre to labours mighty. Trembling in fear
The Spectre weeps, but Los unmov'd by tears or threats
    remains.

59

'I must Create a System, or be enslav'd by another Man's
I will not Reason & Compare; my business is to Create.'
    So Los, in fury & strength, in indignation & burning
        wrath.
Shudd'ring the Spectre howls: his howlings terrify the night.
He stamps around the anvil, beating blows of stern despair.
He curses Heaven & Earth, Day & Night, Sun & Moon.
He curses Forest, Spring and River, Desart and sandy Waste,
Cities and Nations, Families and Peoples, Tongues and Laws,
Driven to desperation by Los's terrors and threat'ning fears.
    Los cries: 'Obey my voice & never deviate from my will,
And I will be merciful to thee! Be thou invisible to all
To whom I make thee invisible, but chief to my own
        Children,
O Spectre of Urthona. Reason not against their dear
        approach,
Nor them obstruct with thy temptations of doubt and
        despair.'
    The Spectre answer'd: 'Art thou not ashamed of those thy
        Sins
That thou callest thy Children? I have kept silent hitherto
Concerning my chief delight, but thou hast broken silence.
Now I will speak my mind. Where is my lovely Enitharmon,
O thou my enemy, where is my Great Sin? She is also thine.'
I said: 'Now is my grief at worst, incapable of being
Surpassed.' But every moment it accumulates more and
        more;
It continues accumulating to eternity. The joys of God
        advance,
For he is Righteous. He is not a Being of Pity and Compas-
        sion.
He cannot feel Distress. He feeds on Sacrifice and Offering,
Delighting in cries and tears, and clothed in holiness &
        solitude.
But my griefs advance also, for ever and ever without end.
O that I could cease to be! Despair! I am Despair,
Created to be the great example of horror and agony. Also my
Prayer is vain. I called for compassion; compassion mock'd.
Mercy and pity threw the grave-stone over me, and with lead
And iron bound it over me for ever. Life lives on my
Consuming, and the Almighty hath made me his Contrary,

To be all evil, all reversed and for ever dead; knowing
And seeing life, yet living not. How can I then behold
And not tremble? How can I be beheld and not abhorr'd?'
  So spoke the Spectre shudd'ring, and dark tears ran down
    his shadowy face,
Which Los wiped off, but comfort none could give, or beam
    of hope.
Yet ceas'd he not from labouring at the roarings of his Forge,
With iron and brass building Golgonooza in great contend-
    ings,
Till his Sons and Daughters came forth from the Furnaces
At the sublime Labours; for Los compelled the invisible
    Spectre
To labours mighty, with vast strength, with his mighty chains,
In pulsations of time and extensions of space,
Striving with Systems, to deliver Individuals from those
    Systems,
That wherever any Spectre began to devour the Dead
He might feel the pain as if a man gnaw'd his own tender
    nerves.

IV

The Golden Builders

  Then Erin came forth from the Furnaces, and all the
    Daughters of Beulah
Came from the Furnaces by Los's mighty power, for
    Jerusalem's
Sake, walking up and down among the Spaces of Erin.
And the Sons and Daughters of Los came forth in perfection
    lovely.
And the Spaces of Erin reach'd from the starry heighth to the
    starry depth.
  Los wept with exceeding joy, and all wept with joy
    together.
They fear'd they never more should see their Father, who
Was built in from Eternity in the Cliffs of Albion.
  But when the joy of meeting was exhausted in loving em-
    brace,

Again they lament: 'O what shall we do for lovely Jerusalem?
Vala is but thy Shadow, O thou loveliest among women,
A shadow animated by thy tears, O mournful Jerusalem!
Why wilt thou give to her a Body whose life is but a Shade,
Her joy and love a shade, a shade of sweet repose?
But animated and vegetated, she is a devouring worm.
What shall we do for thee, O lovely mild Jerusalem?'
And Los said: 'I behold the finger of God in terrors.
Albion is dead; his Emanation is divided from him.
But I am living; yet I feel my Emanation also dividing.
Such a thing was never known. O pity me, thou all-piteous
    one!
What shall I do, or how exist, divided from Enitharmon?
Yet why despair? I saw the finger of God go forth
Upon my Furnaces, from within the Wheels of Albion's Sons,
Fixing their Systems permanent, by mathematic power
Giving a body to Falsehood that it may be cast off for ever,
With Demonstrative Science piercing Apollyon with his own
    bow.
God is within and without; he is even in the depths of
    Hell!'
    Terrified at the sublime Wonder, Los stood before his
    Furnaces,
And they stood around, terrified with admiration at Erin's
    Spaces,
For the Spaces reach'd from the starry heighth to the starry
    depth,
    And they builded Golgonooza, terrible eternal labour!
What are those golden builders doing, near Tyburn's fatal tree,
Near mournful, ever weeping Paddington? Is that Calvary
    and Golgotha
Becoming a building of pity and compassion? Lo!
The stones are pity, and the bricks well wrought affections
Enamel'd with love and kindness; and the tiles engraven
    gold,
Labour of merciful hands; the beams and rafters are for-
    giveness;
The mortar and cement of the work tears of honesty; the
    nails
And the screws and iron braces are well wrought blandish-
    ments

And well contrived words, firm fixing, never forgotten,
Always comforting the remembrance; the floors, humility;
The cielings, devotion; the hearths, thanksgiving.
Prepare the furniture, O Lambeth, in thy pitying looms!
The curtains, woven tears and sighs, wrought into lovely
    forms
For comfort. There the secret furniture of Jerusalem's
    chamber
Is wrought. Lambeth! the Bride, the Lamb's Wife, loveth
    thee.
Thou art one with her, and knowest not of self in thy supreme
    joy.
    Go on, builders, in hope! tho' Jerusalem wanders far away
Without the gate of Los, among the dark Satanic wheels.
    Around Golgonooza lies the land of death eternal, a Land
Of pain and misery and despair and ever brooding melan-
    choly,
From the blue Mundane Shell reaching to the Vegetative
    Earth.
    The Vegetative Universe opens like a flower from the
    Earth's center
In which is Eternity. It expands in Stars to the Mundane
    Shell,
And there it meets Eternity again, both within and without.
And the abstract Voids between the Stars are the Satanic
    Wheels,
(But whatever is visible to the Generated Man
Is a Creation of mercy and love, from the Satanic Void.)
The land of darkness flamed, but no light and no repose;
The land of snows of trembling, and of iron hail incessant;
The land of earthquakes and the land of woven labyrinths;
The land of snares and traps and wheels and pit-falls and
    dire mills;
The Voids, the Solids, and the land of clouds and regions of
    waters;
Self-righteousness conglomerating against the Divine Vision;
A Concave Earth wondrous, Chasmal, Abyssal, Incoherent,
Forming the Mundane Shell, above, beneath, on all sides,
    surrounding Golgonooza.
    Los walks around the walls night and day.
He views the City of Golgonooza, and its smaller cities,

63

And all that has existed in the space of six thousand years,
Permanent and not lost, not lost or vanish'd; and every little
act,
Word, work and wish that has existed, all remaining still,
Shadowy to those who dwell not in them, meer possibilities,
But to those who enter into them they seem the only sub-
stances.
For every thing exists, and not one sigh nor smile nor tear,
One hair nor particle of dust, not one can pass away.
All things acted on Earth are seen in the bright Sculptures
of
Los's Halls, and every Age renews its powers from these
Works,
With every pathetic story possible to happen, from Hate or
Wayward Love; and every sorrow and distress is carved here;
Every Affinity of Parents, Marriages and Friendships are
here,
In all their various combinations, wrought with wondrous
Art,
All that can happen to Man in his pilgrimage of seventy
years.
Such is the Divine Written Law of Horeb and Sinai,
And such the Holy Gospel of Mount Olivet and Calvary.

v

The Children of Light
and the Children of Darkness

And Los beheld his Sons and he beheld his Daughters,
Every one a translucent Wonder, a Universe within,
Increasing inwards into length and breadth and heighth,
Starry and glorious. And they, every one, in their bright loins
Have a beautiful golden gate, which opens into the vegetative
world;
And every one a gate of rubies and all sorts of precious stones
In their translucent hearts, which opens into the vegetative
world;
And every one a gate of iron, dreadful and wonderful,

In their translucent heads, which opens into the vegetative
    world.
And every one has the three regions Childhood, Manhood
    and age.
I see the Four-fold Man: The Humanity in deadly sleep,
And its fallen Emanation, the Spectre and its cruel Shadow.
I see the Past, Present and Future existing all at once
Before me. O Divine Spirit! Sustain me on thy wings,
That I may awake Albion from his long and cold repose!
For Bacon and Newton, sheath'd in dismal steel, their terrors
    hang
Like iron scourges over Albion. Reasonings, like vast
    serpents,
Infold around my limbs, bruising my minute articulations.
   I turn my eyes to the Schools and Universities of Europe,
And there behold the Loom of Locke, whose woof rages dire,
Wash'd by the Water-wheels of Newton. Black the cloth
In heavy wreathes folds over every Nation. Cruel Works
Of many Wheels I view, wheel without wheel, with cogs
    tyrannic
Moving by compulsion each other; not as those in Eden,
    which
Wheel within Wheel in freedom revolve, in harmony and
    peace.
   There is an Outside spread Without, and an Outside spread
    Within,
Beyond the Outline of Identity both ways, which meet in
    One,
An orbèd Void of doubt, despair, hunger and thirst and
    sorrow.
Here the Twelve Sons of Albion, join'd in dark Assembly,
Jealous of Jerusalem's children, asham'd of her little-ones,
(For Vala produc'd the bodies, Jerusalem gave the souls)
Became as Three Immense Wheels, turning upon one-another
Into Non-Entity, and their thunders hoarse appall the Dead,
To murder their own Souls, to build a Kingdom among the
    Dead.
   'Cast! Cast ye Jerusalem forth, the Shadow of delusions,
The Harlot daughter, Mother of pity and dishonourable
    forgiveness,
Our Father Albion's sin and shame! But father now no more,

Nor sons; nor hateful peace and love, nor soft complacencies,
With transgressors meeting in brotherhood around the table,
Or in the porch or garden! No more the sinful delights
Of age and youth, and boy and girl, and animal and herb,
And river and mountain, and city and village, and house and
    family
Beneath the Oak and Palm, beneath the Vine and Fig-tree,
In self-denial! But war and deadly contention between
Father and Son, and light and love! All bold asperities
Of Haters met in deadly strife, rending the house and garden,
The unforgiving porches, the tables of enmity, and beds
And chambers of trembling and suspition; hatreds of age and
    youth,
And boy and girl, and animal and herb, and river and
    mountain,
And city and village, and house and family; that the Perfect
May live in glory, redeem'd by Sacrifice of the Lamb
And of his children before sinful Jerusalem; to build
Babylon, the City of Vala, the Goddess Virgin-Mother.
She is our Mother! Nature! Jerusalem is our Harlot-Sister
Return'd with Children of pollution, to defile our House
With Sin and Shame. Cast, Cast her into the Potter's field!
Her little-ones She must slay upon our Altars, and her aged
Parents must be carried into captivity to redeem her Soul,
To be foɪ a Shame and a Curse, and to be our Slaves for ever.'
    So cry Hand and Hyle, the eldest of the fathers of Albion's
Little-ones, to destroy the Divine Saviour, the Friend of
    Sinners.
                              In a dark and unknown night
Outstretch'd his Giant beauty on the ground in pain and
    tears;
His Children, exil'd from his breast, pass to and fro before
    him.
His birds are silent on his hills; flocks die beneath his
    branches,
His tents are fallen; his trumpet and the sweet sound of his
    harp
Are silent on his clouded hills, that belch forth storms and fire.
His milk of Cows and honey of Bees and fruit of golden
    harvest
Is gathered in the scorching heat and in the driving rain.

Where once he sat, he weary walks, in misery and pain,
His Giant beauty and perfection fallen into dust,
Till from within his wither'd breast, grown narrow with his
   woes,
The corn is turn'd to thistles and the apples into poison,
The birds of song to murderous crows, his joys to bitter
   groans,
The voices of children in his tents to cries of helpless infants,
And, self-exiled from the face of light and shine of morning,
In the dark world, a narrow house, he wanders up and down,
Seeking for rest and finding none; and, hidden far within,
His Eon weeping in the cold and desolated Earth.

   All his Affections now appear withoutside; all his Sons,
His Twelve Sons, Satanic Mill,
Revolve upon his mountains, groaning in pain, beneath
The dark incessant sky, seeking for rest and finding none,
Raging against their Human natures.
And the seven diseases of the soul
Settled around Albion.
Willing the Friends endur'd for Albion's sake, and for
Jerusalem his Emanation, shut within his bosom,
Which harden'd against them more and more, as he builded
   onwards
On the Gulph of Death, in self-righteousness, that roll'd
Before his awful feet in pride of virtue for victory.
And Los was roof'd in from Eternity in Albion's Cliffs
Which stand upon the ends of Beulah; and withoutside all
Appear'd a rocky form against the Divine Humanity.
Albion's Circumference was clos'd; his center began dark'-
   ning
Into the night of Beulah, and the Moon of Beulah rose
Clouded with storms. Los, his strong Guard, walk'd round
   beneath the Moon,
And Albion fled inward.

VI

Jerusalem and Vala

He found Jerusalem upon the River of his City, soft repos'd
In the arms of Vala, assimilating in one with Vala,
The Lilly of Havilah. And they sang soft thro' Lambeth's vales,
In a sweet moony night and silence that they had created,
With a blue sky spread over with wings, and a mild moon,
Dividing and uniting into many female forms, Jerusalem
Trembling; then in one comingling, in eternal tears,
Sighing to melt his Giant beauty on the moony river.
But when they saw Albion fall'n, upon mild Lambeth's vale,
Astonish'd, Terrified, they hover'd over his Giant limbs.
Then thus Jerusalem spoke, while Vala wove the veil of tears,
Weeping, in pleadings of Love, in the web of despair:
'Wherefore hast thou shut me into the winter of human life,
And clos'd up the sweet regions of youth and virgin innocence,
Where we live, forgetting error, not pondering on evil,
Among my lambs and brooks of water, among my warbling birds,
Where we delight in innocence before the face of the Lamb,
Going in and out before him, in his love and sweet affection?'
Vala replied, weeping and trembling, hiding in her veil:
'When winter rends the hungry family, and the snow falls
Upon the ways of men, hiding the paths of man and beast,
Then mourns the wanderer; then he repents his wanderings and eyes
The distant forest; then the slave groans in the dungeon of stone,
The captive in the mill of the stranger, sold for scanty hire.
They view their former life. They number moments over and over,
Stringing them on their remembrance as on a thread of sorrow.
Thou art my sister and my daughter; thy shame is mine also.

Ask me not of my griefs: thou knowest all my griefs.'
　Jerusalem answer'd with soft tears over the valleys:
'O Vala, what is Sin, that thou shudderest and weepest
At sight of thy once lov'd Jerusalem? What is Sin but a little
Error and fault that is soon forgiven? But mercy is not a Sin,
Nor pity, nor love, nor kind forgiveness. O, if I have Sinned
Forgive and pity me! O, unfold thy Veil in mercy and love!
Slay not my little ones, beloved Virgin daughter of Babylon,
Slay not my infant loves and graces, beautiful daughter of
　　Moab.
I cannot put off the human form. I strive, but strive in vain.
When Albion rent thy beautiful net of gold and silver twine
(Thou hadst woven it with art; thou hadst caught me in the
　　bands
Of love; thou refusedst to let me go) Albion beheld thy
　　beauty,
Beautiful thro' our love's comeliness, beautiful thro' pity.
The Veil shone with thy brightness in the eyes of Albion,
Because it inclos'd pity and love, because we lov'd one-
　　another.
Albion lov'd thee; he rent thy Veil; he embraced thee; he
　　lov'd thee!
Astonish'd at his beauty and perfection, thou forgavest his
　　furious love.
I redounded from Albion's bosom in my virgin loveliness;
The Lamb of God reciev'd me in his arms, he smil'd upon us.
He made me his Bride and Wife; he gave thee to Albion.
Then was a time of love. O why is it passed away?'
　Then Albion broke silence and with groans reply'd:
'O Vala! O Jerusalem! do you delight in my groans?
You, O lovely forms, you have prepared my death-cup.
The disease of Shame covers me from head to foot. I have no
　　hope.
Every boil upon my body is a separate and deadly Sin.
Doubt first assailed me; then Shame took possession of me.
Shame divides families; Shame hath divided Albion in
　　sunder.
First fled my Sons, and then my Daughters, then my Wild
　　Animations,
My Cattle next: last ev'n the Dog of my Gate. The Forests
　　fled,

69

The Corn-fields and the breathing Gardens outside separated,
The Sea, the Stars, the Sun, the Moon driv'n forth by my
disease.
All is Eternal Death unless you can weave a chaste
Body over an unchaste Mind! Vala! O that thou wert pure,
That the deep wound of Sin might be clos'd up with the
Needle
And with the Loom, to cover Gwendolen and Ragan with
costly Robes
Of Natural Virtue.
Jerusalem! dissembler Jerusalem! I look into thy bosom,
I discover thy secret places. I hear my Children's voices;
I see their piteous faces gleam out upon the cruel winds.
I see them, distant from my bosom, scourg'd along the roads;
Then, lost in clouds, I hear their tender voices; clouds divide.
    Are the Dead cruel? Are those who are infolded in moral
    Law
Revengeful? O that Death and Annihilation were the same!'
    Then Vala answer'd, spreading her scarlet Veil over
    Albion:
'Albion, thy fear has made me tremble; thy terrors have
surrounded me.
Thy Sons have nail'd me on the Gates, piercing my hands
and feet.
The flesh of multitudes fed and nourish'd me in my child-
hood;
My morn and evening food were prepar'd in Battles of Men.
Great is the cry of the Hounds of Nimrod along the Valley
Of Vision. They scent the odor of War in the Valley of
Vision.
All Love is lost; terror succeeds, and Hatred instead of Love,
And stern demands of Right and Duty instead of Liberty.
Once thou wast to me the loveliest Son of Heaven, but now
Where shall I hide from thy dread countenance and searching
eyes?
I have looked into the secret Soul of him I loved,
And in the dark recesses found Sin, and can never return.'
    Albion again utter'd his voice beneath the silent Moon:
'I brought Love into light of day, to pride in chaste beauty;
I brought Love into light, and fancied Innocence is no more.'
    Then spoke Jerusalem: 'O Albion! my Father Albion!

Why wilt thou number every little fibre of my Soul,
Spreading them out before the Sun, like stalks of flax to dry?
The Infant Joy is beautiful, but its anatomy
Horrible, ghast and deadly. Nought shalt thou find in it
But dark despair and everlasting brooding melancholy!'
   Then Albion turn'd his face toward Jerusalem and spoke:
'Hide thou, Jerusalem, in impalpable voidness, not to be
Touch'd by the hand nor seen with the eye. O Jerusalem,
Would thou wert not, and that they place might never be
   found!
But come, O Vala, with knife and cup! Drain my blood
To the last drop, then hide me in thy Scarlet Tabernacle!
For I see Luvah whom I slew. I behold him in my Spectre,
As I behold Jerusalem in thee, O Vala, dark and cold!'
   Jerusalem then stretch'd her hand toward the Moon and
      spoke:
'Why should Punishment Weave the Veil with Iron Wheels
   of War,
When forgiveness might it Weave with Wings of Cherubim?'

VII

Albion's Struggles to Awake

   Loud groan'd Albion from mountain to mountain and
      replied:
'Jerusalem! Jerusalem! deluding shadow of Albion!
Daughter of my phantasy! unlawful pleasure! Albion's curse!
I came here with intention to annihilate thee. But
My soul is melted away, inwoven within the Veil.
Hast thou again knitted the Veil of Vala which I for thee
Pitying rent in ancient times? I see it whole and more
Perfect and shining with beauty!'
   Jerusalem reply'd, like a voice heard from a sepulcher:
'Father! once piteous! Is pity a Sin?
Thou art my Father and my Brother! Why hast thou hidden me
Remote from the divine Vision, my Lord and Saviour?'
   Trembling stood Albion at her words, in jealous dark
      despair.

71

He felt that Love and Pity are the same, a soft repose,
Inward complacency of soul, a Self-annihilation.
'I have erred. I am ashamed, and will never return more.
I have taught my children sacrifices of cruelty. What shall I
    answer?
I will hide it from Eternals. I will give myself for my Children.
Which way soever I turn, I behold Humanity and Pity!'
    He recoil'd; he rush'd outwards; he bore the Veil whole
    away.
He drew the Veil of Moral Virtue, woven for cruel laws,
And cast it into the Atlantic Deep, to catch the souls of the
    Dead.
He stood between the Palm tree and the Oak of weeping,
Which stand upon the edge of Beulah, and there Albion sunk
Down in sick pallid languor. These were his last words,
    relapsing
Hoarse from his rocks.
'Blasphemous Sons of Feminine delusion! God in the dreary
    Void
Dwells from Eternity, wide separated from the Human Soul.
But thou, deluding Image, by whom imbu'd the Veil I rent,
Lo! here is Vala's Veil whole, for a Law, a Terror and a
    Curse!
And therefore God takes vengeance on me. From my clay-
    cold bosom
My children wander, trembling victims of his Moral Justice.
His snows fall on me and cover me, while in the Veil I fold
My dying limbs. Therefore, O Manhood, if thou art aught
But a meer Phantasy, hear dying Albion's Curse!
May God, who dwells in this dark Ulro and voidness,
    vengeance take
And draw thee down into this Abyss of sorrow and torture,
Like me thy Victim. O that Death and Annihilation were
    the same!
    What have I said? What have I done? O all-powerful
    Human Words!
You recoil back upon me, in the blood of the Lamb slain in
    his Children.
We reared mighty Stones. We danced naked around them,
Thinking to bring Love into light of day, to Jerusalem's
    shame,

72

Displaying our Giant limbs to all the winds of heaven. Sudden,
Shame siez'd us. We could not look on one-another for abhorrence; the Blue
Of our immortal Veins, and all their hosts, fled from our Limbs,
And wander'd distant in a dismal night, clouded and dark.
The Sun fled from the Briton's forehead, the Moon from his mighty loins.
   O what is Life, and what is Man? O what is Death? Wherefore
Are you, my Children, natives in the Grave to where I go?
Or are you born to feed the hungry ravenings of Destruction?
To be the sport of Accident? to waste in Wrath and Love a weary
Life, in brooding cares and anxious labours that prove but chaff!
O Jerusalem! Jerusalem! I have forsaken thy Courts,
Thy Pillars of ivory and gold, thy Curtains of silk and fine
Linen, thy Pavements of precious stones, thy Walls of pearl
And gold, thy Gates of Thansksgiving, thy Windows of Praise,
Thy Clouds of Blessing, thy Cherubims of Tender-mercy
Stretching their Wings sublime over the Little-ones of Albion.
O Human Imagination! O Divine Body I have Crucified!
I have turned my back upon thee, into the Wastes of Moral Law.
There Babylon is builded in the Waste, founded in Human desolation.
   O Babylon! thy Watchman stands over thee in the night;
Thy severe Judge all the day long proves thee, O Babylon,
With provings of destruction, with giving thee thy heart's desire.
   But Albion is cast forth to the Potter, his Children to the Builders,
To build Babylon, because they have forsaken Jerusalem.
The Walls of Babylon are Souls of Men, her Gates the Groans
Of Nations; Her Towers are the Miseries of once happy Families;
Her Streets are paved with Destruction, her Houses built with Death,
Her Palaces with Hell and the Grave, her Synagogues with Torments

Of ever-hardening Despair, squar'd and polish'd with cruel
skill.
Yet thou wast lovely as the summer cloud upon my hills,
When Jerusalem was thy heart's desire, in times of youth and
love.
Thy Sons came to Jerusalem with gifts; she sent them away
With blessings on their hands and on their feet, blessings of
gold
And pearl and diamond. Thy Daughters sang in her Courts;
They came up to Jerusalem; they walked before Albion.
In the Exchanges of London every Nation walk'd,
And London walk'd in every Nation, mutual in love and
harmony.
Albion cover'd the whole Earth, England encompass'd the
Nations
Mutual each within other's bosom, in visions of Regeneration.
Jerusalem cover'd the Atlantic Mountains and the Erythrean,
From bright Japan and China to Hesperia, France and
England.
Mount Zion lifted his head in every Nation under heaven,
And the Mount of Olives was beheld over the whole Earth.
The footsteps of the Lamb of God were there.
                                   But now no more,
No more shall I behold him; he is clos'd in Luvah's Sepulcher.
Yet why these smitings of Luvah, the gentlest, mildest Zoa?
If God was merciful this could not be. O Lamb of God,
Thou art a delusion, and Jerusalem is my Sin! O my Chil-
dren,
I have educated you in the crucifying cruelties of Demonstra-
tion,
Till you have assum'd the Providence of God and slain your
Father.
Dost thou appear before me, who liest dead in Luvah's
Sepulcher?
Dost thou forgive me, thou who wast Dead and art Alive?
Look not so merciful upon me, O thou Slain Lamb of God!
I die! I die in thy arms, tho' Hope is banish'd from me.'

74

Chorus of the Pities

And there was heard a great lamenting in Beulah. All the
    Regions
Of Beulah were moved, as the tender bowels are moved, and
    they said:
'Why did you take Vengeance, O ye Sons of the mighty
    Albion,
Planting these Oaken Groves, erecting these Dragon
    Temples?
Injury the Lord heals; but Vengeance cannot be healed.
As the Sons of Albion have done to Luvah, so they have in
    him
Done to the Divine Lord and Saviour, who suffers with those
    that suffer.
For not one sparrow can suffer, and the whole Universe not
    suffer also,
In all its Regions, and its Father and Saviour not pity and
    weep.
But Vengenace is the destroyer of Grace and Repentance in
    the bosom
Of the Injurer, in which the Divine Lamb is cruelly slain.
    Descend, O Lamb of God, and take away the imputation
    of Sin,
By the Creation of States, and the deliverance of Individuals
    Evermore. Amen.'
    Thus wept they in Beulah over the Four Regions of Albion.
But many doubted and despaired and imputed Sin and
    Righteousness
To Individuals, and not to States. And these Slept in Ulro.

Albion, sunk in Error, rejects the Divine Call

Every ornament of perfection and every labour of love
In all the Garden of Eden and in all the golden mountains
Was become an envied horror, and a remembrance of
    jealousy,
And every Act a Crime, and Albion the punisher and judge.
  And Albion spoke from his secret seat and said:
'All these ornaments are crimes. They are made by the
    labours
Of loves, of unnatural consanguinities and friendships,
Horrid to think of when enquired deeply into; and all
These hills and valleys are accursed witnesses of Sin.
I therefore condense them into solid rocks, stedfast,
A foundation and certainty and demonstrative truth,
That Man be separate from Man. And here I plant my seat.'
  Cold snows drifted around him. Ice covered his loins
    around.
He sat by Tyburn's brook, and underneath his heel shot up
A deadly Tree. He named it Moral Virtue, and the Law
Of God who dwells in Chaos, hidden from the human sight.
The Tree spread over him its cold shadows. (Albion groan'd.)
They bent down; they felt the earth; and again enrooting
Shot into many a Tree, an endless labyrinth of woe.
  From willing sacrifice of Self, to sacrifice of (miscall'd)
    Enemies
For Atonement, Albion began to erect twelve Altars
Of rough unhewn rocks, before the Potter's Furnace.
He nam'd them Justice and Truth. And Albion's Sons
Must have become the first victims, being the first trans-
    gressors,
But they fled to the mountains to seek ransom, building a Strong
Fortification against the Divine Humanity and Mercy,
In Shame and Jealousy to annihilate Jerusalem.
  Then the Divine Vision, like a silent Sun, appear'd above
Albion's dark rocks; and in the Sun a Human Form appear'd.
And thus the Voice Divine went forth upon the rocks of
    Albion.

'I elected Albion for my glory. I gave him to the Nations
Of the whole Earth. He was the Angel of my Presence, and all
The Sons of God were Albion's Sons, and Jerusalem was my
    joy.
The Reactor hath hid himself, thro' envy. I behold him,
But you cannot behold him till he be revealed in his System.
Albion's Reactor must have a place prepar'd. Albion must
    Sleep
The Sleep of Death, till the Man of Sin and Repentance be
    reveal'd.
Hidden in Albion's Forests he lurks. He admits of no Reply
From Albion, but hath founded his Reaction into a Law
Of Action, for Obedience to destroy the Contraries of Man.
He hath compell'd Albion to become a Punisher, and hath
    possess'd
Himself of Albion's Forests and Wilds. And Jerusalem is taken,
The City of the Woods in the Forest of Ephratah is taken,
Her palaces levelled with the dust.
I come that I may find a way for my banished ones to return.
Fear not, O little Flock, I come! Albion shall rise again.'
    Forthwith from Albion's dark'ning locks came two
        Immortal forms,
Saying: 'We alone are escaped, O merciful Lord and
    Saviour.
We flee from the interiors of Albion's hills and mountains,
Beneath his vast ranges of hills surrounding Jerusalem.'

X

Report of the Two that escaped

'Albion walk'd on the steps of fire before his Halls,
And Vala walk'd with him, in dreams of soft deluding
    slumber.
Then Albion ascended mourning into the porches of his
    Palace.
Above him rose a Shadow from his wearied intellect,
Of living gold, pure, perfect, holy. In white linen pure he
    hover'd,

77

Soft exulting in existence, all the Man absorbing.
 Albion fell upon his face prostrate before the wat'ry
  Shadow,
Saying: "O Lord, whence is this change? Thou knowest I
  am nothing!"
And Vala trembled and cover'd her face, and her locks were
  spread on the pavement.
We heard, astonish'd at the Vision, and our hearts trembled
  within us.
We heard the voice of slumberous Albion, and thus he spake
Idolatrous to his own Shadow, words of eternity uttering:
 "O I am nothing, when I enter into judgment with thee!
If thou withdraw thy breath, I die and vanish into Hades.
If thou dost lay thy hand upon me, behold! I am silent.
If thou withhold thy hand, I perish like a fallen leaf.
O I am nothing, and to nothing must return again.
If thou withdraw thy breath, Behold, I am oblivion."
 He ceas'd. The shadowy voice was silent, but the cloud
  hover'd over their heads
In golden wreathes, the sorrow of Man, and the balmy drops
  fell down.
And lo! that son of Man, that Shadowy Spirit of mild Albion,
Luvah, descended from the cloud. In terror Albion rose,
Indignant rose the awful Man, and turn'd his back on Vala.
 We heard the voice of Albion starting from his sleep:
"O cruel pity! O dark deceit! Can love seek for dominion?"
 And Luvah strove to gain dominion over Albion.
They strove together above the Body, where Vala was
  inclos'd,
And the dark Body of Albion left prostrate upon the crystal
  pavement,
Cover'd with boils from head to foot, the terrible smitings of
  Luvah.
 Then frown'd the fallen Man, and put forth Luvah from
  his presence,
'Saying: "Go and Die the Death of Man for Vala the sweet
  wanderer.
I will turn the volutions of your ears outward, and bend your
  nostrils
Downward; and your fluxile eyes, englob'd, roll round in fear;
Your with'ring lips and tongue shrink up into a narrow circle,

Till into narrow forms you creep. Go take your fiery way,
And learn what 'tis to absorb the Man, you Spirits of Pity
and Love!''
They heard the voice and fled, swift as the winter's setting
sun.
And now the human blood foam'd high. The Spirits Luvah
and Vala
Went down the Human Heart, where Paradise and its joys
abounded,
In jealous fears and fury and rage, and flames roll round their
fervid feet,
And the vast form of Nature like a serpent play'd before them.
And as they fled, in folding fires and thunders of the deep,
Vala shrunk in, like the dark sea that leaves its slimy banks,
And from her bosom Luvah fell, far as the east and west;
And the vast form of Nature like a serpent roll'd between,
Whether of Jerusalem's or Vala's ruins congenerated we know
not.
All is confusion. All is tumult. And we alone are escaped.'
So spoke the fugitives. They joined the Divine Family,
trembling.
And the two that escaped were the Emanation of Los and his
Spectre. For where ever the Emanation goes, the Spectre
Attends her as her Guard. And Los's Emanation is named
Enitharmon, and his Spectre is named Urthona. They knew
Not where to flee. They had been on a visit to Albion's
Children,
And they strove to weave a Shadow of the Emanation
To hide themselves, weeping and lamenting for the Vegetation
Of Albion's Children.
Being not irritated by insult, bearing insulting benevo-
lences,
They percieved that corporeal friends are spiritual enemies.
And the Divine hand was upon them, bearing them through
darkness
Back safe to their Humanity, as doves to their windows.
Therefore the Sons of Eden praise Urthona's Spectre in Songs,
Because he kept the Divine Vision in time of trouble.
They wept and trembled: and Los put forth his hand and
took them in,
Into his bosom.

79

XI

Los goes Exploring

The Divine Vision appear'd with Los,
Following Albion into his Central Void among his Oaks.
And Los prayed and said: 'O Divine Saviour, arise
Upon the Mountains of Albion, as in ancient time. Behold!
The Cities of Albion seek thy face. London groans in pain
From hill to hill, and the Thames laments along the Valleys.
The little Villages of Middlesex and Surrey hunger and thirst.
The Twenty-eight Cities of Albion stretch their hands to thee,
Because of the Oppressors of Albion in every City and Village.
They mock at the Labourer's limbs. They mock at his starv'd
    children,
They buy his daughters that they may have power to sell his
    Sons.
They compell the Poor to live upon a crust of bread, by soft
    mild arts.
They reduce the man to want, then give with pomp and
    ceremony.
The praise of Jehovah is chaunted from lips of hunger and
    Thirst.'
    So Los in lamentations follow'd Albion. Albion cover'd
His western heaven with rocky clouds of death and despair.
    Fearing that Albion should turn his back against the
        Divine Vision,
Los took his globe of fire to search the interiors of Albion's
Bosom, in all the terrors of friendship, entering the caves
Of despair and death to search the tempters out, walking
    among
Albion's rocks and precipices, caves of solitude and dark
    despair,
And saw every Minute Particular of Albion degraded and
    murder'd;
But saw not by whom. They were hidden within in the minute
    particulars
Of which they had possess'd themselves. And there they take up
The articulations of a man's soul, and laughing throw it
    down

Into the frame, then knock it out upon the plank; and souls
are bak'd
In bricks, to build the pyramids of Heber and Terah. But Los
Search'd in vain. Clos'd from the minutia he walk'd difficult.
  He came down from Highgate thro' Hackney and Hollo-
    way towards London,
Till he came to old Stratford, and thence to Stepney and the
  Isle
Of Leutha's Dogs, thence thro' the narrows of the River's side,
And saw every minute particular, the jewels of Albion,
  running down
The kennels of the streets and lanes, as if they were abhorr'd.
Every Universal Form was become barren mountains of
  Moral
Virtue, and every Minute Particular harden'd into grains of
  sand,
And all the tendernesses of the soul cast forth as filth and mire;
To where the Tower of London frown'd dreadful over Jeru-
  salem,
A building of Luvah, builded in Jerusalem's eastern gate to be
His secluded Court. Thence to Bethlehem, where was builded
Dens of Despair in the house of bread. Enquiring in vain
Of stones and rocks he took his way, for human form was
  none.
And thus he spoke, looking on Albion's City with many tears:
  'What shall I do? What could I do, if I could find these
    Criminals?
I could not dare to take vengeance. For all things are so
  constructed
And builded by the Divine hand that the sinner shall always
  escape,
And he who takes vengeance alone is the criminal of Provi-
  dence.
If I should dare to lay my finger on a grain of sand
In way of vengeance, I punish the already punish'd. O whom
Should I pity if I pity not the sinner who is gone astray?
O Albion, if thou takest vengeance, if thou revengest thy
  wrongs,
Thou art for ever lost! What can I do to hinder the Sons
Of Albion from taking vengeance, or how shall I them
  perswade?'

So spoke Los, travelling thro' darkness and horrid solitude.
At length he sat on London Stone, and heard Jerusalem's
    voice:
    'Albion, I cannot be thy wife. Thine own Minute Particu-
    lare
Belong to God alone, and all thy little ones are holy.
They are of Faith and not of Demonstration. Wherefore is
    Vala
Cloth'd in black mourning upon my river's currents? Vala,
    awake!
I hear thy shuttles sing in the sky, and round my limbs
I feel the iron threads of love and jealousy and despair.'
    Vala replied: 'Albion is mine! Luvah gave me to Albion,
And now recieves reproach and hate. Was it not said of old,
Set your Son before a man, and he shall take you and your
    sons
For slaves; but set your Daughter before a man and She
Shall make him and his sons and daughters, your slaves for
    ever?
And thou, O harlot daughter, daughter of despair, art all
This cause of these shakings of my towers on Euphrates.
Here is the House of Albion, and here is thy secluded place,
And here we have found thy sins. And hence we turn thee
    forth
For all to avoid thee, to be astonish'd at thee for thy sins,
Because thou art the impurity and the harlot and thy children
Children of whoredoms, born for Sacrifice, for the meat and
    drink
Offering, to sustain the glorious combat and the battle and
    war,
That Man may be purified by the death of thy delusions.'
    So saying she her dark threads cast over the trembling
    River
And over the valleys, from the hills of Hertfordshire to the hills
Of Surrey, across Middlesex, and across Albion's House
Of Eternity. Pale stood Albion at his eastern gate,
Leaning against the pillars, and his disease rose from his
    skirts.
Upon the Precipice he stood, ready to fall into Non-Entity.
    Los was all astonishment and terror. He trembled, sitting
    on the Stone

82

Of London. But the interiors of Albion's fires and nerves were
  hidden
From Los; astonished he beheld only the petrified surfaces.
He siez'd his Hammer and Tongs, his iron Poker and his
  Bellows
Upon the valleys of Middlesex, shouting loud for aid Divine.

XII

The Female Usurper

Turning his back to the Divine Vision, his Spectrous
Chaos before his face appear'd, an Unformed Memory.
Then spoke the Spectrous Chaos to Albion, dark'ning, cold:
'I am your Rational Power, O Albion, and that Human
  Form
You call Divine is but a Worm seventy inches long,
That creeps forth in a night and is dried in the morning sun,
In fortuitous concourse of memorys accumulated and lost.
It ploughs the Earth in its own conceit; it overwhelms the
  Hills
Beneath its winding labyrinths, till a stone of the brook
Stops it in midst of its pride among its hills and rivers.
The ancient Cities of the Earth remove as a traveller;
And shall Albion's Cities remain when I pass over them
With my deluge of forgotten remembrances over the tablet?'
  So spoke the Spectre to Albion. He is the Great Selfhood,
Satan' worship'd as God by the Mighty Ones of the Earth.
  And this is the cause of the appearance in the frowning
    Chaos;
Albion's Emanation, which he had hidden in Jealousy,
Appear'd now in the frowning Chaos, prolific upon the Chaos.
  Albion spoke: 'Who art thou that appearest in gloomy
    pomp,
Involving the Divine Vision in colours of autumn ripeness?
I never saw thee till this time, nor beheld life abstracted,
Nor darkness immingled with light on my furrow'd field.

Whence comest thou? Who art thou, O loveliest? The Divine
   Vision
Is as nothing before thee; faded is all life and joy.'
   Vala replied in clouds of tears, Albion's garment embracing:
'I was a City and a Temple, built by Albion's Children.
I was a Garden planted with beauty. I allured, on hill and
   valley,
The River of Life to flow against my walls and among my
   trees.
Vala was Albion's Bride and Wife in great Eternity,
The loveliest of the daughters of Eternity, when in day-break
I emanated from Luvah, over the Towers of Jerusalem
And in her Courts among her little Children, offering up
The Sacrifice of fanatic love. Why loved I Jerusalem?
Why was I one with her, embracing in the Vision of Jesus?
Wherefore did I, loving, create love, which never yet
Immingled God and Man, when thou and I hid the Divine
   Vision
In cloud of secret gloom, which, behold, involves me round
   about?
   Know me now, Albion! Look upon me! I alone am Beauty!
The Imaginative Human Form is but a breathing of Vala.
I breathe him forth into the Heaven from my secret Cave,
Born of the Woman to obey the Woman, O Albion the
   mighty!
For the Divine appearance is Brotherhood, but I am Love
Elevate into the Region of Brotherhood with my red fires.'
   'Art thou Vala?' replied Albion, 'image of my repose.
O how I tremble! How my members pour down milky fear!
A dewy garment covers me all over; all manhood is gone.
At thy word and at thy look death enrobes me about,
From head to feet, a garment of death and eternal fear.
Is not that Sun thy husband, and that Moon thy glimmering
   Veil?
Are not the stars of heaven thy Children? Art thou not
   Babylon?
Art thou Nature, Mother of all? Is Jerusalem thy Daughter?
Why have thou elevate inward, O dweller of outward
   chambers?
                    O Vala!
In Eternity they neither marry nor are given in marriage.

84

Albion, the high Cliff of the Atlantic, is become a barren
    Land!'
    Los stood at his Anvil, He heard the contentions of Vala.
He heav'd his thund'ring Bellows upon the valleys of
    Middlesex,
He open'd his Furnaces before Vala. Then Albion frown'd
    in anger,
On his Rock, ere yet the Starry Heavens were fled away
From his awful Members. And thus Los cried aloud
To the Sons of Albion, and to Hand the eldest Son of Albion:
    'I hear the screech of Childbirth loud pealing, and the
        groans
Of Death in Albion's clouds, dreadful utter'd over all the
    Earth.
What may Man be? Who can tell? But what may Woman be,
To have power over Man from Cradle to corruptible Grave?
There is a Throne in every Man; it is the Throne of God.
This, Woman has claim'd as her own, and Man is no more.
Albion is the Tabernacle of Vala and her Temple,
And not the Tabernacle and Temple of the Most High.
O Albion! Why wilt thou create a Female Will,
To hide the most evident God in a hidden covert, even
In the shadows of a Woman and a secluded Holy Place,
That we may pry after him as after a stolen treasure,
Hidden among the Dead and mured up from the paths of
    life?'
    So Los spoke.
And many of the Eternal Ones laughed after their manner:
    'Have you known the Judgment that is arisen among the
Sons of Albion, where a Man dare hardly to embrace
His own Wife, for the terrors of Chastity, that they call
By the name of Morality? Their Daughters govern all
In hidden deceit; they are Vegetable, only fit for burning.
Art and Science cannot exist but by Naked Beauty display'd.'

XIII

The Rescuer

Then the Divine hand found the Two Limits, Satan and
    Adam,
In Albion's bosom; for in every Human bosom those limits
    stand.
And the Divine voice came from the Furnaces, as multitudes
    without
Number, the voices of the innumerable multitudes of
    Eternity,
And the appearance of a Man was seen in the Furnaces,
Saving those who have sinned from the punishment of the
    Law,
(In pity of the punisher, whose state is eternal death)
And keeping them from Sin by the mild counsels of his love.
    'Albion goes to Eternal Death. In Me all Eternity
Must pass thro' condemnation, and awake beyond the Grave.
No individual can keep these Laws, for they are death
To every energy of man, and forbid the springs of life.
Albion hath enter'd the State Satan. Be permanent, O State,
And be thou for ever accursed, that Albion may arise again!
And be thou created into a State! I go forth to Create States,
To deliver Individuals evermore. Amen.'
    Then those in Great Eternity who contemplate on Death
Said thus: 'What seems to Be, Is—to those to whom
It seems to Be, and is productive of the most dreadful
Consequences to those to whom it seems to Be, even of
Torments, Despair, Eternal Death. But the Divine Mercy
Steps beyond, and redeems Man in the Body of Jesus. Amen.'
    And One stood forth from the Divine Family and said:
'I feel my Spectre rising upon me. Albion! arouze thyself!
Why dost thou thunder with frozen Spectrous wrath against
    us?
The Spectre is, in Giant Man, insane and most deform'd.
Thou wilt certainly provoke my Spectre against thine in
    fury.'
So Los spoke. But when he saw pale death in Albion's feet,
Again he joined the Divine Body, following merciful,

While Albion fled more indignant, revengeful, covering
His face and bosom with petrific hardness, and his hands
And feet; lest any should enter his bosom and embrace
His hidden heart. His Emanation wept and trembled within
    him.
Uttering not his jealousy, but hiding it as with
Iron and steel, dark and opake, with clouds and tempests
    brooding,
His strong limbs shudder'd upon his mountains high and
    dark.
Turning from Universal Love, petrific as he went,
His cold against the warmth of Eden rag'd with loud
Thunders of deadly war (the fever of the human soul),
Fires and clouds of rolling smoke! But, mild, the Saviour
    follow'd him,
Displaying the Eternal Vision, the Divine Similitude,
In loves and tears of brothers, sisters, sons, fathers and friends,
Which if Man ceases to behold, he ceases to exist;
Saying: 'Albion! Our wars are wars of life and wounds of love,
With intellectual spears, and long-winged arrows of thought.
Mutual in one another's love and wrath all renewing,
We live as One Man. For, contracting our infinite senses,
We behold multitude; or, expanding, we behold as one,
As One Man all the Universal Family; and that One Man
We call Jesus the Christ. And he in us, and we in him,
Live in perfect harmony, in Eden, the land of life,
Giving, receiving, and forgiving each other's trespasses.
He is the Good shepherd, he is the Lord and master;
He is the Shepherd of Albion, he is all in all,
In Eden, in the garden of God, and in heavenly Jerusalem.
If we have offended, forgive us! Take not vengeance against
    us!'
    Thus speaking, the Divine Family follow Albion.
I saw them in the Visions of God upon my pleasant valleys.

XIV

The Friends of Albion

I behold London, a Human awful wonder of God.
He says: 'Return, Albion, return! I give myself for thee.
My Streets are my Ideas of Imagination.
Awake, Albion, awake! And let us awake up together.
My Houses are Thoughts; my Inhabitants, affections,
The children of my thoughts.
For Albion's sake and for Jerusalem thy Emanation
I give myself, and these my brethren give themselves for
    Albion.'
    So spoke London, immortal Guardian. I heard in Lam-
    beth's shades.
In Felpham I heard and saw the Visions of Albion.
I write in South Molton Street what I both see and hear
In regions of Humanity, in London's opening streets.
    I see thee, awful Parent Land, in light. Behold I see
Verulam! Canterbury, venerable parent of men,
Generous immortal Guardian, golden clad! For Cities
Are Men, fathers of multitudes. (And Rivers and Mountains
Are also Men; everything is Human, mighty, sublime.
In every bosom a Universe expands, as wings
Let down at will around, and call'd the Universal Tent)
York, crown'd with loving kindness; Edinburgh, cloth'd
With fortitude, as with a garment of immortal texture,
Woven in looms of Eden, in spiritual deaths of mighty men
Who give themselves in Golgotha, Victims to Justice, where
There is in Albion a Gate of precious stones and gold.
                This Gate cannot be found
By Satan's Watch-fiends. Tho' they search, numbering every
    grain
Of sand on Earth every night, they never find this Gate.
It is the Gate of Los. Withoutside is the Mill, intricate,
    dreadful
And fill'd with cruel tortures. But no mortal man can find
    the Mill
Of Satan in his mortal pilgrimage of seventy years,
For Human beauty knows it not, nor can Mercy find it.

Albion fled through the Gate of Los, and he stood in the Gate.

Los was the friend of Albion who most lov'd him.

Seeing Albion had turned his back against the Divine Vision,

Los said to Albion: 'Whither fleest thou?' Albion reply'd:

   'I die! I go to Eternal Death! The shades of death

Hover within me and beneath, and spreading themselves outside

Like rocky clouds, build me a gloomy monument of woe.

Will none accompany me in my death, or be a Ransom for me

In that dark Valley? I have girded round my cloke, and on my feet

Bound these black shoes of death, and on my hands death's iron gloves.

God hath forsaken me, and my friends are become a burden.

A weariness to me, and the human footstep is a terror to me!'

   Los answered, troubled, and his soul was rent in twain:

'Must the Wise die for an Atonement? Does Mercy endure Atonement?

No! It is moral Severity, and destroys Mercy in its victim.'

So speaking, not yet infected with the Error and Illusion,

Los shuddered at beholding Albion, for his disease

Arose upon him pale and ghastly; and he call'd around

The Friends of Albion. Trembling at the sight of Eternal Death

The four appeared with their Emanations, in fiery Chariots.

   'Albion is sick!' said every valley, every mournful hill

And every river, 'Our brother Albion is sick to death.

He hath leagued himself with robbers; he hath studied the arts

Of unbelief. Envy hovers over him. His Friends are his abhorrence;

Those who give their lives for him are despised.

Those who devour his soul are taken into his bosom.

To destroy his Emanation is their intention.

Arise! Awake! O Friends of the Giant Albion!

They have perswaded him of horrible falshoods;

They have sown errors over all his fruitful fields!'

   The Twenty-four heard. They came trembling, on wat'ry chariots.

O! how the torments of Eternal Death waited on Man,
And the loud-rending bars of the Creation ready to burst
That the wide world might fly from its hinges, and the
    immortal mansion
Of Man for ever be possess'd by monsters of the deeps,
And Man himself become a Fiend, wrap'd in an endless curse,
Consuming and consum'd for ever in flames of Moral Justice.
    For had the Body of Albion fall'n down, and from its
    dreadful ruins
Let loose the enormous Spectre on the darkness of the deep,
At enmity, with the Merciful and fill'd with devouring fire,
A nether-world must have receiv'd the foul enormous spirit,
Under pretence of Moral Virtue fill'd with Revenge and Law,
There to eternity chain'd down, and issuing in red flames
And curses, with mighty arms brandish'd against the heavens,
Breathing cruelty, blood and vengeance, gnashing his teeth
    with pain,
Torn with black storms and ceaseless torrents of his own
    consuming fire;
Within his breast his mighty Sons chain'd down and filled
    with cursings;
And his dark Eon, that once fair crystal form divinely clear,
Within his ribs producing serpents whose souls are flames of
    fire.
    But, glory to the Merciful-One, for he is of tender mercies!
And the Divine Family wept over him as One Man,
And these the Twenty-four in whom the Divine Family
Appear'd. And they were One in Him, a Human Vision,
Human Divine, Jesus, the Saviour, blessed for ever and ever.

XV

*Los and Friends fail to rescue Albion, and are themselves
in danger*

    But Jerusalem cannot be found, hid
By the Daughters of Beulah, gently snatched away and hid
    in Beulah.

There is a Grain of Sand in Lambeth that Satan cannot
     find,
Nor can his Watch Fiends find it. 'Tis translucent and has
     many Angles.
But he who finds it will find Oothoon's palace. For within
Opening into Beulah, every angle is a lovely heaven.
But should the Watch Fiends find it, they would call it Sin,
And lay its Heavens and their inhabitants in blood of
     punishment.
Here Jerusalem and Vala were hid in soft slumberous repose,
Hid from the terrible East, shut up in the South and West.
     The Twenty-eight trembled in Death's dark caves. In cold
          despair
They kneel'd around the Couch of Death, in deep humiliation
And tortures of self-condemnation, while their Spectres rag'd
     within.
The Four Zoas in terrible combustion clouded rage,
Drinking the shuddering fears and loves of Albion's Families,
Destroying by selfish affections the things that they most
     admire,
Drinking and eating, and pitying and weeping, as at a tragic
     scene
The soul drinks murder and revenge and applauds its own
     holiness.
     They saw Albion endeavouring to destroy their Emana-
          tions.
They saw their wheels rising up poisonous against Albion:
Urizen, cold and scientific; Luvah, pitying and weeping;
Tharmas, indolent and sullen; Urthona doubting and des-
     pairing;
Victims to one another and dreadfully plotting against each
     other,
To prevent Albion walking about in the Four Complexions.
     'If we are wrathful, Albion will destroy Jerusalem with
          rooty Groves.
If we are merciful, ourselves must suffer destruction on his
     Oaks.
Why should we enter into our Spectres, to behold our own
     corruptions?
O God of Albion, descend! Deliver Jerusalem from the
     Oaken Groves!'

Then Los grew furious, raging: 'Why stand we here
    trembling around,
Calling on God for help, and not ourselves, in whom God
    dwells,
Stretching a hand to save the falling Man? are we not
    Four
Beholding Albion upon the Precipice, ready to fall into Non-
    Entity?
Seeing these Heavens and Hells conglobing in the Void,
    Heavens over Hells
Brooding in holy hypocritic lust, drinking the cries of pain
From howling victims of Law: building Heavens Twenty-
    seven-fold,
Swell'd and bloated General Forms, repugnant to the Divine-
Humanity who is the only General and Universal Form,
To which all Lineaments tend and seek with love and sym-
    pathy.
All broad and general principles belong to benevolence,
Who protects minute particulars, every one in their own
    identity.
But here the affectionate touch of the tongue is clos'd in by
    deadly teeth,
And the soft smile of friendship and the open dawn of
    benevolence
Become a net and a trap, and every energy rendered cruel,
Till the existence of friendship and benevolence is denied.
The wine of the Spirit, and the vineyards of the Holy-one,
Here turn into poisonous stupor and deadly intoxication,
That they may be condemn'd by Law, and the Lamb of God
    be slain.
And the two Sources of Life in Eternity, Hunting and War,
Are become the Sources of dark and bitter Death, and of
    corroding Hell.
The open heart is shut up in integuments of frozen silence;
A pretence of Art to destroy Art; a pretence of Liberty
To destroy Liberty; a pretence of Religion to destroy Religion.
Oshea and Caleb fight; they contend in the valleys of Peor
In the terrible Family Contentions of those who love each
    other.
The Armies of Balaam weep; no women come to the field;
Dead corses lay before them, and not as in Wars of old.

For the Soldier who fights for Truth calls his enemy his
brother.
They fight and contend for life and not for eternal death.
But here the Soldier strikes, and a dead corse falls at his feet,
Nor Daughter nor Sister nor Mother come forth to embosom
the slain,
But Death, Eternal Death, remains in the Valleys of Peor
The English are scatter'd over the face of the Nations; are
these
Jerusalem's children? Hark? Hear the Giants of Albion cry
at night
'We smell the blood of the English! We delight in their blood
on our Altars.
The living and the dead shall be ground in our rumbling
Mills
For bread of the Sons of Albion, of the Giants Hand and
Scofield!'
Schofield and Kox are let loose upon my Saxons! They
accumulate
A World in which Man is by his Nature the Enemy of Man,
In pride of Selfhood unwieldly stretching out into Non Entity,
Generalizing Art and Science till Art and Science is lost.
Bristol and Bath, listen to my words, and ye Seventeen,
give ear!
It is easy to acknowledge a man to be great and good while we
Derogate from him in the trifles and small articles of that
goodness.
Those alone are his friends who admire his minutest powers,
Instead of Albion's lovely mountains and the curtains of
Jerusalem
I see a Cave, a Rock, a Tree deadly and poisonous, unimag-
inative;
Instead of the mutual Forgivenesses, the Minute Particulars,
I see
Pits of bitumen ever burning, artificial Riches of the
Canaanite,
Like Lakes of liquid lead; instead of heavenly Chapels built
By our dear Lord, I see Worlds crusted with snows and ice.
I see America clos'd apart, and Jerusalem driven in terror
Away from Albion's mountains, far away from London's
spires.

I will not endure this thing! I alone withstand to death
This outrage! Ah me! How sick and pale you all stand round
    me!
Ah me! Pitiable ones! Do you also go to death's vale?
All you, my Friends and Brothers, all you, my beloved
    Companions,
Have you also caught the infection of Sin and stern Repent-
    ance?
I see Disease arise upon you! Yet speak to me, and give
Me some comfort! Why do you all stand silent?'
    So Los spoke. Pale they stood around the House of Death,
In the midst of temptations and despair, among the rooted
    Oaks,
Among reared Rocks of Albion's Sons. At length they rose
With one accord in love sublime, and, as on Cherubs' wings,
They Albion surround, with kindest violence to bear him
    back
Against his will, thro' Los's Gate to Eden, Four-fold, loud,
Their Wings waving over the bottomless Immense, to bear
Their awful charge back to his native home. But Albion,
    dark,
Repugnant, roll'd his Wheels backward into Non-Entity.
Loud roll the Starry Wheels of Albion into the World of
    Death.
And all the Gate of Los clouded, with clouds redounding
    from
Albion's dread Wheels, stretching out spaces immense
    between,
That every little particle of light and air became Opake,
Black and immense, a Rock of difficulty and a Cliff
Of black despair, that the immortal Wings labour'd against,
Cliff after Cliff, and over Valleys of despair and death.
    But, as the Will must not be bended but in the day of
    Divine
Power, Silent, calm and motionless, in the mid-air sublime,
The Family Divine hover around the darkened Albion.

XVI

Come, Great Physician!

Feeling the damps of death, they with one accord delegated
    Los,
Conjuring him by the Highest that he should watch over
    them
Till Jesus shall appear. And they gave their power to Los,
Naming him the Spirit of Prophecy, calling him Elijah.
    Strucken with Albion's disease, they become what they
        behold.
They assimilate with Albion in pity and compassion.
Their Emanations return not. Their Spectres rage in the
    Deep.
The slumbers of Death came over them around the Couch of
    Death,
Before the Gate of Los and in the depths of Non-Entity.
    (Man is adjoined to Man by his Emanative portion
Who is Jerusalem in every individual Man. And her
Shadow is Vala, builded by the reasoning power in Man.
O search and see! Turn your eyes inward! Open, O thou
    World
Of Love and Harmony in Man! Expand thy ever lovely
    Gates!)
    They wept into the deeps a little space. At length was heard
The voice of Bath, faint as the voice of the Dead in the House
    of Death.
Bath, healing City, whose wisdom, in midst of Poetic
Fervor, mild spoke through the Western Porch, in soft gentle
    tears:
    'O Albion, mildest Son of Eden! clos'd is thy Western
        Gate.
Brothers of Eternity, this Man, whose great example
We all admir'd and lov'd, whose all benevolent countenance,
    seen
In Eden, in lovely Jerusalem, drew even from envy
The tear, and the confession of honesty open and undisguis'd
From mistrust and suspition, the Man is himself become
A piteous example of oblivion; to teach the Sons

Of Eden that however great and glorious, however loving
And merciful the Individuality, however high
Our palaces and cities, and however fruitful are our fields,
In Selfhood we are nothing, but fade away in morning's
    breath.
Our mildness is nothing; the greatest mildness we can
    use
Is incapable and nothing. None but the Lamb of God can
    heal
This dread disease, none but Jesus. O Lord! Descend and
    Save!
Albion's Western Gate is clos'd. His death is coming apace.
Jesus alone can save him. For, alas, we none can know
How soon his lot may be our own.
    Nothing but mercy can save him! Nothing but mercy
        interposing
Lest he should slay Jerusalem in his fearful jealousy.
O God, descend! Gather our brethren, deliver Jerusalem!
But that we may omit no office of the friendly spirit,
Oxford, take thou these leaves of the Tree of Life; with
    eloquence
That thy immortal tongue inspires, present them to Albion.
Perhaps he may receive them, offer'd from thy loved hands.'
    So spoke, unheard by Albion, the merciful Son of Heaven
To those whose Western Gates were open, as they stood
    weeping
Around Albion. But Albion heard him not. Obdurate, hard,
He frown'd on all his Friends, counting them enemies in his
    sorrow.
    Oxford, immortal Bard, with eloquence
Divine he wept over Albion, speaking the words of God
In mild perswasion, bringing leaves of the Tree of Life.
    'Thou art in Error, Albion, the Land of Ulro.
One error not remov'd will destroy a human Soul.
Repose in Beulah's night till the Error is remov'd.
Reason not on both sides. Repose upon our bosoms
Till the Plow of Jehovah and the Harrow of Shaddai
Have passed over the Dead, to awake the Dead to Judgment.'
    But Albion turn'd away, refusing comfort.
Alas! The time will come when a man's worst enemies
Shall be those of his own house and family, in a Religion

Of Generation, to destroy, by sin and atonement, happy
    Jerusalem,
The Bride and Wife of the Lamb.
                O God! Thou art not an Avenger!

XVII

Destroy not these Little Ones

Thus Albion sat, studious of others in his pale disease,
Brooding on evil. But when Los open'd the Furnaces before
    him
He saw that the accursed things were his own affections
And his own beloveds. Then he turned sick; his soul died
    within him.
Also Los, sick and terrified, beheld the Furnaces of Death,
And must have died, but the Divine Saviour descended
Among the infant loves and affections, and the Divine Vision
    wept
Like evening dew on every herb upon the breathing ground.
    Albion spoke, in his dismal dreams: 'O thou deceitful
    friend,
Worshipping mercy and beholding thy friend in such afflic-
    tion!
Los! Thou now discoverest thy turpitude to the heavens.
I demand righteousness and justice, O thou ingratitude!
Give me my Emanations back, food for my dying soul.
My daughters are harlots; my sons are accursed before me.
O! I have utterly been wasted! I have given my daughters to
    devils!'
    So spoke Albion, in gloomy majesty; and deepest night
Of Ulro roll'd round his skirts from Dover to Cornwall.
    Los answered: 'Righteousness and justice I give thee in
    return
For thy righteousness. But I add mercy also, and bind
Thee from destroying these little ones. Am I to be only
Merciful to thee, and cruel to all that thou hatest?
Thou wast the Image of God, surrounded by the Four Zoas.

G   97

Three thou hast slain. I am the Fourth; thou canst not
    destroy me.
I have innocence to defend, and ignorance to instruct:
I have no time for seeming, and little arts of compliment,
In morality and virtue, in self-glorying and pride.
There is a limit of Opakeness, and a limit of Contraction
In every Individual Man, and the limit of Opakeness
Is named Satan, and the limit of Contraction is named Adam.
But when Man sleeps in Beulah, the Saviour in mercy takes
Contraction's limit, and of the limit he forms Woman, that
Himself may in process of time be born Man to redeem.
But there is no limit of Expansion. There is no limit of
    Translucence
In the bosom of Man for ever, from eternity to eternity.
    Therefore I break thy bonds of righteousness, I crush thy
        messengers,
That they may not crush me and mine. Do thou be righteous
And I will return it; otherwise I defy thy worst revenge.
Consider me as thine enemy, on me turn all thy fury;
But destroy not these little ones, nor mock the Lord's
    anointed.
Destroy not by Moral Virtue the little ones whom he hath
    chosen,
The little ones whom he hath chosen in preference to thee.
He hath cast thee off for ever. The little ones he hath
    anointed!
Thy Selfhood is for ever accursed from the Divine presence.'
    So Los spoke: then turn'd his face and wept for Albion.
Albion replied: 'Go, Hand and Hyle! Seize the abhorred
    friend
As you have seized the Twenty-four rebellious ingratitudes,
To atone for you, for spiritual death. Man lives by deaths of
    Men.
Bring him to justice before heaven, here upon London Stone.
All that they have is mine! From my free gen'rous gift
They now hold all they have. Ingratitude to me,
To me their benefactor, calls aloud for vengeance deep.'
    Los stood before his furnaces awaiting the fury of the
        Dead;
And the Divine hand was upon him, strengthening him
    mightily.

The Spectres of the Dead cry out from the deeps beneath.
They curse their human kindness and affection.
They rage like wild beasts in the forests of affliction.
In the dreams of Ulro they repent of their human kindness.
  'Come up, build Babylon, Rahab is ours, and all her
    multitudes
With her in pomp and glory of victory. Depart,
Ye twenty-four, into the deeps! Let us depart to glory!'
  Their Human majestic forms sit up upon their Couches
Of death. They curb their Spectres, as with iron curbs.
They enquire after Jerusalem, in the regions of the dead,
With the voices of dead men, low, scarcely articulate;
And with tears cold on their cheeks they weary repose.
  'O when shall the morning of the grave appear? and when
Shall our salvation come? We sleep upon our watch,
We cannot awake! and our Spectres rage in the forests.
O God of Albion, where art thou? Pity the watchers!'
  Thus mourn they.

XVIII

Mercy prepares a retreat for Jerusalem

Loud the cries of War on the Rhine and Danube with Albion's
    Sons.
Away from Beulah's hills and vales break forth the souls of
    the Dead,
With cymbal, trumpet, clarion and the scythed chariots of
    Britain.
  Hark! and record the terrible wonder, that the Punisher
Mingles with his Victim's Spectre, enslaved and tormented,
To him whom he has murder'd bound in vengeance and
    enmity.
  Shudder not, but write; and the hand of God will assist
    you!
Therefore I write Albion's last words: 'Hope is banish'd
    from me!'
  These were his last words; and the merciful Saviour in his
    arms

99

Receiv'd him, in the arms of tender mercy, and repos'd
The pale limbs of his Eternal Individuality
Upon the Rock of Ages. Then, surrounded with a cloud,
In silence the Divine Lord builded with immortal labour,
Of gold and jewels, a sublime Ornament, a Couch of repose,
With sixteen pillars canopied with emblems and written
    verse,
Spiritual Verse, order'd and measur'd, from whence time
    shall reveal
The five books of the Decalogue, the books of Joshua and
    Judges,
Samuel a double book, and Kings a double book, the Psalms
    and Prophets,
The four-fold Gospels, and the Revelations everlasting.
Eternity groan'd and was troubled at the image of Eternal
    Death.
    There is a place where Contrarieties are equally true;
From this sweet place Maternal Love awoke Jerusalem.
With pangs she forsook Beulah's pleasant lovely shadowy
    Universe
Where no dispute can come, created for those who Sleep.
    Weeping was in all Beulah, and all the Daughters of Beulah
Wept for their sister, the daughter of Albion, Jerusalem,
When out of Beulah the Emanation of the Sleeper descended
With solemn mourning, out of Beulah's moony shades and
    hills
Within the Human Heart, whose Gates closed with solemn
    sound.
    And this the manner of the terrible Separation.
The Emanations of the grievously afflicted Friends of Albion
Concenter in one Female form, an Aged pensive Woman.
Astonish'd, lovely, embracing the sublime shade, the
    Daughters of Beulah
Beheld her with wonder. With awful hands she took
A Moment of Time, drawing it out with many tears and
    afflictions
Into a Rainbow of jewels and gold, a mild Reflection from
Albion's dread Tomb, eight thousand and five hundred years
In its extension. Every two hundred years has a door to Eden.
    She also took an Atom of Space, with dire pain opening it
    a Center

Into Beulah. Trembling the Daughters of Beulah dried
Her tears. She ardent embrac'd her sorrows, occupied in
 labours
Of sublime mercy. Perusing Albion's Tomb
She sat: she walk'd among the ornaments, solemn mourning.
The Daughters attended her shudderings, wiping the death
 sweat.
 Los also saw her in his seventh Furnace. He also, terrified,
Saw the finger of God go forth upon his seventh Furnace,
Away from the Starry Wheels, to prepare Jerusalem a place,
When with a dreadful groan the Emanation mild of Albion
Burst from his bosom in the Tomb, like a pale snowy cloud,
Female and lovely, struggling to put off the Human Form,
Writhing in pain. The Daughters of Beulah in kind arms
 received
Jerusalem, weeping over her, among the Spaces of Erin
In the Ends of Beulah.

XIX

The Mourning for Albion

And thus Erin spoke to the Daughters of Beulah, in soft tears:
   'Albion the Generous,
Albion the mildest son of Heaven, the Place of Holy Sacrifice
Where Friends die for each other, will become the Place
Of Murder, and unforgiving, never-awaking Sacrifice of
 Enemies.
The children must be sacrific'd (a horror never known
Till now in Beulah), unless a Refuge can be found
To hide them from the wrath of Albion's Law, that freezes
 sore
Upon his Sons and Daughters, self-exiled from his bosom.
Draw ye Jerusalem away from Albion's Mountains,
To give a Place for Redemption. O Daughters of Beulah,
Come and mourn over Albion, the white cliff of the Atlantic,
The Mountain of Giants. All the Giants of Albion are become
Weak, wither'd, darken'd; and Jerusalem is cast forth from
 Albion.

101

They deny that they ever knew Jerusalem, or ever dwelt in
  Shiloh.
  The Visions of Eternity, by reason of narrowed percep-
  tions,
Are become weak Visions of Time and Space, fix'd into
  furrows of death,
Till deep dissimulation is the only defence an honest man has
  left.
  O Polypus of Death! O Spectre over Europe and Asia,
Withering the Human Form by Laws of Sacrifice for Sin!
By Laws of Chastity and Abhorrence I am wither'd up,
Striving to Create a Heaven in which all shall be pure and
  holy
In their own Selfhoods, in Natural Selfish Chastity, to banish
  Pity
And dear Mutual Forgiveness, and to become One Great
  Satan,
Inslav'd to the most powerful Selfhood; to murder the Divine
  Humanity,
In whose sight all are as the dust, and who chargeth his
  Angels with folly!
  Ah! Weak and wide astray! Ah, Shut in narrow doleful
  form,
Creeping in reptile flesh upon the bosom of the ground!
The Eye of Man, a little narrow orb, clos'd up and dark,
Scarcely beholding the Great Light, conversing with the
  ground;
The Ear, a little shell, in small volutions shutting out
True Harmonies, and comprehending great as very small;
The Nostrils, bent down to the earth and clos'd with senseless
  flesh,
That odours cannot them expand, nor joy on them exult;
The Tongue a little moisture fills, a little food it cloys,
A little sound it utters, and its cries are faintly heard.
  Rush on! Rush on! Rush on, ye vegetating Sons of Albion!
The Sun shall go before you in Day: the Moon shall go
Before you in Night. Come on! Come on! Come on! The
  Lord
Jehovah is before, behind, above, beneath, around!
He has builded the arches of Albion's Tomb, binding the stars
In merciful order, bending the Laws of Cruelty to Peace.

Remove from Albion, far remove these terrible surfaces.
They are beginning to form Heavens and Hells in immense
Circles, the Hells for food to the Heavens, food of torment,
Food of despair. They drink the condemn'd Soul, and rejoice
In cruel holiness, in thir Heavens of Chastity and Uncir-
      cumcision.
Yet they are blameless, and Iniquity must be imputed only
To the State they are entered into, that they may be deliver'd.
Satan is the State of Death, and not a Human existence;
A World where Man is by nature the enemy of Man,
Because the Evil is created into a State, that Men
May be deliver'd time after time, evermore. Amen.
Learn therefore, O Sisters, to distinguish the Eternal
      Human,
That walks about among the stones of fire, in bliss and woe
Alternate, from those States or Worlds in which the Spirit
      travels.
This is the only means to the Forgiveness of Enemies.
Therefore remove from Albion these terrible Surfaces,
And let wild seas and rocks close up Jerusalem, away from
The Atlantic Mountains, where Giants dwelt in Intellect,
Now given to stony Druids and Allegoric Generation,
To the Twelve Gods of Asia, the Spectres of those who Sleep,
Sway'd by a Providence oppos'd to the Divine Lord Jesus,
A murderous Providence, a Creation that groans, living on
      Death,
Where Fish and Bird and Beast and Man and Tree and Metal
      and Stone
Live by devouring, going into Eternal Death continually.
Albion is now possess'd by the War of Blood; the Sacrifice
Of envy Albion is become, and his Emanation cast out.
Come, Lord Jesus, Lamb of God, descend! for if, O Lord,
If thou hadst been here, our brother Albion had not died.
Arise, Sisters! Go ye and meet the Lord, while I remain.
Behold the foggy mornings of the Dead on Albion's cliffs!
Ye know that if the Emanation remain in them
She will become an Eternal Death, an Avenger of Sin,
A Self-righteousness, the proud Virgin-Harlot, Mother of
      War,
And we also, and all Beulah, consume beneath Albion's
      curse.'

So Erin spoke to the Daughters of Beulah,
And Erin's lovely Bow enclos'd the Wheels of Albion's Sons.
　Expanding on wing, the Daughters of Beulah replied in
　　sweet response:
'Come, O thou Lamb of God and take away the remembrance
　of Sin.
To Sin, and hide the Sin in sweet deceit, is lovely;
To Sin in the open face of day is cruel and pitiless. But
To record the Sin for a reproach, to let the Sun go down
In a remembrance of the Sin, is a Woe and a Horror,
A Brooder of an Evil Day, and a Sun rising in Blood!
　Come then, O Lamb of God, and take away the remem-
　　brance of Sin.'

XX

Los labours for Albion

But Los, who is the Vehicular Form of strong Urthona,
Wept vehemently over Albion, where Thames' currents
　spring
From the Rivers of Beulah—pleasant river, soft, mild, parent
　stream.
And the roots of Albion's Tree enter'd the Soul of Los
As he sat before his Furnaces, clothed in sackcloth of hair,
In gnawing pain dividing him from his Emanation,
Inclosing all the Children of Los time after time,
Their Giant Forms condensing into Nations and Peoples and
　Tongues.
Here, on the banks of the Thames, Los builded Golgonooza,
Outside of the Gates of the Human Heart, beneath Beulah,
In the midst of the rocks of the Altars of Albion. In fears
He builded it, in rage and fury. It is the Spiritual Fourfold
London, continually building and continually decaying
　desolate.
　In eternal labours loud the Furnaces, and loud the Anvils
Of Death thunder incessant, around the flaming Couches of
The Twenty-four Friends of Albion, and round the awful
　Four,

For the protection of the Twelve Emanations of Albion's Sons,
The Mystic Union of the Emanation in the Lord. Because
Man divided from his Emanation is a dark Spectre,
His Emanation is an ever-weeping melancholy Shadow;
But she is made receptive of Generation thro' mercy.
   In Great Eternity every particular Form gives forth, or
      Emanates
Its own peculiar Light. And the Form is the Divine Vision,
And the Light is his Garment. This is Jerusalem in every
      Man,
A Tent and Tabernacle of Mutual Forgiveness, Male and
      Female Clothings.
And Jerusalem is called Liberty among the Children of
      Albion.
   But Albion fell down, a Rocky fragment, from Eternity
      hurl'd
By his own Spectre, who is the Reasoning Power in every
      Man,
Into his own Chaos, which is the Memory between Man and
      Man.
He tosses like a cloud outstretch'd among Jerusalem's ruins
Which overspread all the Earth; he groans among his ruin'd
      porches.
   But the Spectre like a hoar-frost and a mildew rose over
      Albion,
Saying: 'I am God, O Sons of Men! I am your Rational
      Power!
Am I not Bacon and Newton and Locke, who teach Humility
      to Man,
Who teach Doubt and Experiment; and my two Wings,
      Voltaire, Rousseau?
Where is that Friend of Sinners, that Rebel against my Laws,
Who teaches Belief to the Nations, and an unknown Eternal
      Life?
Come hither into the Desart, and turn these stones to bread!
Vain foolish Man, wilt thou believe without Experiment?
And build a World of Phantasy upon my Great Abyss,
A World of Shapes, in craving lust and devouring appetite?'
   So spoke the hard, cold, constrictive Spectre

XXI

The Great Voice of Eternity

When those who disregard all Mortal Things saw a Mighty-
    One
Among the Flowers of Beulah still retain his awful strength,
They wonder'd, checking their wild flames; and Many
    gathering
Together into an Assembly, they said, 'Let us go down
And see these changes.' Other said, 'If you do so, prepare
For being driven from our fields; what have we to do with the
    Dead?
To be their inferiors or superiors we equally abhor.
Superior none we know, inferior none. All equal share
Divine Benevolence and Joy; for the Eternal Man
Walketh among us, calling us his Brothers and his Friends,
Forbidding us that Veil which Satan puts between Eve and
    Adam,
By which the Princes of the Dead enslave their Votaries,
Teaching them to form the Serpent of precious stones and
    gold,
To sieze the Sons of Jerusalem and plant them in One Man's
    Loins,
To make One Family of Contraries, that Joseph may be sold
Into Egypt for Negation,—a Veil the Saviour, born and
    dying, rends!'
    But others said, 'Let us to him who only Is, and who
Walketh among us, give decision. Bring forth all your fires!'
    So saying, an eternal deed was done: in fiery flames
The Universal Concave raged, such thunderous sounds as
    never
Were sounded from a mortal cloud, nor on Mount Sinai old,
Nor in Havilah, where the Cherub roll'd his redounding
    flame.
Loud, loud the Mountains lifted up their voices, loud the
    Forests.
Rivers thunder'd against their banks. Loud Winds furious
    fought.
The Seas raised up their voices, and lifted their hands on high.

The Stars in their courses fought, the Sun, Moon, Heaven,
  Earth,
Contending for Albion and for Jerusalem his Emanation,
And for Shiloh the Emanation of France, and for lovely Vala.
  Then far the greatest number were about to make a
  Separation,
And they elected Seven, call'd the Seven Eyes of God,
Lucifer, Molech, Elohim, Shaddai, Pahad, Jehovah, Jesus.
They nam'd the Eighth; he came not, he hid in Albion's
  Forests.
But first they said (and their Words stood in Chariots in
  array,
Curbing their Tygers with golden bits and bridles of silver
  and ivory):
  'Let the Human Organs be kept in their perfect Integrity,
At will contracting into Worms, or expanding into Gods,
And then, behold! what are these Ulro Visions of Chastity?
Then as the moss upon the tree, or dust upon th plow,
Or as sweat upon the labouring shoulder, or as the chaff
Of the wheat-floor, or as the dregs of the sweet wine-press.
Such are these Ulro Visions. For tho' we sit down within
The plowed furrow, list'ning to the weeping clods, till we
Contract or expand Space at will; or if we raise ourselves
Upon the chariots of the morning, contracting or expanding
  Time,
Everyone knows we are One Family, One Man blessed for
  ever.'
  Silence remain'd, and everyone resum'd his Human
  Majesty.
And many conversed on these things, as they labour'd at the
  furrow,
Saying: 'It is better to prevent misery than to release from
  misery;
It is better to prevent error than to forgive the criminal.
Labour well the Minute Particulars, attend to the Little-ones,
And those who are in misery cannot remain so long,
If we but do our duty. Labour well the teeming Earth!'
  They plow'd in tears. The trumpets sounded before the
  golden Plow,
And the voices of the Living Creatures were heard in the
  clouds of Heaven,

Crying, 'Compel the Reasoner to Demonstrate with un-
hewn Demonstrations.
Let the Indefinite be explored, and let every Man be judged
By his own Works! Let all Indefinites be thrown into
Demonstrations,
To be pounded to dust, and melted in the Furnaces of
Affliction.
He who would do good to another, must do it in Minute
Particulars.
General Good is the plea of the scoundrel, hypocrite and
flatterer.
For Art and Science cannot exist but in minutely organized
Particulars,
And not in generalizing Demonstrations of the Rational
Power.
The Infinite alone resides in Definite and Determinate
Identity.
Establishment of Truth depends on destruction of Falsehood
continually,
On Circumcision, not on Virginity, O Reasoners of Albion!'
So cried they at the Plow. Albion's Rock frowned above.
And the Great Voice of Eternity rolled above, terrible in
clouds,
Saying, 'Who will go forth for us, and Who shall we send
before our face?'

XXII

The Great Refusal of Albion's Daughters

Then Los heaved his thund'ring Bellows on the Valley of
Middlesex
And thus he chaunted his Song; the Daughters of Albion
reply.
'What may Man be? Who can tell? But what may Woman
be,
To have power over Man from Cradle to corruptible Grave?
He who is an Infant, and whose Cradle is a Manger,

Knoweth the Infant sorrow, whence it came and where it
    goeth,
And who weave it a Cradle of the grass that withereth away.
This World is all a Cradle for the erred wandering phantom,
Rock'd by Year, Month, Day and Hour; and, every two
    Moments
Between, dwells a Daughter of Beulah, to feed the Human
    Vegetable.
Entune, Daughters of Albion, your hymning Chorus mildly,
Cord of affection thrilling extatic on the iron Reel
To the golden Loom of Love, to the moth-labour'd Woof,
A Garment and Cradle weaving for the infantine Terror,
For fear, at entering the Gate into our World of cruel
Lamentation, it flee back and hide in Non-Entity's dark wild,
Where dwells the Spectre of Albion, destroyer of Definite
    Form.
The Sun shall be a Scythed Chariot of Britain, the Moon a
    Ship
In the British Ocean, Created by Los's Hammer, measured
    out
Into Days & Nights & Years & Months, to travel with my
    feet
Over these desolate rocks of Albion. O daughters of despair,
Rock the Cradle, and in mild melodies tell me where found
What you have enwoven with so much tears and care, so
    much
Tender artifice, to laugh, to weep, to learn, to know!
Remember! Recollect! what dark befel in wintry days.'
    'O it was lost for ever, and we found it not; it came
And wept at our wintry Door. Look! Look! Behold, Gwen-
    dolen
Is become a Clod of Clay! Merlin is a Worm of the Valley!'
    Then Los uttered with Hammer and Anvil: 'Chaunt!
    revoice!
I mind not your laugh, and your frown I not fear; and
You must my dictate obey. From your gold-beam'd Looms
    trill
Gentle to Albion's Watchman. On Albion's mountains
    re-echo,
And rock the Cradle while—Ah me!—Of that Eternal Man,
And of the cradled Infancy in his bowels of compassion,

Who fell beneath his instruments of husbandry and became
Subservient to the clods of the furrow; the cattle and even
The emmet and earth-worm are his superiors and his lords.'
　　Then the response came warbling from trilling Looms in
　　　Albion;
'We women Tremble at the light, therefore hiding fearful
The Divine Vision with Curtain and Veil and fleshly Taber-
　　nacle.'
　　Los utter'd, swift as the rattling thunder upon the moun-
　　　tains,
'Look back into the Church, Paul! Look! Three Women
　　around
The Cross! O Albion, why didst thou a Female Will Create?'

XXIII

Albion's Friends still seek to save Him

And the voices of Bath and Canterbury and York and
　　Edinburgh cry,
'What is a Wife and what is a Harlot? What is a Church and
　　what
Is a Theatre? Are they Two, and not One? Can they exist
　　separate?
Are not Religion and Politics the same thing? Brotherhood
　　is Religion,
O demonstrations of Reason, dividing families in cruelty and
　　pride!'

　　But Albion fled from the Divine Vision, with the Plow of
　　　Nations enflaming,
The Living Creatures madden'd. And Albion fell into the
　　furrow, and
The Plow went over him, and the Living was plowed in
　　among the Dead.
But his Spectre rose over the starry Plow; Albion fled beneath
　　the Plow,
Till he came to the Rock of Ages, and he took his seat upon
　　the Rock.

And one Daughter of Los sat at the fiery Reel, and another
Sat at the shining Loom, with her sisters standing round.
Terrible their distress, and their sorrow cannot be utter'd.
And another Daughter of Los sat at the Spinning Wheel.
Endless their labour, with bitter food, void of sleep.
Tho' hungry, they labour. They rouse themselves anxious,
Hour after hour labouring at the whirling Wheel—
Many Wheels—and as many lovely Daughters sit weeping.
Yet the intoxicating delight they take in their work
Obliterates every other evil. None pities their tears;
Yet they regard not pity, and they expect no one to pity,
For they labour for life and love, regardless of any one
But the poor Spectres that they work for incessantly.
They are mock'd by everyone that passes by; they regard not.
They labour; and when their Wheels are broken by scorn and
          malice
They mend them, sorrowing with many tears and afflictions.
    Other Daughters of Los, labouring at Looms less fine,
Create the Silk-worm and the Spider and the Catterpiller,
To assist in their most grievous work of pity and compassion.
And others create the wooly Lamb, and the downy Fowl
To assist in the work; the Lamb bleats, the Sea-fowl cries.
Men understand not the distress and the labour and sorrow
That in the Interior Worlds is carried on in fear and trem-
          bling,
Weaving the shudd'ring fears and loves of Albion's Families.

XXIV

Jerusalem Comforted

    In flaming fire within the Furnaces the Divine Vision
          appear'd
On Albion's hills, often walking from the Furnaces in clouds
And flames among the Druid Temples and the Starry Wheels;
Gather'd Jerusalem's Children in his arms, and bore them
          like
A Shepherd, in the night of Albion which overspread all the
          Earth.

'I gave thee liberty and life, O lovely Jerusalem,
And thou hast bound me down upon the Stems of Vegetation.
Why wilt thou rend theyself apart, Jerusalem,
And build this Babylon, and sacrifice in secret Groves
Among the Gods of Asia, among the fountains of pitch and
  nitre?
Therefore thy Mountains are become barren, Jerusalem,
Thy Valleys, Plains of burning sands, thy Rivers, waters of
  death.
Thy Villages die of the Famine, and thy Cities
Beg bread from house to house, lovely Jerusalem.
Why wilt thou deface thy beauty, and the beauty of thy
  little-ones,
To please thy Idols, in the pretended chastities of Uncircum-
  cision?
Thy sons are lovelier than Egypt or Assyria; wherefore
Dost thou blacken their beauty, by a secluded place of rest
And a peculiar Tabernacle, to cut the integuments of beauty
Into veils of tears and sorrows, O lovely Jerusalem?
They have perswaded thee to this; therefore their end shall
  come,
And I will lead thee thro' the Wilderness, in shadow of my
  cloud.
And in my love I will lead thee, lovely Shadow of Sleeping
  Albion.'
    This is the song of the Lamb, sung by Slaves in evening time.
But Jerusalem faintly saw him. Clos'd in the dungeaons of
  Babylon,
Her Form was held by Beulah's Daughters; but all within,
  unseen,
She sat at the Mills, her hair unbound, her feet naked,
Cut with the flints. Her tears run down, her reason grows like
The Wheel of Hand, incessant turning day and night without
  rest,
Insane she raves upon the winds, hoarse, inarticulate.
    All night Vala hears; she triumphs in pride of holiness
To see Jerusalem deface her lineaments with bitter blows
Of despair, while the Satanic Holiness triumph'd in Vala,
In a religion of Chastity and Uncircumcised Selfishness,
Both of the Head and Heart and Loins, clos'd up in Moral
  Pride.

But the Divine Lamb stood beside Jerusalem; oft she saw
The lineaments Divine, and oft the voice heard, and oft she
    said:
'O Lord and Saviour, have the Gods of the Heathen pierced
    thee,
Or hast thou been pierced in the House of thy Friends?
Art thou alive? And livest thou for evermore? Or art thou
Not, but a delusive shadow, a thought that liveth not?
Babel mocks, saying there is no God, or Son of God,
That thou, O Human Imagination, O Divine Body, art all
A delusion. But I know thee, O Lord, when thou arisest upon
My weary eyes, even in this dungeon and this iron mill.
The Stars of Albion cruel rise; thou bindest to sweet influ-
    ences.
For thou also sufferest with me, altho' I behold thee not;
And altho' I sin and blaspheme thy holy name, thou pitiest
    me,
Because thou knowest I am deluded by the turning mills,
And by these visions of pity and love, because of Albion's
    death!'
    Thus spake Jerusalem, and thus the Divine Voice replied:
'Mild Shade of Man, pitiest thou these Visions of terror and
    woe?
Give forth thy pity and love! Fear not! lo, I am with thee
    always
Only believe in me, that I have power to raise from death
Thy Brother who sleepeth in Albion. Fear not, trembling
    Shade,
Repose on me till the morning of the Grave. I am thy life.'

XXV

The Holy Spirit is—Forgiveness

'Behold! In the Visions of Elohim Jehovah, behold Joseph
    and Mary,
And be comforted, O Jerusalem, in the Visions of Jehovah
    Elohim.'

She looked and saw Joseph, the Carpenter in Nazareth,
and Mary

His espoused wife. And Mary said, 'If thou put me away
from thee

Dost thou not murder me?' Joseph spoke in anger and fury,
'Should I

Marry a Harlot and an Adulteress?' Mary answer'd, 'Art
thou more pure

Than thy Maker, who forgiveth Sins and calls again Her
that is Lost?

Tho' She hates, he calls her again in love. I love my dear
Joseph,

But he driveth me away from his presence; yet I hear the
voice of God

In the voice of my Husband. Tho' he is angry for a moment,
he will not

Utterly cast me away. If I were pure, never could I taste the
sweets

Of the Forgiveness of Sins; if I were holy, I never could behold
the tears

Of love of him who loves me in the midst of his anger, in
furnace of fire.'

   'Ah my Mary!' said Joseph, weeping over, and embracing
her closely in

His arms, 'Doth he forgive Jerusalem, and not exact Purity
from her who is

Polluted? I heard a voice in my sleep, and his angel in my
dream,

Saying, "Doth Jehovah forgive a Debt only on condition that
it shall

Be Payed? Doth he forgive Pollution only on conditions of
Purity?

That Debt is not Forgiven! That Pollution is not Forgiven!

Such is the Forgiveness of the Gods, the Moral Virtues
of the

Heathen, whose tender Mercies are Cruelty. But Jehovah's
Salvation

Is without Money and without Price, in the Continual
Forgiveness of Sins,

In the Perpetual Mutual Sacrifice in Great Eternity; for
behold,

There is none that liveth and Sinneth not. And this is the
    Covenant
Of Jehovah: If you Forgive one-another, so shall Jehovah
    Forgive You,
That He Himself may Dwell among You. Fear not then to
    take
To thee Mary thy wife, for she is with Child by the Holy
    Ghost".'
  Then Mary burst forth into a Song; she flowed like a
    River of
Many Streams into the arms of Joseph, and gave forth her
    tears of joy
Like many waters.
                      And I heard the voice among
The Reapers, saying, 'Am I Jerusalem the lost Adulteress? or
    am I
Babylon come up to Jerusalem?' And another voice answer'd
    saying,
  'Does the voice of my Lord call me again? Am I pure thro'
    his Mercy
And Pity? Am I become lovely as a Virgin in his sight, who
    am
Indeed a Harlot drunken with the Sacrifice of Idols? Does he
Call her pure as he did in the days of her infancy, when She
Was cast out to the loathing of her person? The Chaldean
    took
Me from my Cradle. The Amalekite stole me away upon his
    Camels
Before I had ever beheld with love the face of Jehovah, or
    known
That there was a God of Mercy. O Mercy, O Divine Hu-
    manity!
O Forgiveness and Pity and Compassion! If I were pure I
    should never
Have known Thee; if I were Unpolluted I should never have
Glorified thy Holiness, or rejoiced in thy great Salvation.'
  Mary leaned her side against Jerusalem. Jerusalem
    recieved
The Infant into her hands, in the visions of Jehovah. Times
    passed on.
Jerusalem fainted over the Cross and Sepulcher.

XXVI

'*I am the Resurrection*'

'Repose on me till the morning of the Grave. I am thy life.'
  Jerusalem replied: 'I am an outcast; Albion is dead;
I am left to the trampling foot and the spurning heel;
A Harlot I am call'd; I am sold from street to street;
I am defac'd with blows and with the dirt of the Prison;
And wilt thou become my Husband, O my Lord and
    Saviour?
Shall Vala bring thee forth? Shall the Chaste be ashamed
    also?
I see the Maternal Line, I behold the seed of the Woman;
Cainah and Ada and Zillah, and Naamah, Wife of Noah,
Shuah's daughter and Tamar and Rahab the Canaanitess,
Ruth the Moabite, and Bathsheba of the daughters of Heth,
Naamah the Ammonite, Zibeah the Philistine, and Mary.
These are the Daughters of Vala, Mother of the Body of death.
But I, thy Magdalen, behold thy Spiritual Risen Body.
Shall Albion arise? I know he shall arise at the Last Day.
I know that in my flesh I shall see God. But Emanations
Are weak; they know not whence they are, nor whither tend.'
  Jesus replied: 'I am the Resurrection and the Life.
I die, and pass the limits of possibility, as it appears
To individual perception. Luvah must be created,
And Vala, for I cannot leave them in the gnawing Grave,
But will prepare a way for my banished-ones to return.
  Come now with me into the villages; walk through all the
    cities;
Tho' thou art taken to prison and judgment, starved in the
    streets,
I will command the cloud to give thee food, and the hard rock
To flow with milk and wine. Tho' thou seest me not a season,
Even a long season, and a hard journey, and a howling
    wilderness,
Tho' Vala's cloud hide thee, and Luvah's fires follow thee,
Only believe and trust in me. Lo! I am always with thee.'
  So spoke the Lamb of God, while Luvah's cloud, reddening
    above

Burst forth in streams of blood upon the heavens, and dark
     night
Involv'd Jerusalem, and the Wheels of Albion's Sons turn'd
     hoarse
Over the Mountains, and the fires blaz'd on Druid Altars,
And the Sun set in Tyburn's Brook, where Victims howl and
     cry.
   But Los beheld the Divine Vision among the flames of the
     furnaces.
Therefore he lived and breathed in hope. But his tears fell
     incessant,
Because his Children were clos'd from him apart, and Eni-
     tharmon
Dividing in fierce pain. Also the Vision of God was clos'd in
     clouds
Of Albion's Spectres, that Los in despair oft sat and often
     ponder'd
On Death Eternal, in fierce shudders upon the mountains of
     Albion
Walking, and in the vales in howlings fierce. Then, to his
     Anvils
Turning, anew began his labours, tho' in terrible pains.

NOTE

From this point onwards the course of the poem seems to become even more disconnected and difficult. Some sub-myths are
given prominence, variations of the main theme, but not always
easily made consistent with one another. The story of the
crucifixion of love (Luvah) through the ages is often prominent.
The Daughters of Albion, accepting Vala the deceiver as their
mother, grow mad in their cruelty to the victim. Some of the
details of their tortures are linked in Blake's mind, not only
with the human sacrifices of Moloch-worshippers or Druids, and
the horrors of all the wars of history, but also with the recent
massacres and wars of the French revolution. The tragedy of
Luvah had been re-enacted in Paris.
   It is clear that Blake had an immense amount of written
material, vision after vision, to draw upon in writing *Jerusalem*,
and that he was unable to fit the pieces together in consecutive
logical form. Maybe he did not try very hard to do so, for he

would have regarded a submission to any rigid logical order as a 'spectral' betrayal of truth and imagination.

What is added in this latter part of the poem consists mostly of fresh statements and illustrations of the great story of Man's pilgrimage, as seen from the temporal and the eternal side. I have omitted a great deal because of its lack of clarity and continuity and its repetitiveness of ideas. What I have retained has still plenty of difficulties, but also much of stimulating value, jewels dropped by the wayside as Blake pursues his journey into the world of imagination, into the *inside* of human experience, opening into infinity.

XXVII

The Dark Hermaphrodite: and Human Miseries

Then all the Daughters of Albion become One before Los, even Vala.
And she put forth her hand upon the Looms, in dreadful howlings,
Till she vegetated into a hungry Stomach and a devouring Tongue.
Her Hand is a Court of Justice; her feet two Armies in Battle;
Storms and Pestilence in her Locks; and in her Loins Earthquake
And Fire and the Ruin of Cities and Nations and Families and Tongues.
She cries: 'The Human is but a Worm, and thou, O Male, thou art
Thyself Female, a Male, a breeder of Seed, a Son and Husband. And lo!
The Human Divine is Woman's Shadow, a Vapor in the summer's heat.
Go, assume Papal dignity, thou Spectre, thou Male Harlot. Arthur,
Divide into the Kings of Europe in times remote, O Womanborn

And Woman-nourish'd and Woman-educated and Woman-
scorn'd!'
'Wherefore art thou living?' said Los, 'and Man cannot
live in thy presence.
All Quarrels arise from Reasoning. The secret Murder and
The violent Man-slaughter, these are the Spectre's double
Cave,
The Sexual Death, living on accusation of Sin and Judgment,
To freeze Love and Innocence into the gold and silver of the
Merchant.
Without Forgiveness of Sin, Love is itself Eternal Death.'
Then the Spectre drew Vala into his bosom, magnificent,
terrific,
Glittering with precious stones and gold, with Garments of
blood and fire.
He wept in deadly wrath of the Spectre, in self-contradicting
agony,
Crimson with wrath and green with Jealousy, dazzling with
Love
And Jealousy mingled.
A dark Hermaphrodite they stood, frowning, upon Lon-
don's River,
And the Distaff and Spindle in the hands of Vala, with the
Flax of
Human Miseries, turn'd fierce with the lives of Men along
the valley.
In the depths of Albion's bosom, in the eastern heaven,
They sound the clarions strong, they chain the howling
Captives,
They cast lots into the helmet, they give the oath of blood in
Lambeth,
They vote the death of Luvah, and they nail'd him to Albion's
Tree in Bath,
They stain'd him with poisonous blue, they inwove him in
cruel roots,
To die a death of six thousand years, bound round with
vegetation.
The sun was black and the moon roll'd a useless globe thro'
Britain.
Then left the Sons of Urizen the plow and harrow, the
loom,

The hammer and the chisel and the rule and compasses.
From London fleeing,
They forg'd the sword on Cheviot, the chariot of war and the
battle-axe,
The trumpet fitted to mortal battle; and the flute of summer
in Annandale,
And all the Arts of Life, they chang'd into the Arts of Death
in Albion.
The hour-glass contemn'd because its simple workmanship
Was like the workmanship of the plowman; and the water-
wheel
That raises water into cisterns, broken and burn'd with fire,
Because its workmanship was like the workmanship of the
shepherd.
And in their stead, intricate wheels invented, wheel without
wheel,
To perplex youth in their outgoings, and to bind to labours
in Albion
Of day and night the myriads of eternity, that they may
grind
And polish brass and iron, hour after hour, laborious task,
Kept ignorant of its use; that they might spend the days of
wisdom
In sorrowful drudgery to obtain a scanty pittance of bread;
In ignorance to view a small portion, and think that All,
And call it Demonstration!—blind to all the simple rules of
life.
  'Now, now the battle rages, round thy tender limbs, O
Vala!
Now smile among thy bitter tears; now put on all thy beauty.
Is not the wound of the sword sweet, and the broken bone
delightful?
Wilt thou now smile among the scythes, when the wounded
groan in the field?
  We were carried away in thousands from London, and in
tens
Of thousands from Westminster and Marybone, in ships
closed up,
Chain'd hand and foot, compelled to fight under the iron
whips
Of our captains, fearing our officers more than the enemy.

Lift up thy blue eyes, Vala, and put on thy sapphire shoes,
Scatter the blood from thy golden brow, the tears from thy
silver locks;
Shake off the waters from thy wings, and the dust from thy
white garments.
Remember all thy feigned terrors on the secret couch of
Lambeth's Vale
When the sun rose in glowing morn with arms of mighty
hosts
Marching to battle, who was wont to rise with Urizen's harps,
Girt as a sower with his seed, to scatter life abroad over
Albion.
Arise, O Vala! Bring the bow of Urizen, bring the swift
arrows of light.
How raged the golden horses of Urizen, compelled to the
chariot of love!
Compell'd to leave the plow to the ox, to snuff up the winds
of desolation,
To trample the corn fields in boastful neighings. This is no
gentle harp,
This is no warbling brook, nor shadow of a mirtle tree,
But blood and wounds and dismal cries, and shadows of the
oak;
And hearts laid open to the light by the broad, grizly sword,
And bowels, hid in hammer'd steel, ripp'd quivering on the
ground.
Call forth thy smiles of soft deceit; call forth thy cloudy tears.
We hear thy sighs in trumpets shrill, when morn shall blood
renew.'
  So sang the Spectre sons of Albion, round Luvah's Stone
of Trial,
Mocking and deriding at the writhings of their Victim.

XXVIII

The Self-tormented

While they rejoice over Luvah in mockery and bitter scorn
Sudden they become like what they behold, in howlings and
deadly pain.
Spasms smite their features, sinews and limbs. Pale they look
on one another;
They turn, contorted; their iron necks bend unwilling
towards
Luvah; their lips tremble; their muscular fibres are cramp'd
and smitten;
They become like what they behold!
Yet, immense in strength and power,
In awful pomp and gold, in all the precious unhewn stones
of Eden,
They build a stupendous building on the Plain of Salisbury,
with chains
Of rocks round London Stone, of Reasonings, of unhewn
Demonstrations,
In labyrinthine arches (mighty Urizen the Architect) thro'
which
The Heavens might revolve, and Eternity be bound in their
chain.
Labour unparallell'd! A wondrous rocky World of cruel
destiny,
Rocks piled on rocks, reaching the stars, stretching from pole
to pole.
The building is Natural Religion, and its altars Natural
Morality,
A building of eternal death, whose proportions are eternal
despair.
Here Vala stood, turning the iron spindle of destruction
From heaven to earth.
    The Daughters of Albion, clothed in garments of needle
    work,
Strip them off from their shoulders and bosoms. They lay
aside
Their garments, they sit naked upon the Stone of trial.

The knife of flint passes over the howling Victim. His blood
Gushes, and stains the fair side of the fair Daughters of Albion.
They put aside his curls, they divide his seven locks upon
His forehead, they bind his forehead with thorns of iron,
They put into his hand a reed, they mock, sayjng, 'Behold
The King of Canaan whose are seven hundred chariots of
    iron!'
They take off his vesture whole, with their knives of flint,
But they cut asunder his inner garments, searching with
Their cruel fingers for his heart; and there they enter in pomp,
In many tears, and there they erect a temple and an altar.
They pour cold water on his brain in front, to cause
Lids to grow over his eyes, in veils of tears, and caverns
To freeze over his nostils.
    Ah! Alas! at the sight of the Victim, and at sight of those
        who are smitten,
All who see become what they behold. Their eyes are cover'd
With veils of tears, and their nostrils and tongues shrunk up,
Their ear bent out wards. As their Victim, so are they; in the
        pangs
Of unconquerable fear, amidst delights of revenge earth-
    shaking.
And as their eye and ear shrunk, the heavens shrunk away.
The Divine Vision became first a burning flame, then a
    column
Of fire, then an awful fiery wheel surrounding earth and
    heaven,
And then a globe of blood, wandering distant in an unknown
    night.
Afar into the unknown night the mountains fled away.
    The Human Form began to be alter'd by the Daughters
        of Albion
And the perceptions to be dissipated into the Indefinite,
    becoming
A mighty Polypus, nam'd Albion's Tree.
    They look forth; the Sun is shrunk; the Heavens are shrunk
Away into the far remote; and the Trees and Mountains
    wither'd
Into indefinite cloudy shadows, in darkness and separation.
By invisible Hatreds adjoin'd, they seem remote and separate
From each other—and yet are a mighty Polypus in the Deep!

As the mistletoe grows on the oak, so Albion's Tree upon
Eternity. Lo!
He who will not commingle in Love must be adjoined by
Hate.
  Plinlimmon shrunk away; Snowdon trembled; the moun-
tains
Of Wales and Scotland beheld the descending War, the
routed flying;
Red run the streams of Albion; Thames is drunk with blood,
The Humber and the Severn are drunk with the blood of the
slain.
The Sun forgets his course. Like a drunken man he hesitates
Upon the Cheseldon hills, thinking to sleep on the Severn.
In vain! He is hurried afar into an unknown Night.
He bleeds, in torrents of blood, as he rolls thro' heaven above.
He chokes up the paths of the sky. The Moon is leprous as
snow,
Trembling, and descending down, seeking to rest on high
Mona,
Scattering her leprous snows in flakes of disease over Albion.
The Stars flee remote. The heaven is iron. The earth is
sulphur.
And all the mountains and hills shrink up, like a withering
gourd,
As the Senses of Men shrink together under the knife of flint
In the hands of Albion's Daughters, among the Druid
Temples.

XXIX

The Torments of Love and Desire

And the Twelve Daughters of Albion united in Rahab and
Tirzah,
A Double Female. And they drew out from the Rocky Stones
Fibres of Life to weave; for every Female is a Golden Loom.
The Rocks are opake hardnesses covering all Vegetated
things.

They cut the fibres from the Rocks; groaning in pain they
    Weave,
Calling the Rocks Atomic Origins of Existence; denying
    Eternity
By the Atheistical, Epicurean Philosophy of Albion's Tree.
They call the Rocks Parents of Men, and adore the frowning
    Chaos,
Dancing around in howling pain, clothed in the bloody Veil,
Hiding Albion's Sons within the Veil, closing Jerusalem's
Sons without; to feed with their Souls the Spectres of Albion;
Ashamed to give love openly to the piteous and merciful
    Man,
Counting him an imbecile mockery; but the Warrior
They adore, and his revenge cherish, with the blood of the
    Innocent.
                             Loud the Warriors rage
Beneath the iron whips of their Captains, and consecrated
    banners;
Loud the Sun and Moon rage in the conflict; loud the Stars
Shout in the night of battle; and their spears grow to their
    hands
With blood, weaving the deaths of the mighty into—a
    Tabernacle
For Rahab and Tirzah; till the Great Polypus of Generation
    covered the Earth.
In Verulam the Polypus's Head; winding around his bulk
Thro' Rochester and Chichester and Exeter and Salisbury
To Bristol; and his Heart beat strong on Salisbury Plain,
Shooting out Fibres round the Earth, thro' Gaul and Italy
And Greece, and along the Sea of Rephaim into Judea,
To Sodom and Gomorrha; thence to India, China and
    Japan.
  Tirzah sits weeping to hear the shrieks of the dying; her
    Knife
Of flint is in her hand; she passes it over the howling Victim.
'O thou poor Human Form!' said she, 'O thou poor child of
    woe!
Why wilt thou wander away from Tirzah? Why me compel
    to bind thee?
If thou dost go away from me, I shall consume upon these
    Rocks.

These fibres of thine eyes, that used to beam in distant
    heavens
Away from me, I have bound down with a hot iron.
These nostrils, that expanded with delight in morning skies,
I have bent downward with lead melted in my roaring
    furnaces
Of affliction, of love, of sweet despair, of torment unendurable.
Come, circumscribe this tongue of sweets, and with a screw
    of iron
Fasten this ear into the rock.
Weep not so, Sisters, weep not so! Our life depends on this,
Or mercy and truth are fled away from Shechem and Mount
    Gilead,
Unless my beloved is bound down upon the Stems of
    Vegetation.'
    And thus the Warriors cry, in the hot day of Victory, in
    Songs:
'Look! the beautiful Daughter of Albion sits naked upon the
    Stone,
Her panting Victim beside her. Her heart is drunk with blood,
Tho' her brain is not drunk with wine. She goes forth from
    Albion
In pride of beauty, in cruelty of holiness, in the brightness
Of her tabernacle and her ark and secret place; the beautiful
    Daughter
Of Albion delights the eyes of the Kings; their hearts and the
Hearts of their Warriors glow hot before Thor and Friga.
    O Molech!
O Chemosh! O Bacchus! O Venus! O Double God of
    Generation!
    Why trembles the Warrior's limbs, when he beholds thy
    beauty,
Spotted with Victims' blood, by the fires of thy secret taber-
    nacle
And thy ark and holy place? At thy frowns, at thy dire
    revenge,
Smitten as Uzzah of old, his armour is soften'd, his spear
And sword faint in his hand.
                    I am drunk with unsatiated love,
I must rush again to War, for the Virgin has frown'd and
    refus'd.

Sometimes I curse, and sometimes bless thy fascinating
  beauty.
Once Man was occupied in intellectual pleasures and
  energies,
But now my Soul is harrow'd with grief and fear and love and
  desire,
And now I hate, and now I love; and Intellect is no more.
There is no time for anything but the torments of love and
  desire.'

XXX

A mighty, threatening Form

Then all the Males conjoined in One Male, and every one
Became a ravening, eating cancer growing in the Female,
A Polypus of Roots of Reasoning, Doubt, Despair and Death,
Going forth and returning from Albion's Rocks to Canaan,
Devouring Jerusalem from every Nation of the Earth.
  Envying stood the enormous Form, at variance with Itself
In all its Members, in eternal torment of love and jealousy,
Driven forth by Los time after time from Albion's cliffy shore,
Drawing the free loves of Jerusalem into infernal bondage,
That they might be born in contentions of Chastity, and in
Deadly hate between Leah and Rachel, Daughters of deceit
  and Fraud,
Bearing the Images of various species of Contention
And Jealousy and Abhorrence and Revenge and deadly
  Murder,
Till they refuse liberty to the male; and not like Beulah
Where every Female delights to give her maiden to her hus-
  band.
The Female searches sea and land for gratifications to the
Male Genius, who in return clothes her in gems and gold,
And feeds her with the food of Eden; hence all her beauty
  beams.
She Creates, at her will, a little moony night and silence,
With Spaces of sweet gardens, and a tent of elegant beauty,
Closed in by a sandy desart, and a night of stars shining,

And a little tender moon, and hovering angels on the wing.
And the Male gives a Time and Revolution to her space,
Till the time of love is passed in ever varying delights.
For All Things Exist in the Human Imagination;
And thence in Beulah they are stolen in secret amorous theft,
Till they have had punishment enough to make them commit
    Crimes.
Hence rose the Tabernacle in the Wilderness and all its
    offerings,
From Male and Female Loves in Beulah and their Jealousies.
But no one can consummate Female bliss in Los's World
    without
Becoming a Generated Mortal, a Vegetating Death.
And now the Spectres of the Dead awake in Beulah. All
The Jealousies become Murderous, uniting together in
    Rahab,
A Religion of Chastity, forming a Commerce to sell Loves,
With Moral Law an Equal Balance, not going down with
    decision.
Therefore the Male, severe and cruel, fill'd with stern
    Revenge,
Mutual Hate returns, and mutual Deceit and mutual fear.
  Hence the Infernal Veil grows in the disobedient Female,
Which Jesus rends, and the whole Druid Law removes away
From the Inner Sanctuary, a false Holiness hid within the
    Center.
For the Sanctuary of Eden is in the Camp, in the Outline,
In the Circumference, and every Minute Particular is Holy.
Embraces are Comminglings from the Head even to the
    Feet,
And not a pompous High Priest entering by a Secret Place.
  And this the form of mighty Hand, sitting on Albion's cliffs
Before the face of Albion, a mighty, threat'ning Form.
His bosom wide and shoulders huge, overspreading won-
    drous,
Bear Three strong, sinewy Necks, and Three awful and
    terrible Heads,
Three Brains, in contradictory council brooding incessantly,
Neither daring to put in act its councils, fearing each other,
Therefore rejecting Ideas as nothing, and holding all Wisdom
To consist in the agreements and disagreements of Ideas,

Plotting to devour Albion's Body of Humanity and Love.
Imputing Sin and Righteousness to Individuals, Rahab
Sat, deep within him hid, his Feminine Power unreveal'd,
Brooding Abstract Philosophy, to destroy Imagination, the Divine-
Humanity. Her Brain enlabyrinths the whole heaven of her bosom and loins,
To put in act what her Heart wills. O who can withstand her power?
Her name is Vala in Eternity; in time her name is Rahab.

XXXI

What is Above is Within

The Starry Heavens all were fled from the mighty limbs of Albion.
And above Albion's Land was seen the Heavenly Canaan,
As the Substance is to the Shadow; and above Albion's Twelve Sons
Were seen Jerusalem's Sons, and all the Twelve Tribes spreading
Over Albion. As the Soul is to the Body, so Jerusalem's Sons
Are to the Sons of Albion; and Jerusalem is Albion's Emanation.
   What is Above is Within, for everything in Eternity is translucent.
The Circumference is Within; Without is formed the Selfish Center;
And the Circumference still expands, going forward to Eternity;
And the Center has Eternal States; these States we now explore.
   And these the names of Albion's Twelve Sons, and of his Twelve Daughters,
With their districts: Hand dwelt in Selsey, and had Sussex and Surrey
And Kent and Middlesex, all their Rivers and their Hills of flocks and herds

Their Villages, Towns, Cities, Sea-Ports, Temples, Sublime
  Cathedrals.
All were his Friends, and their Sons and Daughters inter-
  marry in Beulah.
For all are Men in Eternity, Rivers, Mountains, Cities,
  Villages;
All are Human, and when you enter into their Bosoms you
  walk
In Heavens and Earths, as in your own Bosom you bear your
  Heaven
And Earth. And all you behold, tho' it appears without, it is
  Within,
In your Imagination, of which this World of Mortality is
  but a Shadow.

(Here followed thirty-six lines describing how all the English
counties were assigned to the particular sons and daughters of
Albion.)

　　And Los shouted with ceaseless shoutings, and his tears
  poured down
His immortal cheeks, rearing his hands to heaven for aid
  Divine!
But he spoke not to Albion, fearing lest Albion should turn
  his back
Against the Divine Vision, and fall over the Precipice of
  Eternal Death;
But he receded before Albion, and before Vala weaving the
  Veil
With the iron shuttle of War, among the rooted Oaks of
  Albion;
Weeping and shouting to the Lord day and night; and his
  Children
Wept around him.
　　Where Luvah's World of Opakeness grew to a period, it
Became a Limit, a Rocky hardness, without form and void,
Accumulating without end. Here Los, who is of the Elohim,
Opens the furnaces of affliction, in the Emanation,
Fixing the Sexual into an ever-prolific Generation,
Naming the Limit of Opakeness, Satan, and the Limit of
  Contraction, Adam.

Voltaire insinuates that these Limits are the cruel work of
    God,
Mocking the Remover of Limits, and the Resurrection of the
    Dead,
Setting up Kings in wrath, in holiness of Natural Religion,
(which Los with his mighty Hammer demolishes time on
    time
In miracles and wonders in the four-fold Desart of Albion),
Permanently Creating (to be in Time reveal'd and demol-
    ish'd)
Satan, Cain, Tubal, Nimrod, Pharoh, Priam, Bladud, Belin,
Arthur, Alfred, the Norman Conqueror, Richard, John,
And all the Kings and Nobles of the Earth and all their
    Glories.
These are Created by Rahab and Tirzah, in Ulro. But,
    around
These, to preserve them from Eternal Death, Los Creates
Adam, Noah, Abraham, Moses, Samuel, David, Ezekiel,
Dissipating the rocky forms of Death by his thunderous
    Hammer.
As the Pilgrim passes, while the Country permanent remains,
So Men pass on, but States remain permanent for ever.
    The Spectres of the Dead howl round the porches of Los,
In the terrible Family feuds of Albion's cities and villages,
To devour the Body of Albion, hung'ring and thirsting and
    rav'ning.
The Sons of Los clothe them, and feed, and provide houses
    and gardens.
And every Human Vegetated Form in its inward recesses
Is a house of pleasantness, and a garden of delight, built by
    the
Sons and Daughters of Los.
    And the four Zoas are Urizen and Luvah and Tharmas
    and Urthona,
In opposition deadly; and their Wheels in poisonous
And deadly stupor turn'd against each other, loud and fierce.
Entering into the Reasoning Power, forsaking Imagination,
They became Spectres; and their Human Bodies were
    reposed
In Beulah by the Daughters of Beulah, with tears and
    lamentations.

The Spectre is the Reasoning Power in man, and when separated
From Imagination, and closing itself, as in steel, in a Ratio
Of the Things of Memory, It thence frames Laws and Moralities
To destroy Imagination, the Divine Body, by Martyrdoms and Wars.
  Teach me, O Holy Spirit, The Testimony of Jesus! Let me
Comprehend Wonderous things out of the Divine Law.
I behold Babylon in the opening Streets of London. I behold
Jerusalem in ruins, wandering about from house to house.
This I behold; the shudderings of death attend my steps.
I walk up and down in Six Thousand Years; their Events are present before me;
To tell how Los, in grief and anger, whirling his Hammer on high,
Drave the Sons and Daughters of Albion from their ancient mountains.
They became the Twelve Gods of Asia, Opposing the Divine Vision.
  And Rahab, Babylon the Great, hath destroyed Jerusalem,
And all her Twenty-seven Heavens, now hid and now reveal'd,
Appear in strong delusive light of Time and Space, drawn out
In shadowy pomp, by the Eternal Prophet created evermore.
For Los in Six Thousand Years walks up and down continually,
That not one Moment of Time be lost, and every revolution
Of Space he makes permanent.
                                   Thus Rahab is revealed,
Mystery, Babylon the Great, the Abomination of Desolation,
Religion hid in War, a Dragon red and hidden Harlot.
But Jesus, breaking thro' the Central Zones of Death and Hell,
Opens Eternity in Time and Space, Triumphant in Mercy!

  But now the Starry Heavens are fled from the mighty limbs of Albion.

XXXII

Los fights on. Jerusalem mourns in Exile

The Spectres of Albion's Twelve Sons revolve mightily
Over the Tomb and over the Body, rav'ning to devour
The Sleeping Humanity. Los, with his mace of iron,
Walks round. Loud his threats; loud his blows fall
On the rocky Spectres, as the Potter breaks the potsherds,
Dashing in pieces Self-righteousnesses, driving them from
    Albion's
Cliffs. Loud howl the Spectres in his iron Furnace.

While Los laments at his dire labours, viewing Jerusalem
Sitting before his Furnaces clothed in sackcloth of hair,
Albion's Twelve Sons surround the Forty-two gates of Erin
In terrible armour, raging against the Lamb and against
    Jerusalem,
Surrounding them with armies, to destroy the Lamb of God.
They took their Mother Vala and they crown'd her with
    gold.
They named her Rahab, and gave her power over the Earth,
Even to the stars exalting her Throne, to build beyond the
    Throne
Of God and the Lamb, to destroy the Lamb, and usurp the
    Throne of God,
Drawing their Ulro Voidness round the Four-fold Humanity.
  Naked Jerusalem lay, before the Gates upon Mount Zion,
The Hill of Giants, all her foundations levell'd with the dust,
Her Twelve Gates thrown down, her children carried into
    captivity,
Herself in chains;
And thus her voice went forth in the darkness of Philisthea:
                'God hath forsaken me!
The arrows of the Almighty pour upon me and my children!
I have sinned, and am an outcast from the Divine Presence!
My tents are fall'n! My pillars are in ruins! My children
    dash'd
Upon Egypt's iron floors and the marble pavements of Assyria.
I melt my soul in reasonings among the towers of Heshbon.

Mount Zion is become a cruel rock, and no more dew
Nor rain, no more the spring of the rock appears, but cold
Hard and obdurate are the furrows of the mountain of wine
    and oil.
The mountain of blessing is itself a curse and an astonishment.
The hills of Judea are fallen with me into the deepest hell.
Away from the Nations of the Earth, and from the Cities of
    the Nations,
I walk to Ephraim; I seek for Shiloh; I walk like a lost sheep
Among precipices of despair; in Goshen I seek for light
In vain, and in Gilead for a physician and a comforter.
Goshen hath follow'd Philistia, Gilead hath joined with Og.
They are become narrow places in a little and dark land,
How distant far from Albion! His hills and his valleys no
    more
Receive the feet of Jerusalem. They have cast me quite away,
And Albion is himself shrunk to a narrow rock, in the midst
    of the sea!
The plains of Sussex and Surrey, their hills of flocks and herds
No more seek to Jerusalem, nor to the sound of my Holy-ones.
The fifty-two Counties of England are harden'd against me,
As if I was not their Mother; they despise and cast me out.
   London cover'd the whole Earth; England encompass'd
    the Nations,
And all the Nations of the Earth were seen in the Cities of
    Albion.
My pillars reach'd from sea to sea. London beheld me come
From my east and from my west. He blessed me and gave
His children to my breasts, his sons and daughters to my
    knees.
His aged parents sought me out in every city and village;
They discern'd my countenance with joy; they shew'd me to
    their sons,
Saying, 'Lo, Jerusalem is here! She sitteth in our secret
    chambers.
Levi and Judah and Issachar, Ephraim, Manasseh, Gad
    and Dan
Are seen in our hills and valleys; they keep our flocks and
    herds,
They watch them in the night; and the Lamb of God appears
    among us!'

The river Severn stay'd his course at my command;
Thames poured his waters into my basons and baths;
Medway mingled with Kishon; Thames receiv'd the heavenly
Jordan.
  Albion gave me to the whole Earth, to walk up and down,
  to pour
Joy upon every mountain, to teach songs to the shepherd and
plowman.
I taught the ships of the sea to sing the songs of Zion.
Italy saw me, in sublime astonishment; France was wholly
mine,
As my garden and as my secret bath; Spain was my heavenly
couch;
I slept in his golden hills; the Lamb of God met me there;
There we walked, as in our secret chamber, among our little
ones.
They looked upon our loves with joy; they beheld our secret
joys
With holy raptures of adoration—rap'd sublime in the
Visions of God.
Germany, Poland, and the North, wooed my footsteps; they
found
My gates in all their mountains, and my curtains in all their
vales.
The furniture of their houses was the furniture of my chamber.
Turkey and Grecia saw my instruments of music; they
arose,
They seiz'd the harp, the flute, the mellow horn of Jerusalem's
joy.
They sounded thanksgivings in my courts. Egypt and Lybia
heard;
The swarthy sons of Ethiopia stood round the Lamb of God,
Enquiring for Jerusalem; he led them up my steps to my
altar.
And thou, America! I once beheld thee, but now behold no
more
Thy golden mountains, where my Cherubim and Seraphim
rejoic'd
Together among my little-ones. But now my Altars run with
blood,
My fires are corrupt, my incense is a cloudy pestilence

Of seven diseases! Once a continual cloud of salvation rose
From all my myriads. Once the Four-fold World rejoic'd
    among
The pillars of Jerusalem, between my winged Cherubim;
But now I am clos'd out from them, in the narrow passages
Of the valleys of destruction, into a dark land of pitch and
    bitumen,
From Albion's Tomb afar; and from the four-fold wonders of
    God
Shrunk to a narrow doleful form in the dark land of Cabul.
I walk and count the bones of my beloveds
Along the Valley of Destruction, among these Druid Temples,
Which overspread all the Earth in patriarchal pomp and
    cruel pride.

XXXIII

Vala also Suffers and Laments

'Tell me, O Vala, thy purposes; tell me wherefore thy
    shuttles
Drop with the gore of the slain; why Euphrates is red with
    blood;
Wherefore in dreadful majesty and beauty, outside, appears
Thy Masculine from thy Feminine, hardening against the
    heavens
To devour the Human! Why dost thou weep upon the wind,
    among
Those cruel Druid Temples? O Vala! Humanity is far above
Sexual organization, and the Visions of the Light of Beulah,
Where Sexes wander in dreams of bliss among the Emana-
    tions;
Where the Masculine and Feminine are nurs'd into Youth
    and Maiden
By the tears and smiles of Beulah's Daughters, till the time of
    Sleep is past.
Wherefore then do you realize these nets of beauty and
    delusion
In open day, to draw the souls of the Dead into the light,

Till Albion is shut out from every Nation under Heaven,
Encompass'd by the frozen Net and by the rooted Tree.'
  Beside her Vala howl'd upon the winds, in pride of beauty,
Lamenting among the timbrels of the Warriors, among the
    Captives,
In cruel holiness; and her lamenting songs were from Arnon
And Jordan to Euphrates. Jerusalem follow'd, trembling,
Her children in captivity, listening to Vala's lamentation
In the thick cloud and darkness. And the voice went forth
    from
The cloud: 'O rent in sunder from Jerusalem, the Harlot
    daughter,
In an eternal condemnation, in fierce burning flames
Of torment unendurable! And if once a Delusion be found
Woman must perish, and the Heavens of Heavens remain no
    more!
  My Father gave to me command to murder Albion
In unreviving death; my Love, my Luvah, order'd me in
    night
To murder Albion, the King of Men.
                        Luvah fram'd the knife and Luvah gave
The Knife into his daughter's hand. Such a thing was never
    known
Before in Albion's land, that one should die a death never to
    be reviv'd!
For, in our battles, we the Slain men view with pity and
    love;
We soon revive them in the secret of our tabernacles.
But I, Vala, Luvah's daughter, keep his body embalm'd in
    moral laws
With spices of sweet odours of lovely jealous stupefaction,
Within my bosom, lest he arise to life and slay my Luvah.
Pity me then, O Lamb of God! O Jesus, pity me!
Come into Luvah's Tents, and seek not to revive the Dead!'
  So sang she, and the Spindle turn'd furious as she sang.
The Children of Jerusalem, the Souls of those who sleep,
Were caught into the flax of her Distaff and in her Cloud,
To weave Jerusalem a body according to her will,
A Dragon form on Zion Hill's most ancient promontory.
The Spindle turn'd in blood and fire: loud sound the trum-
    pets

Of war; the cymbals play loud before the Captains.
  The Serpent Temples thro' the Earth, from the wide Plain
    of Salisbury,
Resound with cries of Victims, shouts and songs and dying
    groans.
And Rahab, like a dismal and indefinite hovering Cloud,
Refus'd to take a definite form. She hover'd over all the
    Earth,
Calling the definite, sin, defacing every definite form
Invisible or Visible; stretch'd out in length or spread in
    breadth
Over the Temples, drinking groans of victims, weeping in
    pity
And joying in the pity, howling over Jerusalem's walls.

XXXIV

*Interlude. Cambel and Gwendolen, daughters of Albion: their
Pride, Jealousy and Repentance*

This rather complicated sub-myth, which interrupts the main
narrative, is omitted.

XXXV

*Los dedicates himself afresh to the salvation of Albion, and calls
on his fellow-workers for aid*

  Los saw, and was comforted at his Furnaces, uttering thus
    his voice:
'I know I am Urthona, keeper of the Gates of Heaven,
And that I can at will expatiate in the Gardens of bliss;
But pangs of love draw me down to my loins, which are
Become a fountain of veiny pipes. O Albion! my brother!
Corruptibility appears upon thy limbs, and never more
Can I arise and leave thy side, but labour here incessant
Till thy awaking. Yet alas, I shall forget Eternity!
Against the Patriarchal pomp and cruelty labouring incessant

I shall become an Infant horror. O Albion, my brother!
Jerusalem hungers in the desert.
The scorn'd and contemn'd youthful girl, where shall she fly?
Sussex shuts up her villages; Hants, Devon and Wilts
Surrounded with masses of stone in order'd forms. Determine
    then
A Form for Vala and a Form for Luvah, here on the Thames,
Where the Victim nightly howls beneath the Druid's knife;
A Form of Vegetation; nail them down on the stems of
    Mystery.
O when shall the Saxon return with the English, his redeemed
    brother?
O when shall the Lamb of God descend among the Repro-
    bate?
Woden and Thor and Friga wholly consume my Saxons
On their enormous altars built in the terrible north.
    Found ye London! Enormous city, weeps thy River?
Upon his parent bosom lay thy little ones, O land
Forsaken! Surrey and Sussex are Enitharmon's Chamber,
Where I will build her a Couch of repose, and my pillars
Shall surround her in beautiful labyrinths.
    Let Cambel and her Sisters sit within the Mundane shell,
Forming the fluctuating Globe according to their will.
According as they weave the little embryon nerves and veins,
The Eye, the little Nostrils and the delicate Tongue, and
    Ears
Of labyrinthine intricacy, so shall they fold the World;
That whatever is seen upon the Mundane Shell, the same
Be seen upon the fluctuating Earth, woven by the sisters.
And sometimes the Earth shall roll in the Abyss, and some-
    times
Stand in the Center, and sometimes stretch flat in the Ex-
    panse,
According to the will of the lovely Daughters of Albion.
Sometimes it shall assimilate with mighty Golgonooza,
Touching its summits; and sometimes, divided, roll apart.
As a beautiful Veil, so these Females shall fold and unfold,
According to their will, the outside surface of the Earth,
An outside shadowy surface, superadded to the real Surface,
Which is unchangeable for ever and ever. Amen, so be it!
    Separate Albion's Sons gently from their Emanations,

Weaving bowers of delight on the current of infant Thames,
Where the old Parent still retains his youth. As I, alas!
Retain my youth eight thousand and five hundred years,
The labourer of ages in the Valleys of Despair!
    The land is mark'd for desolation, and unless we plant
The seeds of Cities and of Villages in the Human bosom
Albion must be a rock of blood. Mark ye the points
Where Cities shall remain, and where Villages. For the rest,
It must lie in confusion till Albion's time of awaking.
Place the Tribes of Llewellyn in America, for a hiding place,
Till sweet Jerusalem emanates again into Eternity.
    The night falls thick: I go upon my watch: be attentive.
The Sons of Albion go forth. I follow from my Furnaces,
That they return no more, that a place be prepar'd on
    Euphrates.
Listen to your Watchman's voice. Sleep not before the
    Furnaces.
Eternal Death stands at the door. O God, pity our labours!'
    So Los spoke to the Daughters of Beulah, while his Emanation
Like a faint rainbow waved before him, in the awful gloom
Of London City on the Thames, from Surrey hills to High-
    gate.
Swift turn the silver spindles and the golden weights play soft
And lulling harmonies beneath the Looms, from Caithness
    in the north
To Lizard-point and Dover in the south. His Emanation
Joy'd in the many weaving threads in bright Cathedron's
    Dome,
Weaving the Web of life for Jerusalem. The Web of life,
Down-flowing into Entuthon's Vales, glistens with soft
    affections.

XXXVI

Los hears a cry from Babylon, and has a vision of Jerusalem

    Los arose upon his watch and, down from Golgonooza,
Putting on his golden sandals to walk from mountain to
    mountain,

He takes his way, girding himself with gold, and in his hand
Holding his iron mace. The Spectre remains attentive;
Alternate they watch in night, alternate labour in day,
Before the Furnaces labouring, while Los all night watches
The stars rising and setting, and the meteors and terrors of
    night.
  And thus he heard the voice of Albion's daughters on
    Euphrates:
'Our Father Albion's land, O, it was a lovely land! and the
    Daughters of Beulah
Walked up and down in its green mountains. But Hand is fled
Away, and mighty Hyle; and after them Jerusalem is gone.
    Awake!
We builded Jerusalem as a City and a Temple. From
    Lambeth
We began our foundations, lovely Lambeth. O lovely Hills
Of Camberwell, we shall behold you no more in glory and
    pride.
For Jerusalem lies in ruins; and the Furnaces of Los are
    builded there.
You are now shrunk up to a narrow Rock in the midst of the
    Sea.
  But here we build Babylon on Euphrates, compell'd to
    build
And to inhabit, our Little-ones to clothe in armour of the
    gold
Of Jerusalem's Cherubims, and to forge them swords of her
    altars.
I see London, blind and age-bent, begging thro' the Streets
Of Babylon, led by a child; his tears run down his beard.
  The night falls thick. Hand comes from Albion in his
    strength.
He combines into a Mighty-one, the Double Molech and
    Chemosh,
Marching thro' Egypt in his fury. The East is pale at his
    course.
But we woo him all the night in songs. O Los! Come forth,
    O Los!
Divide us from these terrors, and give us power them to
    subdue.
Arise upon thy Watches! Let us see thy Globe of Fire

On Albion's Rocks; and let thy voice be heard upon
   Euphrates.'
Thus sang the Daughters in lamentation.
                              List'ning to their lamentation
Los walks upon his ancient Mountains, in the deadly dark-
   ness,
Among his Furnaces, directing his laborious Myriads, watch-
   ful,
Looking to the East. And his voice is heard over the whole
   Earth,
As he watches the Furnaces by night, and directs the
   labourers.
   And thus Los replies upon his Watch. The Valleys listen
   silent;
The Stars stand still to hear; Jerusalem and Vala cease to
   mourn.
His voice is heard from Albion; the Alps and Appenines
Listen; Hermon and Lebanon bow their crowned heads;
Babel and Shinar look toward the Western Gate, they sit
   down
Silent at his voice. They view the red Globe of Fire in Los's
   hand
As he walks from Furnace to Furnace, directing the
   Labourers.
   And this is the Song of Los, the Song he sings on his
   Watch:
'O lovely, mild Jerusalem! O Shiloh of Mount Ephraim!
I see thy Gates of Precious stones, thy Walls of gold and
   silver.
Thou art the soft reflected Image of the Sleeping Man,
Who, stretch'd on Albion's rocks, reposes among his Twenty-
   eight
Cities, where Beulah lovely terminates in the hills and valleys
   of Albion;
Cities not yet embodied in Time and Space. Plant ye
The Seeds, O Sisters, in the bosom of Time and Space's
   womb,
To spring up for Jerusalem, lovely Shadow of Sleeping
   Albion.
   Why wilt thou rend theyself apart, and build an Earthly
   Kingdom,

To reign in pride and to oppress and to mix the cup of
    Delusion?
O thou that dwellest with Babylon, come forth, O lovely-one!
I see thy form, O lovely mild Jerusalem, wing'd with six
    Wings,
In the opacous Bosom of the Sleeper, lovely, Three-fold
In Head and Heart and Reins, three Universes of Love and
    Beauty.
Thy forehead bright—Holiness to the Lord—with Gates of
    pearl,
Reflects Eternity. Beneath, thy azure wings of feathery down,
Ribb'd, delicate and cloth'd with feather'd gold and azure
    and purple,
From thy white shoulders shadowing purity in holiness;
Thence, feather'd with soft crimson of the ruby, bright as
    fire,
Spreading into the azure, Wings which like a canopy
Bends over thy immortal Head, in which Eternity dwells.
Albion, beloved Land! I see thy mountains and thy hills
And valleys, and thy pleasant cities—Holiness to the Lord.
    Thy Bosom white, translucent, cover'd with immortal
    gems,
A sublime ornament, not obscuring the outlines of beauty,
Terrible to behold for thy extreme beauty and perfection.
Twelve-fold here all the Tribes of Israel I behold,
Upon the Holy Land. I see the River of Life, and Tree of
    Life;
I see the New Jerusalem descending out of Heaven,
Between thy Wings of gold and silver, feather'd, immortal,
Clear as the rainbow, as the cloud of the Sun's tabernacle.
Thy Reins, cover'd with Wings translucent, sometimes
    covering
And sometimes spread abroad, reveal the flames of holiness,
Which like a robe covers, and like a Veil of Seraphim
In flaming fire unceasing burns, from Eternity to Eternity.
Twelve-fold I there behold Israel in her Tents.
A Pillar of Cloud by day, a Pillar of Fire by night
Guides them; there I behold Moab and Ammon and Amalek.
There, Bells of silver round thy knees, living, articulate
Comforting sounds of love and harmony; and on thy feet
Sandals of gold and pearl'.

Thus Los sings upon his Watch, walking from Furnace to
   Furnace.
He seizes his Hammer every hour. Flames surround him as
He beats. Seas roll beneath his feet. Tempests muster
Around his head. The thick hailstones stand ready to obey
His voice in the black cloud. His Sons labour in thunders
At his Furnaces. His Daughters at their Looms sing woes.

XXXVII

The Spectre's last fling. The Jealousies of Enitharmon

Nor can any consummate bliss without being Generated
On Earth, of those whose Emanations weave the loves
Of Beulah for Jerusalem and Shiloh, in immortal Golgonooza,
Concentering in the majestic form of Erin, in eternal tears,
Viewing Los in his shudderings, pouring balm on his sorrows.
So dread is Los's fury that none dare him to approach
Without becoming his Children, in the Furnaces of affliction.
   And Enitharmon like a faint rainbow waved before him,
Filling with Fibres from his loins, which redden'd with desire,
Into a Globe of Blood beneath his bosom, trembling in
   darkness
Of Albion's clouds. He fed it with his tears and bitter groans,
Hiding his Spectre in invisibility from the timorous Shade,
Till it became a separated cloud of beauty, grace and love
Among the darkness of his Furnaces; dividing asunder till
She, separated, stood before him, a lovely Female, weeping,
Even Enitharmon separated outside. And his Loins closed
And heal'd after the separation. His pains he soon forgot,
Lured by her beauty outside of himself, in shadowy grief.
Two wills they had, two Intellects; and not as in times of old.
   Silent they wandered, hand in hand like two Infants, terri-
   fied at each other's beauty,
Envying each other, yet desiring, in all-devouring Love.
   Los first broke silence, and began to utter his love:
'O lovely Enitharmon! I behold thy graceful forms
Moving beside me till, intoxicated with the woven labyrinth

144

Of beauty and perfection, my wild fibres shoot in veins
Of blood thro' all my nervous limbs. Soon, overgrown in
     roots,
I shall be closed from thy sight. Seize therefore in thy hand
The small fibres as they shoot around me; draw out in pity
And let them run on the winds of thy bosom. I will fix them
With pulsations. We will divide them into Sons and
     Daughters,
To live in thy bosom's translucence, as in an eternal morning.'
     Enitharmon answer'd: 'No! I will seize thy Fibres and
     weave
Them, not as thou wilt, but as I will! for I will Create
A round Womb beneath my bosom, lest I also be overwoven
With Love. Be thou assured, I never will be thy slave!
Let Man's delight be Love, but Woman's delight be Pride.
In Eden our Loves were the same; here they are opposite.
I have Loves of my own; I will weave them, in Albion's
     Spectre.
While Jerusalem divides thy care, while thou carest for
     Jerusalem
Know that I never will be thine. Also, thou hidest Vala!
From her these fibres shoot, to shut me in a Grave.
You are Albion's Victim; he has set his Daughter in your
     path!'
     Los answer'd, sighing like the bellows of his furnaces,
'I care not! The swing of my Hammer shall measure the
     starry round.
When, in Eternity, Man converses with Man, they enter
Into each other's Bosom (which are Universes of delight)
In mutual interchange. And first their Emanations meet,
Surrounded by their Children. If they embrace and com-
     mingle,
The Human Four-fold Forms mingle also, in thunders of
     Intellect.
But if the Emanations mingle not, with storms and agitations
Of earthquakes and consuming fires they roll apart, in fear.
For Man cannot unite with Man but by their Emanations,
Which stand both Male and Female at the Gates of Each
     Humanity.
How then can I ever again be united as Man with Man
While thou, my Emanation, refusest my Fibres of dominion?

When Souls mingle and join thro' all the Fibres of Brother-
　　hood
Can there be any secret joy on Earth greater than this?'
　　Enitharmon answer'd: 'This is Woman's World, nor need
　　she any
Spectre to defend her from Man. I will Create secret places;
A triple Female Tabernacle for Moral Law I weave;
That he who loves Jesus may loathe, terrified, Female love,
Till God himself becomes a Male subservient to the Female.'
　　She spoke in scorn and jealousy, alternate torments.
A sullen smile broke from the Spectre, in mockery and scorn,
Knowing himself the author of their divisions and shrinkings.
Gratified at their contentions, he wiped his tears, he wash'd
　　his visage.
'The Man who respects Woman shall be despised by Woman,
And deadly cunning and mean abjectness only shall enjoy them.
For I will make their places of joy and love excrementitious.
Continually building, continually destroying, in family feuds,
While you are under the domination of a jealous Female,
Unpermanent for ever because of love and jealousy,
You shall want all the Minute Particulars of Life.'
　　Thus joy'd the Spectre, in the dusky fires of Los's Forge,
　　eyeing
Enitharmon, who at her Looms sings lulling cadences,
While Los stood at his Anvil in wrath, the victim of their
　　love and hate.
The blow of his Hammer is Justice, the swing of his Hammer
　　Mercy,
The force of Los's Hammer is eternal Forgiveness. But
His rage or his mildness were vain; she scatter'd his love on
　　the wind.

XXXVIII

'The Covering Cherub'—a vision of Antichrist

A terrible, indefinite, Hermaphroditic form,
A Wine-press of Love and Wrath; double, Hermaphroditic,
Twelvefold in Allegoric pomp, in selfish holiness:

Thus was the Covering Cherub reveal'd, majestic image
Of Selfhood, Body put off, the Antichrist accursed;
Covered with precious stones, a Human Dragon, terrible
And bright, stretch'd over Europe and Asia, gorgeous.

His Head, dark, deadly, in its brain incloses a reflexion
Of Eden all perverted; Egypt on the Gihon many-tongued
And many-mouth'd; Ethiopia; Lybia; the Sea of Rephaim.
Minute Particulars in slavery I behold, among the brick-
      kilns
Disorganiz'd. And there is Pharoh in his iron Court,
And the Dragon of the River, and the Furnaces of iron.

His bosom wide reflects Moab and Ammon, on the River
Pison, since called Arnon, There is Heshbon beautiful,
The Rocks of Rabbath on the Arnon, and the Fish-pools of
      Heshbon,
Whose currents flow into the Dead Sea by Sodom and
      Gomorra.

Above his head high arching Wings, black, fill'd with Eyes,
Spring upon iron sinews from the Scapulae and Os Humeri;
There Israel in bondage to his Generalizing Gods,
Molech and Chemosh. And in his left breast is Philistea,
In Druid Temples over the whole Earth with Victim's
      sacrifice,
From Gaza to Damascus, Tyre and Sidon, and the Gods
Of Javan, thro' the Isles of Grecia, and all Europe's Kings,
Where Hiddekel pursues his course among the rocks.
Two Wings spring from his ribs of brass, starry, black as night,
But translucent their blackness, as the dazzling of gems.

His loins enclose Babylon on Euphrates beautiful,
And Rome in sweet Hesperia. There Israel, scatter'd abroad
In martyrdoms and slavery, I behold—ah, vision of sorrow!
Inclosed by eyeless Wings, glowing with fire as the iron
Heated in the Smith's forge, but cold the wind of their dread
      fury.

But in the midst of a devouring Stomach, Jerusalem,
Hidden within the Covering Cherub, as in a Tabernacle
Of threefold workmanship, in allegoric delusion and woe.

A Double Female now appeared within the Tabernacle,
Religion hid in War; a Dragon red and hidden Harlot,
Each within other; but without, a Warlike Mighty-one
Of dreadful power, sitting upon Horeb, pondering dire

And mighty preparations, mustering multitudes innumerable
Of warlike sons, among the sands of Midian and Aram.
For multitudes of those who sleep in Alla descend,
Lured by his warlike symphonies of tabret, pipe and harp;
They become One with the Antichrist and are absorbed in
    him.

xxxix

The Demonstrations of Los

The Feminine separates from the Masculine, and both from
    Man,
Ceasing to be His Emanations, Life to themselves assuming.
                No more the Masculine mingles
With the Feminine, but the Sublime is shut out from the
    Pathos
In howling torment, to build walls of separation, compelling
The Pathos to weave curtains of hiding secrecy from the
    torment.
   Los cries: 'No Individual ought to appropriate to Himself,
Or to his Emanation, any of the Universal Characteristics.
Those who dare appropriate to themselves Universal
    Attributes
Are the blasphemous Selfhoods, and must be broken asunder.
A Vegetated Christ, and a Virgin Eve, are the Hermaphro-
    ditic
Blasphemy. By his Material Birth he is that Evil-one,
And his Maternal Humanity must be put off Eternally,
Lest the Sexual Generation swallow up Regeneration.
Come, Lord Jesus, take on thee the Satanic Body of Holiness.'
   So Los cried, in the valleys of Middlesex, in the Spirit of
    Prophecy,
While in Selfhood Hand and Hyle and Bowen and Skofeld
    appropriate
The Divine Names, seeking to vegetate the Divine Vision
In a corporeal and ever dying Vegetation and Corruption.
   For Los said: 'When the Individual appropriates Univer-
    sality

He divides into Male and Female, and when the Male and
Female
Appropriate Individuality they become an Eternal Death.
Hermaphroditic worshippers of a God of cruelty and law,
Your Slaves and Captives you compel to worship a God of
Mercy!
These are the Demonstrations of Los, and the blows of my
mighty Hammer.'
So Los spoke. And the Giants of Albion, terrified and
ashamed
With Los's thunderous words, began to build trembling
rocking Stones,
Plotting to devour Albion and Los the friend of Albion;
Denying in private, mocking God and Eternal Life; and in
public
Collusion calling themselves Deists, worshipping the Mater-
nal
Humanity, calling it Nature and Natural Religion.
But still the thunder of Los peals loud, and thus the
thunders cry:
'It is easier to forgive an Enemy than to forgive a Friend.
The man who permits you to injure him deserves your
vengeance;
He will also receive it. Go, Spectre; obey my most secret
desire,
Which thou knowest without my speaking. Go to these Fiends
of Righteousness,
Tell them to obey their Humanities and not pretend Holiness
When they are murderers, as far as my Hammer and Anvil
permit.
Go, tell them that the Worship of God is honouring his gifts
In other men, and loving the greatest men best, each
according
To his Genius, which is the Holy Ghost in Man: there is no
other
God than that God who is the intellectual fountain of
Humanity.
He who envies or calumniates (which is murder and cruelty)
Murders the Holy-one. Go, tell them this; and overthrow
their cup.
Their bread, their altar-table, their incense and their oath,

Their marriage and their baptism, their burial and consecra-
tion.
I have tried to make friends by corporeal gifts, but have
only
Made enemies. I never made friends but by spiritual gifts,
By severe contentions of friendship, and the burning fire of
thought.
He who would see the Divinity must see him in his Children,
One first, in friendship and love, then a Divine Family, and
in the midst
Jesus will appear. So he who wishes to see a Vision, a perfect
Whole,
Must see it in its Minute Particulars, organized; and not as
thou,
O Fiend of Righteousness, pretendest. Thine is a disorganised
And snowy cloud, brooder of tempests and destructive War.
You smile with pomp and rigor; you talk of benevolence and
virtue.
I act with bevolence and virtue, and get murder'd time after
time.
You accumulate Particulars, and murder by analyzing, that
you
May take the aggregate: and you call the aggregate Moral
Law,
And you call that swell'd and bloated Form a Minute
Particular!
But General Forms have their vitality in Particulars; and
every
Particular is a Man, a Divine Member of the Divine Jesus.'
So Los cried at his Anvil, in the horrible darkness, weeping.

XL

The Signal of the Morning

The Spectre builded stupendous Works, taking the Starry
Heavens
Like to a curtain, and folding them according to his will;

Repeating the Smaragdine Table of Hermes to draw Los
 down
Into the Indefinite; refusing to believe without demonstra-
 tion.
Los reads the Stars of Albion; the Spectre reads the Voids
Between the Stars, among the arches of Albion's Tomb
 sublime;
Rolling the Sea in rocky paths; forming Leviathan
And Behemoth, the War by Sea enormous and the War
By Land astounding; erecting pillars in the deepest Hell
To reach the heavenly arches. Los beheld, undaunted,
 furious.
His heav'd Hammer, he swung it round, and at one blow
In unpitying ruin driving down the pyramids of pride,
Smiting the Spectre on his Anvil, and the integuments of his
 Eye
And Ear unbinding, in dire pain, with many blows
Of strict severity, self-subduing, and with many tears
 labouring.
  Then he sent forth the Spectre. All his pyramids were
   grains
Of sand, and his pillars dust on the fly's wing, and his starry
Heavens a moth of gold and silver, mocking his anxious
 grasp!
Thus Los alter'd his Spectre; and every Ratio of his reason
He alter'd time after time, with dire pain and many tears,
Till he had completely divided him into a separate space.
  Terrified Los sat to behold, trembling and weeping and
   howling:
'I care not whether a Man is Good or Evil; all that I care
Is whether he is a Wise Man or a Fool. Go, put off Holiness
And put on Intellect, or my thund'rous Hammer shall drive
 thee
To wrath which thou condemnest, till thou obey my voice.'
  'What do I see? The Briton, Saxon, Roman, Norman,
   amalgamating
In my furnaces into One Nation, the English, and taking
 refuge
In the Loins of Albion.
This sinful Nation created in our Furnaces and Looms is
 Albion!'

So Los spoke. Enitharmon answer'd in great terror, in
Lambeth's Vale;
'The Poet's Song draws to its period, and Enitharmon is no
more.
For if he be that Albion, I can never weave him in my Looms,
But when he touches the first fibrous thread, like filmy dew
My Looms will be no more, and I, annihilate, vanish for
ever.
Then thou wilt Create another Female according to thy
will.'
Los answer'd, swift as the shuttle of gold: 'Sexes must
vanish and cease
To be, when Albion arises from his dread repose, O lovely
Enitharmon;
When all their Crimes, their Punishments, their Accusations
of Sin,
All their Jealousies, Revenges, Murders, hidings of Cruelty in
deceit,
Appear only in the Outward Spheres of Visionary Time and
Space,
In the shadows of Possibility, by Mutual Forgiveness for
evermore,
And in the Vision and the Prophecy; that we may foresee
and avoid
The terrors of Creation and Redemption and Judgment.'
Enitharmon heard. She raised her head like the mild
Moon:
'O Rintrah! O Palamabron! What are your dire and awful
purposes?
Enitharmon's name is nothing before you: you forget all my
Love.
The Mother's love of obedience is forgotten, and you seek a
Love
Of the pride of dominion.
Pride meets with Pride upon the mountains in the stormy
day,
In that terrible Day of Rintrah's plow, and of Satan's driving
the Team.
Ah! then I heard my little ones weeping along the Valley,
Ah! then I saw my beloved ones fleeing from my Tent.
How can I hear my little ones weeping along the Valley,

Or how upon the distant hills see my beloveds' Tents?'
  Then Los again took up his speech, as Enitharmon ceast:
'Fear not, my Sons, this Waking Death; he is become One
    with me.
Behold him here! We shall not Die! We shall be united in
    Jesus.
Will you suffer this Satan, this Body of Doubt that Seems but
    Is Not,
To occupy the very threshold of Eternal Life? If Bacon,
    Newton, Locke
Deny a Conscience in Man, and the Communion of Saints
    and Angels
Contemning the Divine Vision and Fruition, Worshipping
    the Deus
Of the Heathen, the God of This World, and the Goddess
    Nature,
Mystery, Babylon the Great, the Druid Dragon and hidden
    Harlot,
Is it not that Signal of the Morning which was told us in the
    Beginning?'

XLI

The Awakening

Albion, cold, lies on his Rock. Storms and Snows beat round
    him,
Beneath the Furnaces and the starry Wheels and the Immor-
    tal Tomb.
Howling winds cover him. Roaring seas dash furious against
    him.
In the deep darkness broad lightnings glare, long thunders
    roll.
The Weeds of Death inwrap his hands and feet, blown inces-
    sant
And wash'd incessant by the for-ever restless sea-waves
    foaming abroad
Upon the white Rock. England, a Female Shadow, as deadly
    damps

Of the Mines of Cornwall and Derbyshire, lies upon his
   bosom, heavy,
Moved by the wind in volumes of thick cloud, returning,
   folding round
His loins and bosom, unremovable by swelling storms and
   loud rending
Of enraged thunders. Around them the Starry Wheels of their
   Giant Sons
Revolve; and over them the Furnaces of Los: and the
   Immortal Tomb around;
Erin sitting in the Tomb to watch them, unceasing, night
   and day;
And the Body of Albion was closed apart from all
   Nations.
Over them the famish'd Eagle screams on bony wings, and
   around
Them howls the Wolf of famine. Deep heaves the Ocean,
   black, thundering
Around the wormy Garments of Albion; then pausing in
   deathlike silence.
   Time was Finished! The Breath Divine Breathed over
   Albion,
Beneath the Furnaces and starry Wheels, and in the Immortal
   Tomb;
And England, who is Britannia, awoke from Death on
   Albion's Bosom.
She awoke, pale and cold; she fainted seven times on the
   Body of Albion.
   'O piteous Sleep! O piteous Dream! O God, O God,
   awake! I have slain
In Dreams of Chastity and Moral Law, I have murdered
   Albion! Ah!
In Stonehenge and on London Stone and in the Oak Groves
   of Malden
I have slain him in my Sleep, with the Knife of the Druid. O
   England,
O all ye Nations of the Earth, behold ye the Jealous Wife!'
   Her voice pierc'd Albion's clay-cold ear. He moved upon
   the Rock.
The Breath Divine went forth upon the morning hills. Albion
   mov'd

Upon the Rock. He open'd his eyelids in pain, in pain he mov'd
His stony Members. He saw England; Ah! shall the Dead live again?
  The Breath Divine went forth over the morning hills. Albion rose
In anger; the wrath of God, breaking bright, flaming on all sides around
His awful limbs. Into the Heavens he walked, clothed in flames,
Loud thund'ring, with broad flashes of flaming lightning and pillars
Of fire; speaking the Words of Eternity in Human Forms, in direful
Revolutions of Action and Passion, thro' the Four Elements on all sides
Surrounding his awful Members.
  Thou seest the Sun, in heavy clouds
Struggling to rise above the Mountains. In his burning hand
He takes his Bow, then chooses out his arrows of flaming gold.
Murmuring the Bowstring breathes with ardour! Clouds roll round the
Horns of the wide Bow; loud sounding winds sport on the mountain brows,
Compelling Urizen to his Furrow and Tharmas to his Sheep-fold
And Luvah to his Loom; Urthona he beheld, mightily labouring at
His Anvil, in the Great Spectre Los, unwearied labouring and weeping.
Therefore the Sons of Eden praise Urthona's Spectre in songs,
Because he kept the Divine Vision in time of trouble.
  As the Sun and Moon lead forward the Visions of Heaven and Earth
England, who is Britannia, enter'd Albion's bosom rejoicing,
Rejoicing in his indignation, adoring his wrathful rebuke.
She who adores not your frowns will only loathe your smiles.

XLII

The Offering of Self

As the Sun and Moon lead forward the Visions of Heaven
and Earth,
England, who is Britannia, entered Albion's bosom rejoicing.
Then Jesus appeared, standing by Albion as the Good
Shepherd
By the lost sheep that he hath found; and Albion knew that it
Was the Lord, the Universal Humanity. And Albion saw his
Form,
A Man; and they conversed as Man with Man in Ages of
Eternity.
And the Divine Appearance was the likeness and similitude
of Los.
Albion said: 'O Lord, what can I do? my Selfhood cruel
Marches against thee, deceitful, from Sinai and from Edom
Into the Wilderness of Judah, to meet thee in his pride.
I behold the Visions of my deadly sleep of Six Thousand
Years,
Dazzling around thy skirts like a serpent of precious stones
and gold.
I know it is my Self, O my Divine Creator and Redeemer.'
Jesus replied: 'Fear not, Albion. Unless I die thou canst not
live;
But if I die I shall arise again, and thou with me.
This is Friendship and Brotherhood; without it Man Is Not.'
So Jesus spoke. The Covering Cherub coming on in dark-
ness
Overshadow'd them, and Jesus said: 'Thus do Men in
Eternity
One for another, to put off, by forgiveness, every sin.'
Albion reply'd: 'Cannot Man exist without mysterious
Offering of Self for Another? Is this Friendship and Brother-
hood?
I see thee in the likeness and similitude of Los, my Friend.'
Jesus said: 'Wouldest thou love one who never died
For thee? Or ever die for one who had not died for thee?
And if God dieth not for Man, and giveth not himself

Eternally for Man, Man could not exist; for Man is Love
As God is Love; every kindness to another is a little Death
In the Divine Image, nor can Man exist but by Brotherhood.'
   So saying, the Cloud overshadowing divided them asunder.
Albion stood in terror, not for himself, but for his Friend
Divine. And Self was lost in the contemplation of faith,
And wonder at the Divine Mercy, and at Los's sublime
   honour.
   'Do I sleep amidst danger to Friends? O my Cities and
   Counties,
Do you sleep? Rouze up! Rouze up! Eternal Death is
   abroad!'
   So Albion spoke: and threw himself into the Furnaces of
   affliction.
All was a Vision, all a dream! The Furnaces became
Fountains of Living Waters, flowing from the Humanity
   Divine.
And all the Cities of Albion rose from their slumbers, and all
The Sons and Daughters of Albion, on soft clouds, waking
   from sleep.
Soon all around, remote, the Heavens, burnt with flaming
   fires;
And Urizen and Luvah and Tharmas and Urthona arose into
Albion's bosom. Then Albion stood before Jesus in the clouds
Of Heaven,—Fourfold, among the Visions of God, in
   Eternity!

XLIII

The Vision of Albion Redeemed

'Awake, Awake, Jerusalem! O lovely Emanation of Albion
Awake, and overspread all Nations as in Ancient Time.
For lo! the Night of Death is past, and the Eternal Day
Appears upon our hills. Awake, Jerusalem, and come away!'
   So spake the Vision of Albion; and in him so spake, in my
   hearing,
The Universal Father. Then Albion stretch'd his hand into
   Infinitude

And took his Bow.

Fourfold the Vision; for bright-beaming Urizen

Lay'd his hand on the South and took a breathing Bow of carved gold:

Luvah his hand stretch'd to the East and bore a silver Bow, bright shining:

Tharmas Westward a Bow of brass, pure flaming, richly wrought:

Orthona Northward, in thick storms, a Bow of iron, terrible thundering.

And the Bow is a Male and Female, and the Quiver of the Arrows of Love

Are the Children of his Bow, a Bow of Mercy and Loving-kindness, laying

Open the hidden Heart, in Wars of mutual Benevolence, Wars of Love.

And the Hand of Man grasps firm, between the Male and Female Loves.

And he clothed himself in Bow and Arrows, in awful state, Fourfold,

In the midst of his Twenty-eight Cities, each with his Bow breathing.

Then each an Arrow flaming from his Quiver fitted carefully;

Then drew, fourfold, the unreprovable String, bending thro' the wide Heavens

The horned Bow, fourfold. Loud sounding flew the flaming Arrow, fourfold.

Murmuring, the Bowstring breathes with ardour; Clouds roll round the horns

Of the wide Bow; loud sounding Winds sport on the Mountains' brows.

The Druid Spectre was Annihilate; loud thund'ring, rejoicing, terrific, vanishing,

Fourfold Annihilation! And at the clangor of the Arrows of Intellect

The innumerable Chariots of the Almighty appear'd in Heaven,

And Bacon and Newton and Locke, and Milton and Shakspear and Chaucer.

And every Man stood Fourfold. Each four Faces had.

South stood the nerves of the Eye; East, in rivers of bliss, the Nerves of the

Expansive Nostrils; West flow'd the Parent Sense, the Tongue; North stood
The labyrinthine Ear; Circumscribing and circumcising the excrementitious
Husk and Covering—into Vacuum evaporating; revealing the lineaments of Man;
Driving outward the Body of Death in an Eternal Death and Resurrection,
Awaking it to Life, among the Flowers of Beulah; rejoicing in Unity
In the Four Senses, in the Outline, the Circumference and Form; for ever
In Forgiveness of Sins, which is Self-annihilation; it is the Covenant of Jehovah.
　The Four Living Creatures, Chariots of Humanity, Divine, incomprehensible,
In beautiful Paradises expand. These are the Four Rivers of Paradise
And the Four Faces of Humanity, fronting the Four Cardinal Points
Of Heaven; going forward, forward, irresistible, from Eternity to Eternity.

XLIV

They walked in Eternity

And they conversed together in Visionary forms dramatic, which bright
Redounded from their tongues in thunderous majesty, in Visions,
In new Expanses; creating exemplars of Memory and of Intellect;
Creating Space, creating Time, according to the wonders Divine
Of Human Imagination, throughout all the three Regions immense
Of Childhood, Manhood and Old Age. And the all-tremendous, unfathomable Non-Ens

Of Death was seen in regenerations, terrific or complacent, varying

According to the subject of discourse. And every Word and every Character

Was Human. According to the Expansion or Contraction, the translucence or

Opakeness of nervous fibres, such was the variation of Time and Space,

Which vary according as the Organs of Perception vary. And they walked

To and fro in Eternity as One Man, reflecting each in each, and clearly seen

And seeing, according to fitness and order.

                                        And I heard Jehovah speak

Terrific from his Holy Place, and saw the Words of the Mutual Covenant Divine

On chariots of gold and jewels, with Living Creatures, starry and flaming

With every colour. Lion, Tyger, Horse, Elephant, Eagle, Dove, Fly, Worm,

And the all-wondrous Serpent, clothed in gems and rich array, Humanize

In the Forgiveness of Sins, according to thy Covenant, Jehovah.

  They cry:

'Where is the Covenant of Priam, the Moral Virtues of the Heathen?

Where is the Tree of Good and Evil, that rooted beneath the cruel heel

Of Albion's Spectre, the Patriarch Druid? Where are all his Human Sacrifices

For Sin, in War, and in the Druid Temples of the Accuser of Sin, beneath

The Oak Groves of Albion, that cover'd the whole Earth beneath his Spectre?

Where are the Kingdoms of the World, and all their glory, that grew on Desolation?'

  Such is the Cry from all the Earth, from the Living Creatures of the Earth,

And from the Thirty-two Nations of the Earth among the Living Creatures.

All Human Forms identified; even Tree, Metal, Earth and
 Stone, all
Human Forms identified, living, going forth, and returning,
 wearied,
Into the Planetary lives of Years, Months, Days and Hours;
 reposing,
And then Awaking into his Bosom, in the Life of Immortality.
 And I heard the Name of their Emanations; they are
 named Jerusalem.

The End of the Song of Jerusalem.

Commentary and Notes

Commentary

In reading *Jerusalem* we must remember that Blake was not primarily concerned to write a good poem. He certainly claimed a real inspiration, stating that whole passages were written quickly, under the dictation of the spirit. He maintained that the free verse form which he adopted released him from the needless fetters and labours of rhyme and regular metre. Yet it is plain that he worked over, altered and re-arranged much of what he wrote. He asserts that 'every word, every letter, is studied and put into its fit place; the terrific numbers are reserved for the terrific parts, the mild and gentle for the mild and gentle parts, and the prosaic for inferior parts; all are necessary to each other.' His high claims we certainly cannot accept in fullness, though we must acknowledge the moving energy of most passages, the frequent strength and beauty of individual lines, and his skill of vocabulary. We may note that he speaks of himself in his introduction as an 'Orator', and admits that a long poem cannot always soar.

Essentially, Blake wrote as a prophet and seer, commissioned to deliver an urgent message, which he knows is of vital importance to all. 'Mark well my words! They are of your eternal salvation.' He seeks to make deep contact with his readers, to open their inward eyes, and to awake their slumbering humanity. Albion is Everyman. *De te fabula narratur*. In one of the illustrations to *Jerusalem* is shown a gigantic figure seated in the utmost misery and despair, with head sunk between his knees, and refusing to look at the scroll on which Blake inscribes one of his condensed gnomic quatrains:

> Each Man is in his Spectre's power
> Until the arrival of that hour
> When his Humanity awake
> And cast his Spectre into the Lake.

We do well to try to read the work with the same immediacy as that with which he wrote it. It will then prove to be not a merely interesting literary pleasure, but a rousing, stirring spiritual experience.

In this commentary I shall try, section by section, to give a brief analysis of subject-matter, and add notes on lines or words which present special difficulties.

I

ALBION REJECTS THE CALL OF THE DIVINE
HUMANITY AND CHAOS IS COME AGAIN

The prophet declares the compulsion under which he writes, and prays for continued inspiration by the spirit of Jesus.

The call of Jesus, as an indwelling presence, to the lost Man, is rejected by him, with expressions of unbelief, rationalism, selfishness, possessiveness and jealousy—the 'spectral' qualities. This rejection means that his 'Emanation', his power to love and forgive, leaves him, though his jealousy tries to hide and keep her, as a man might his wife.

Albion—Everyman, Britain, the human race—has fallen asleep, spiritually, sunk into the delusion of 'Ulro', a living death in blind materialism and egoism. This is the cosmic tragedy, played out over the course of ages, as well as within each individual human soul.

Fallen Man has refused to use his imagination, and has only his sceptical reason to rely upon. The result is blindness, indefiniteness, mechanism and sterility. Blake's vision of this state is to see the whole of space round our globe as if filled with changing indefinite forms of clouds or rocks, with glimpses of fiery plains, tangled forests and barren mountains—the confused domain of 'abstract philosophy'. There are also huge iron wheels, grating and grinding against each other with harsh cogs—the workings of hard logic and of an order in which 'man is the enemy of man'. These 'Starry Wheels', in contrast to the living wheels seen by Ezekiel, constitute together the mechanism of the great inhuman 'Satanic Mills'.

The whole phantasmagoria is that of an illusory, inverse world, ringing the whole earth with what Blake calls a 'Mundane Shell, cavernous in length, bredth and highth'. In such a

163

world Jerusalem cannot live. Albion's choice of it means that she is driven away from her children; she is seen departing as a pillar of smoke disappearing eastward.

Man's fall also means, of course, continual wars upon earth. But there is a limit to the fall, and forces making for restoration are also continually active among men. The Daughters of Beulah minister with rest and inspiration, for they have not forgotten Jerusalem. They represent all the promptings and experiences of human love and loyalty still to be found among men and women, even if they have forgotten God. And above all, the fiery labours of Los have never ceased, Los who has been faithful to his vision, Los who will never leave his friend Albion to perish.

II

THE TEMPTATION OF LOS AND HIS CONTENTIONS WITH HIS SPECTRE

Los is the imaginative, creative spirit in man. Blake possibly gave him this name as the inverse of Sol; he is the source of spiritual energy just as the sun is the source of physical energy. ' 'Twas outward the Sun, inward Los in his might.'

All down the ages prophets, poets, inspirers and redeemers have kept alive, and fanned into flame, the spark of divine energy within mankind, which is his assurance of a spiritual life. The great mythical, Promethean figure of Los is that of one who works with fire, who burns out errors and forges forms of truth. Beneath the Starry Wheels of abstract reasoning his Furnaces are seen to be ever burning, signals of hope and salvation.

Yet each of the 'living' men, who collectively constitute Los, is subject to all the temptations to which his fellows are falling victims all around him. And so Los himself is shown as continually tempted to go astray like Albion, tempted to yield, like his friend, to the domination of his rationalizing Spectre, and to lose his own Emanation, to whom Blake gave the name of Enitharmon.

This long section of *Jerusalem* is devoted mainly to a detailed account of Los's struggle to preserve his integrity, to prevent

164

his Spectre from finally separating off and becoming his master. One has always to remember that Blake was exploring not only into the whole history of man's soul, but also at the same time into his own specific personal experiences. I feel sure that Los's struggle is here given so much space and detail, often repetitious, because Blake is describing a specially stern and critical inner struggle which he had recently been through. On his removal from London to the Sussex seacoast in 1800 he felt at first a revival of his powers and inspiration, as a son of Los, and started work on his projected great epic poem. But doubts and difficulties soon pressed hard upon him. His neighbour and patron, the minor poet William Hayley, disapproved of his prophetic pictures and writings, and called upon him, in the name of common sense and financial advantage, to devote himself to producing miniature portraits and commercial engravings. He had continually to listen to the voice of his Spectre, speaking to him through the lips of Hayley. But there came to him also at Felpham decisive visionary experiences, impelling him to new spiritual labours. Some account of these is given in his very personal poem *Milton*, at which we shall be looking later. At length he knew that victory was won, that he must break away from Hayley and hack-work and return to London. Having made this resolve he wrote to his friend and confidant Thomas Butts, in the exuberance of a newly found freedom:

'I have been very unhappy, but am so no longer. I am again emerged into the light of day. I still, and shall to eternity, embrace Christianity, and adore Him who is the express image of God; but I have travelled through perils and darkness not unlike a champion. I have conquered and shall go on conquering. Nothing can withstand the fury of my course among the stars of God and in the abysses of the accuser.' And a year later, after a further illumination in London, he wrote, to Hayley himself, in the very language of the *Jerusalem* at which he was working, 'For now, O Glory! and O Delight! I have entirely reduced that spectrous fiend to his station, whose annoyance has been the ruin of my labours. . . . I was a slave bound in a mill among beasts and devils . . . I thank God with entire confidence that it shall be so no longer—he is become my servant who domineered over me, he is even as a brother who was my enemy.' So it was finally with Los and his Spectre.

The course of the argument between Los and his Spectre is in general plain enough, but one or two passages require some explanation. An illustration shows Los as the mighty-muscled smith, resting upon his long-handled hammer in front of his furnace fire, listening to the temptation being poured into his ear by the beaked, bat-winged figure of his Spectre hovering over him. At the end of the section we see Los's Spectre—his Pride, his Ego and his Reason—compelled, though unwillingly, to labour at the creative forges of the spirit.

Note 1. *Generation and Regeneration*

Generation is the state of existence in the physical world of the senses, of sex and birth and time. *Regeneration* is the new birth, the annihilation of the spectre-self, and the entering into the life of the spirit, the rising into Beulah and eventually into Eden. Generation has its own religion, full of blindness and error, with a history stretching from Druidism to Deism, and always denying the true forgiving religion of Jesus, thereby trying to destroy Jerusalem. And yet 'Time is the Mercy of Eternity', and the chain of physical births on earth was designed to give opportunity for the Divine Birth, the Incarnation. Generation itself is holy, in so far as it is a type and a foretelling of the birth of the Lamb of God.

Note 2. '*Thy Uncircumcised pretences to Chastity*'

Blake uses the word 'circumcision' in its original sense of 'cutting round'. He thinks of a designer or sculptor cutting away meaningless masses and fragments in order to reveal a beautiful form. So Man's true form is not revealed until the falsehoods and errors that hide it have been cut away. Blake calls this 'circumscribing and circumcising the excrementitious husk and Covering, revealing the lineaments of Man'.

'Chastity' is one of Blake's shorthand words, standing for the false religion of the spectral world, which seeks to restrain man's energies and desires by negative and restrictive commandments and to achieve a sham purity through timid conventions and a refusal to venture and create.

Note 3. '*Hand has absorbed all his brethren*'

'Hand' is taken as representative of the twelve sons of Albion, just as one might take 'Judah' as representing the twelve tribes

166

of Israel. There may also be a reference to the fact that the sons are all in the assertive, warlike state, in which every man's hand is against his brother and the strongest becomes a tyrant over the rest. Hand shows the characteristics of the proud and selfish heart of fallen man. His generous impulses and insights are narrowed and condensed into errors, hates and jealousies which bring war upon earth and persecutions of the prophets. His forging is the inverse of that of Los and the two are eternal opponents.

Note 4. *The Daughters of Albion*

The desires and emotions of Albion, in his divided state, become cruel and jealous, his loves carnal and possessive. Blake allows that these 'Daughters of Albion' have a fierce attractive beauty, but he fears it, for it obscures the true beauty of mercy and humanity. So he represents Los as keeping out of their reach and sending forth his reason to expose their falsity.

Note 5. *Negations are not Contraries*

Blake taught, as many others have done, that man's life is always lived in tension, polarity, struggle. In the *Marriage of Heaven and Hell* he laid down that 'Without Contraries there is no progression. Attraction and Repulsion, Reason and Energy, Love and Hate are necessary to human existence'. But to take the negative pole of any such a pair alone and impute reality to it results in a 'Negation', a mere emptiness. Unbelief, denial, or any other negative, can never be a foundation to build upon.

III

LOS CONQUERS THE SPECTRE

Los comes through his temptation successfully, continuing to labour creatively, rejecting the abstractions and systems constructed by the unenlightened reasoners. The results of his labours begin to appear. His spectre would still like to obstruct, but falls into despair when he finds that he has no life or strength of his own, but must work under the direction of Los.

Note 1. *The joys of God advance*

The God here described is the falsely-imagined God made by the spectre in his own image, the God of hard justice, who demands sacrifice and punishment, finding his joy therein.

Note 2. *Building Golgonooza*

Those who on earth keep faithful to their spiritual vision, the children of Los, produce works of love and loveliness. Their labours, seen as a whole, are described as the building of a great city of refuge and joy, the 'spiritual fourfold London'. To this city Blake gave the curious name of Golgonooza— possibly implying that it was the seat of life, the converse of Golgotha the place of death. Thus Los is builder and architect, as well as smith.

IV

THE GOLDEN BUILDERS

The artists and builders of the spiritual life of vision recognize each other as forming one family—the children of Los— engaged in a great common work. They live together in joy, in a world they themselves are building, like a blessed island of the West (here called Erin). They are preparing a place for Jerusalem, when she returns. But on Earth Vala has taken the place of Jerusalem, Vala with her physical beauty and erotic attraction, the shadow and completion of Jerusalem in the days of innocence, but now become a false goddess, a soul-less devouring force.

Los sees that though Albion is spiritually dead, God's providence is still at work for him. The fallen man will shape and materialize his false beliefs, in experience, into such forms of horror that when he sees them he will himself cast them off. Los and his children therefore go on building their city of beauty and affections in hope, while the children of Albion are building the great hollow Pandemonic World-shell of error and war. The works of Los have a timeless reality; the works of the selfhood are unreal and will eventually vanish.

Note 1. *Eternity—both within and without*

Explore into the recesses of an atom, or into the depths of stellar space, and in both cases you come upon Eternity, Infinity—as modern science is beginning to discover. It is the same with a human being; explore the inmost recesses of his soul, or the furthest outreach of his brain-power, and you come upon Eternity, at both extremes. God is 'within and without'.

Note 2. *Not one can pass away*

The significance, or real being, of anything, is something beyond its appearance in Time. All things acted on earth have a meaning in eternity, and can therefore never pass into nothingness (unless that meaning is a pure negation). When Blake goes on to speak of 'the bright sculptures of Los's Halls', he is thinking of the whole historic roll of human experience, with its archetypes and discoveries, which repeat the same essential story from age to age, because men share the same 'Human Form'. Records of this story of the soul of man are preserved for us in great works of art, and in particular in the great works of imaginative literature, such (says Blake here) as we find embedded in the Old and the New Testaments.

V

THE CHILDREN OF LIGHT AND THE
CHILDREN OF DARKNESS

The children of Los live in the light of Eternity, creating glory in the world around them by their energy, their love and their thought—'loins, heart and head'.

Blake breaks off here to describe his own vision of humanity's age-long 'cold repose' of spiritual sleep and mortal error. He uses the names of Bacon, Newton and Locke as typical of the false philosophy of his own day, which he hated and sought to destroy—a philosophy which put its trust in experiment, sense impressions and reason, and had no place for faith, imaginative vision, and realities beyond the reach of sense.

The sons of Albion, possessed by this creed of 'the Dead', profess their belief in antagonisms among men, and in the

169

Goddess-Mother Nature, while they utterly reject Jerusalem, 'mother of pity and dishonourable forgiveness'.

Again we see Albion as the giant stretched out in deadly sleep, and the consequent desolation brought upon the whole earth. Yet Los and his other friends still undertake to suffer for his redemption.

Note 1. *There is an outside* . . .

Just as the eye of vision sees a real, eternal 'Inside' in the heart of all things and in their furthest extension, so also the eye of the selfish materialistic reasoner sees a false 'outside' both at the centre and the circumference of being. And thus he constructs his own dead world of doubt, mechanism and destruction.

Note 2. *The Friends* . . .

These are all those who, like Los, preserve their spiritual vision. They see Albion's blindness and sickness, and are willing to suffer in order to help him. They stay with Albion in his prisoning world, and while he loses touch with the eternal both within and without, they must forgo the joys of Beulah and endure the darkness for his sake. But the whole passage is by no means clear.

VI

JERUSALEM AND VALA

We are now shown some of the divisions and disasters which arise from the loss of innocence and the growth of a sense of sin. We must, as usual, read them, with their sudden changes of time and attitude, as scenes in the story of the results of false thought and false morals both in human history and at the same time in the fluctuating darkness within a single human soul— yours or mine.

We first behold Jerusalem and Vala, the spiritual and temporal beauties, united in the golden days of innocence, when London was the earthly Paradise. Then Albion's fall drives them apart. Jerusalem, with her impulses of spontaneous pity, love and joy, is held to be a false immoral delusion; man shuts his eyes to her loveliness and banishes her from his breast. Vala shares in Albion's fall, in his sense of sin and shame. Her net of woven earthly beauty becomes now an enclosing net of restrictions, unforgivingness and self-righteousness. She too turns away from Jerusalem.

Albion now joins the discussion, revealing both his false religion and his sufferings. His past delights with Vala and Jerusalem together he now regards as shameful impurity. He will try to 'weave a chaste body over an unchaste mind', that is, to repress his natural desires and hide them beneath an outward, formal purity. He recognizes that his sin has driven away his own children into slavery, and warped the whole creation. He longs for extinction rather than for the death-in-life which he is experiencing.

Vala laments that she is being tortured, driven to wars and hatreds and stern duties in place of the freedom of love. Albion retorts that he is showing what love really is—pride in the exclusive possession of some enjoyed beauty; innocence and shared love are delusions. Jerusalem warns him against the analysing and rationalizing of joy. But he demands punishments—for himself as for others; Jerusalem cries 'not punishment, but forgiveness!'

Note 1. *I see Luvah, whom I slew*

Luvah, as one of the four immortal realities, or 'Zoas,' represents man's pure affections and emotions. But the fall of man replaces the spiritual and emanative by the rational and selfish. Then Albion sees Luvah as the ally of his Spectre and of the earthly Vala, that is, he has killed the real Luvah of self-giving love, and replaced it by lust and possessive attachments. Luvah is always being sacrificed in the sensual, logical world, as is finally shown in the death of Jesus. Albion, in his heart, knows that he has murdered a holy one and deserves death for the deed.

VII

ALBION'S STRUGGLES TO AWAKE

In this section we overhear something of the critical debate always going on in man's soul. Is Albion to fix his gaze on

Jerusalem, learn pity, and cast off the entangling 'Veil of Vala', or is he to turn his eyes away from her, as a delusive and impossible ideal, to cling to his self-assertion and his 'crucifying cruelties' of thought and action, to go on building Babylon instead of Jerusalem? We see him swinging first one way and then the other; on the point of repentance, and then hardening his heart again. At the close he feels himself hopelessly involved in his world of death, and yet we feel that he may still be saved, for he sees the figure of a saviour who has passed through death into life, and cannot in his heart believe that this is but an illusion.

Note 1. *Complacency*

Blake uses this word to mean, not self-satisfaction, but peace and harmony.

Note 2. *Cast it into the Atlantic Deep*

The 'Atlantic Deep' is another symbol for the illusory world of space and time, which drowned the primal earthly Paradise of Atlantis. In this ocean live the 'Dead', who believe in matter and in the harsh 'Moral Law'. When Albion (here only temporarily) cast off the net or veil of illusion, it returns to its own place, to catch more dead souls.

VIII

CHORUS OF THE PITIES

The Daughters of Beulah are spirits and intuitions that inspire man to trust to love, to make friendships, true marriages and homes, founded on understanding and forgiveness, entering thus into the quiet joys of the state of 'Beulah'. Here they watch in sorrow how men worship false gods, make wars, and take vengeance upon each other, bringing suffering to the whole linked universe. They call upon the Saviour to descend to the rescue.

This passage ends the first chapter, a quarter, of the poem. Various attempts have been made to trace a definite pattern and progression in the four chapters, but it is not clear to see.

We must be content to treat the pages and episodes as 'flash-backs' and illustrations of the inclusive story, with which we are now becoming familiar, all leading towards an apocalypse to come. Each of the many repetitions adds some new insight or image, and takes us further into the soul of man, which can be explored for ever.

IX

ALBION, SUNK IN ERROR, REJECTS THE DIVINE CALL

The second chapter begins with a varied repetition of the opening scene of the first chapter, showing Albion, in his self-will, turning a deaf ear to the inward calling of the Divine Humanity. He rejects the beauty of love and brotherhood in favour of egoism, jealousy and lordship. The system of punitive morality which he accepts encloses him in deadly shades; his altars of unforgiving 'Justice' demand human sacrifices. He teaches his children also to deny Humanity and Mercy, and men fortify their dwellings against each other.

But the Divine Vision (called also by the names of the Human Form, Human Family, Divine Family, or Lord and Saviour) continues to call on the self-banished to return, and although Albion, the once glorious, refuses to listen, the Saviour's voice speaks of his ultimate redemption as assured.

And yet something in Albion's dark heart did respond. Two immortal figures leave it and join the Divine Family. They represent all those individuals in mankind, and all the nascent impulses of love in a man's soul, which are true to the vision of Eternity. Here they are called the Emanation of Los (named Enitharmon) who has been seeking to redeem the children of Albion, and the corresponding Spectre, now her obedient servant and guard. They come to report the failure of their mission, and the tragic events they have seen enacted in Mansoul.

Note 1. *Atonement. Man of Sin and Repentance*

Blake regards the theory that forgiveness of sins is conditional upon the prior repentance of the sinner, and also upon someone 'atoning' by paying the allotted penalty for the sin, as the

173

doctrine of Satan and not of Jesus, and he rejects it with loathing. The 'Man of Sin and Repentance' (or the 'Reactor') is the man who accepts and acts upon this false doctrine.

Note 2. *The Reactor*

This is the only place in which Blake uses this term. It is evidently equivalent to a man's 'Selfhood' or 'Satan', who reacts in opposition to the Divine Humanity, and sets up his rival throne in the heart. Fallen man with his unenlightened eyes cannot see how false and dangerous the usurper is, until in course of time his nature is revealed plainly by the sheer horror of the forms of living which he establishes. Then man will recognize the evil and cast it off.

X

REPORT OF THE TWO THAT ESCAPED

Nearly fifty lines of this section are taken bodily from a scene in *The Four Zoas*, as are several other passages in *Jerusalem*. Here the clear-sighted representatives of Los describe some of the errors and struggles of Albion, which they have seen and have been unable to prevent.

We have to be very careful, in reading Blake, to note whether his characters are speaking in their original, or in their fallen, state. As they change from one to the other, words and values reverse their meanings; devils must now be described as angels and angels as devils. 'I read black where you read white'.

Here Albion, still in spiritual slumber, sets up his own shadow, his own empty reason, as God, worshipping it with words which are rightly due only to the eternal. The whole passage is of course an ironic description of a parody of real worship.

There follows a difficult passage dealing with Albion's struggles with his emotions and passions, that part of his being which Blake personifies as Luvah. Luvah in his pure state represents pity and self-giving love. But with man's fall his emotions fall also. His love becomes restricted and possessive, affections are replaced by 'jealous fears, fury and rage'. Blake describes such change (as so often in other passages) as the constriction of the senses, and of life in general, from widest vision to a narrow selfish materialism.

Similarly Vala, the beauty of earth, and especially of woman, when set up as a Goddess in her own right, shrinks to a delusion and a temptation.

In such a condition, Nature appears as cruel and monstrous, and the life of man becomes mere tumult and confusion.

The last few lines of this section contain no doubt a reminiscence of Blake's recent experiences at Felpham. Hayley, a good friend on the material plane, had shown himself as an enemy and hindrance to the artist's spiritual life. But Blake and his wife had kept true to their vision and had fled back like doves to their little home in London.

Note 1. *Urthona*

Blake never became quite consistent in his use of the names of Los and Urthona, and used them almost interchangeably. But most often Urthona is the name of the 'Zoa' in eternity, and Los is Urthona's representative in time.

Note 2. *The Vegetation of Albion's Children*

The symbol of 'Vegetation' is very often used by Blake as a reference to man's birth into the material world, and especially to his acceptance of this world as reality, instead of as a 'shadow' of the spiritual world as seen by the Imagination. In some of his illustrations he expresses the same idea by showing the feet or the fingers of his human figures as extending and growing as roots into the ground.

XI

LOS GOES EXPLORING

Los, as Albion's friend, bent on his redemption, now starts out to try to discover who and what is responsible for the confusion and misery. The manifoldness of the Myth is shown by the way in which Los's journey can be thought of as an exploration of the social evils of London and of the Home Counties, that part of

England which Blake knew, and at the same time as a deep exploring of man's psychology, his motives, fears and errors.

To enter Albion's bosom and to explore the recesses of London was to make one and the same journey, for the errors of man's soul are externalized in the social conditions which he creates. Blake saw clearly the evils and cruelties of the new industrial civilization which was developing around him, in which men and women and children—the 'jewels of Albion'—were being exploited and oppressed. But his indignation stopped short of seeking out the oppressors in order to punish them. To revenge wrongs, in his view, did spiritual injury to the avenger; the wrong-doer was already doomed to the punishment of Providence, and should be an object of pity rather than of hate.

Los, in his contemplation of London, overhears a conversation between Jerusalem and Vala, the weaver of the deceptive web of 'love, jealousy and despair', who has usurped the place of Jerusalem on the Thames, and in man's heart. Vala mocks Jerusalem as a delusive and sinful deceiver, and claims Albion, the proud warrior, as her own. Los is terrified to see Albion so petrified into hardness and error, and takes up his task of creative redemption with new energy.

Note 1. *Los took his globe of fire*

This line is illustrated in the frontispiece to *Jerusalem*. The globe of fire represents the light of spiritual energy and vision, which will enable its bearer to discover the secrets of the grave. For to enter the heart of fallen man is to descend into the grave. A similar design is used elsewhere by Blake, for example in two illustrations to Blair's poem *The Grave*, and in the fifteenth emblem of *The Gates of Paradise*. In the *Jerusalem* illustration Los is not shown as the usual heroic naked figure, but as some anonymous prophet or pilgrim, with perhaps a hint of Blake's own figure. For he regarded this poem as being such an exploration, and himself as inspired by the spirit of Los.

Note 2. *Minute Particulars*

This is a very favourite phrase of Blake's. He had a horror of vague and cloudy generalizations, describing them as the refuge of scoundrels and hypocrites. The infinite could not be seen in abstract generalizations, but only in 'grains of sand', in definite forms with outline and individuality. Mankind could only be known in individual men; and men only in their 'little nameless, unremembered acts of kindness and of love'. Beauty is not revealed by indefinite blotches and masses, but in naked forms and loving detail. Blake carried out to the full his own rule of 'labour well the Minute Particulars'.

Note 3. *Dens of Despair in the House of Bread*

In his vision of London Blake is appalled not only by the sight of wretched ragged children in the gutter-kennels of East London's riverside slums, but also by the cruel conditions of the treatment of the lunatics in the 'Bedlam' institute in Lambeth. 'Bedlam' is a corruption of 'Bethlehem', which means 'the House of Bread'. It is as if Blake were saying 'My house shall be called a House of Bread, but ye have made it a Den of Despair'.

XII

THE FEMALE USURPER

Here we are given another picture of Albion listening to the voice of his Spectre, whose reasoning tells him that this world is just a chaos of fortuitous passing events; man is just a biological creature, born to look after himself; and that the greatest cities of the world are doomed to vanish into the mists of memory.

Albion, accepting this, falls into further error. Vala appears to him and stakes out her claim to be worshipped. She reminds him of their union in the days of primal innocence, but now had not she and Albion rejected Jerusalem and dreams of universal brotherhood, and accepted the discovery that the highest experience of love is that of passion with its red fires? Was not Vala now his ideal of woman and of Love? But Albion feels that this invitation is a deadly one; Nature, however beautiful, is not a final revelation. Babylon can never replace Jerusalem.

Los overhears the temptation and breaks out into loud protests at the power of Woman to usurp the place of God in the depths of a man's soul. To Blake such idolatry was the cause of the furtiveness, possessiveness and jealousy which he saw in the sex relationships of his society. The Eternals laughed scornfully at a so-called morality which labelled natural desires as sinful, and drove both men and women into shame, secrecy and deceit.

XIII

THE RESCUER

The first few lines of this section are engraved on a plate which has no direct continuity with the preceding or the following page. Most of the page is covered by a vigorous picture of the creation of Eve. The agent in this creation is shown as Jesus, the Word, who is calling the woman forth from the body of the sleeping Adam, the whole scene being framed in a setting of red fire, representing intense spiritual energy. As in so many other pages, the reader is left to work out the connection between picture and text. The poem is now setting out to deal with the redeeming work of the God-Man, the climax of history. The picture reminds us of the promise of 'the seed' and of the part assigned to woman in the story. Woman, who can be temptress, is also the mother of every man, through whom all lovers, artists and seers, and finally the Divine Redeemer, will be brought into this world to rescue the fallen race.

The innumerable activities within 'Los's Furnaces', that is, all the imaginative, prophetic, forgiving acts in history, culminate in 'the appearance of a Man' (a reminiscence from the Book of Daniel) in the furnace. This Human Form Divine is seen by Blake as identical with Jesus, whose mission is explained. In union with him man will pass through condemnation and awake 'beyond the Grave'. Jesus reveals to each individual the true nature of the 'State' of Selfhood into which he had fallen, and leads him out of it into the 'eternal' type of living. The Heavenly Ones who watch the course of events on earth rejoice to see this deliverance from the torments of illusion.

Los, who now takes up the word again, resumes his argument with Albion, who blind, jealous and rebellious, plunges onward in his self-will. But the Saviour ever follows him, pleading with him to open his eyes to the Divine Vision shown 'in loves and tears of brothers, sisters, sons, fathers and friends'. To close his eyes to these evidences of spiritual life is, in effect, to be dead.

Note 1. *The Two Limits, Satan and Adam.*
For an explanation of this see page 187 following, Note 2.

Note 2. *Jesus, the Christ*
The Divine Family, the Divine Vision, the Human Divine, the Saviour, the Eternal Man, the One Man—we are asked by Blake to see the reality hidden behind all these equivalent names in the figure of Jesus the Christ, who is 'all in all, in Eden', in Eden which He would have called the Kingdom of Heaven, entered by the pathway of compassion and forgiveness.

XIV

THE FRIENDS OF ALBION

The innumerable 'loves and tears' of human compassion and affection, wherever displayed, have all been part of the redeeming influence working upon Albion. And now Blake sees all this spiritual power as exemplified in the inner history of the cathedral cities of Britain. He personifies them as the spiritual Friends of Albion, continually seeking to rescue him from his errors, sins and despairs. 'Cities are the fathers of multitudes.'

He begins, naturally enough, with a vision of the spiritual being of London, the whole pattern of the endless self-giving of its citizens through the long course of its history. Blake himself was a son of London and a lover of London. This vision of London with its 'opening streets' is the happy counterpart to the terrible vision of sinful, fallen London, with its 'chartered' (bound) streets and manacled inhabitants given to us in the *Songs of Experience.*

From London Blake's eyes pass over the whole land, bathed in the light of loving-kindness, and pause on the four holy cities of Verulam (St Albans), Canterbury, York and Edinburgh, all of them homes of a succession of saints and martyrs who had entered through the same secret gate into the eternal country. This is the gate of imaginative energy and vision, which is here named the gate of Los. But Albion has fled the other way through this gate, into the Satanic dead land, and feels himself a lost soul.

For his reclamation Los calls together the Friends of Albion, the twenty-eight cathedral cities who represent in our country the Divine Family, the Mercy of God, the spirit of Jesus. They are among the agents used by the Divine Mercy, which will never suffer Albion to be finally lost, and to sink down into an eternal Hell.

Note 1. *I heard in Lambeth's shades*

To Blake Lambeth was a place of vision, the spiritual centre of London. This was not only because the Archbishop had his seat there, but also because Blake was living in Lambeth during a time of inspiration, when his earlier prophetic books were written. In Felpham by the sea he had had greater illumination, seeing as well as hearing; and now, back in London in a lodging in South Molton Street, he continues to see and hear, and is also writing down the prophet's message.

Note 2. *Rivers and Mountains are also Men*

The sight of rivers and mountains awake thoughts and emotions in us; they speak to us. If they can so communicate with us there must be something common in their natures and in ours. We are able to give them reverence, to see something of their essential, eternal 'forms', deriving from the same Creative Spirit that has made us. The ultimate cosmic unity is not of mankind only, but of all created things. One is reminded of St Francis saluting them all as brothers and sisters. Like St Paul, Blake thought of the whole creation as suffering with man in his fall, groaning together until all are saved together, into the liberty of Sons of God.

Note 3. *Does Mercy endure Atonement?*

Here once more Blake takes the opportunity to denounce the common religious theory of his day that Divine Justice needs a victim (a Ransom, as Albion here calls it, in his dark error), to undergo the necessary punishment before mercy can be shown to an offender. Such a demand, says Blake, is 'heathen cruelty'.

Note 4. *His dark Eon*

Eon is here a contraction for *Emanation*. If a soul could fall irretrievably (which is not possible) it would mean that even the Emanation would be corrupted and would breed corruption.

XV

LOS AND THE FRIENDS FAIL TO RESCUE ALBION, AND ARE THEMSELVES IN DANGER

The Friends of Albion are overwhelmed by the sight of his condition of death. Instead of taking any action they gaze upon him with despair, and thereby begin to be infected with his spiritual disease; their own Spectres begin to run wild, and they are in peril of losing their own Emanations.

The sight of this weakness infuriates Los. He breaks out into a long and indignant description of what he beholds in Albion, a speech in which, after Blake's fashion, symbol after symbol for man's life in selfishness and constriction come crowding together. The Friends of Albion now respond to Los's call to action, and together they raise Albion on their wings and endeavour to bear him back home through the visionary gate. But Albion will not co-operate. His blindness, self-will and pride are like giant wheels which roll him back into the outer darkness; his Satanic state turns every particle of light and air into great obstructing rocks and hills.

Since it is a divine law that no one can be saved by force against his own will, Albion cannot be rescued until a day arrives when he will turn and deny himself and receive divine power. But he is not forgotten by the Holy Ones, who watch above him, waiting for the day of redemption to dawn.

Note 1. *There is a grain of sand in Lambeth*

Even though Albion, humanity in general, is fallen and imprisoned in his own false state, yet individual men and women still have individual experiences of felicity, love and illumination. These take place each in its own particular 'Lambeth', or place of vision. Each is an entry into 'Beulah', the land of true affections and repose, where is the palace of

181

'Oothoon', the innocent soul (a character in the *Vision of the Daughters of Albion*). It is the inhabitants of Beulah who know that Jerusalem still lives and who cherish her until Albion's awakening.

Such spiritual experience can never be found or understood by those who are in the state of materialism and selfishness, the state called Satan. They hear of it, but regard it as a delusion and a sin. They cannot find the hidden entry (called in the preceding section the Gate of Los) even though 'they number every grain of sand on earth every night'. For they cannot 'see a world in a grain of sand'; to them it is nothing but—a grain of sand!

There is a parallel passage in *Milton* which tells how an instant in time, just as a point in space, may be a gate opening into the infinite—'Eternity in an hour'. It runs:

'There is a Moment in each Day that Satan cannot find
Nor can his Watch-Fiends find it. But the Industrious find
This Moment, and it multiply, and when it ever is found
It renovates every Moment of the Day.'

One instant of insight may illuminate and purify all our daily living.

Note 2. *In deep humiliation*

Albion's Friends are humiliated because they find that they are not ready to sacrifice themselves for his salvation—'if we are merciful, ourselves must suffer destruction'—yet their refusal will mean death for Jerusalem. This means that they too are infected with Albion's disease, and that there is a state of war arising among their four inward life-powers—the reason becoming hard and cold, the pity sentimental, the body indolent, and the spirit doubting; they are on the brink of joining Albion in spiritual death.

Note 3. *Rooty, oaken Groves*

One invariable sign of man's fall is his readiness to judge, punish and execute his fellows. One of Blake's favourite symbols for this state is that of the dark forest or Grove. As usual, a number of allusions are combined in one word or phrase. The Grove is, like the 'high place', that place of worship of cruel heathen gods, so often forbidden to the Israelites; it is also the oak forest in Britain, in whose recesses the Druids performed their human sacrifices; it is not only a place of gloom in which lost souls wander, but its mighty intertwining roots provide, together with the rocks in which they grow, an underground labyrinth of woe from which escape is almost impossible. Man's enlacement in these roots is a symbol also of his enslavement to the materialsism of 'vegetated' life. In many of Blake's plates this underground entombment and enrootment is vividly pictured.

Note 4. *Then Los grew furious*

Blake's own indignations and leading ideas come pouring out together whenever, as here, he gives Los the word; and Los's final cry at the end of this speech—that, like Elijah, he is the only one who has remained faithful to the divine vision—no doubt expresses Blake's own sense of loneliness in continually giving out a prophetic message to which none would listen.

Blake–Los here sees, combined in one inclusive vision, Albion on the Couch of Death which mercy has provided for him, the whole of space filled with the indefinite forms created by his false religion—clouds and caves and rocks and poisonous trees and burning lakes; and the whole earth a scene of divisions, oppressions and cruel wars, the outward expressions of man's false pride and blind hatred. For all the terrors and cruelties, though they fill the great circles of all space and all time, yet originate and are enacted within the little circle of the human skull.

Note 5. *Heavens twenty-seven-fold*

These 'Heavens' are the successive and interlacing forms of religion which mankind, in the long course of its history, has constructed or accepted. With his usual adherence to some unimportant number-system and his desire to be specific and definite, Blake gives us in a later page the names of these twenty-seven Heavens or Churches. The first is named after Adam; the next nine after various antediluvian patriarchs; then follow eleven more, from Noah to Abraham; and the last six bear the names of Moses, Solomon, Paul, Constantine, Charlemaine and Luther. A good mixture, representing in general the substitutes for, or perversions of, the Everlasting

Gospel of pure love and continual forgiveness which Jesus came to reveal.

Note 6. *Hunting and War*

I think that Blake is here concerned to emphasize that spiritual life is something very active, not a matter of mere acceptance and enjoyment, but involving eager search for new truths and achievements, and 'severe contentions of Friendship'. The following Biblical references are not made clear in detail but the general sense is plain. Oshea (the original name of Joshua) and Caleb represent the faithful and imaginative servants of God, who 'fight, as in the wars of old', living in the golden age of innocence, in which 'our wars are wars of life and wounds of love, with intellectual spears and long-winged arrows of thought'. But the 'armies of Balaam', and all subsequent armies of men, have waged physical and mental wars of death and hate.

Note 7. *I smell the blood of the English*

The cruel giant sons of Albion adopt here, rather comically, the cry of the nursery-tale giant

> Fee! Fo! Fi! Fum!
> I smell the blood of an Englishman!
> Be he alive or be he dead
> I'll grind his bones to make my bread!

XVI

COME, GREAT PHYSICIAN!

The Friends of Albion are still standing round his couch of death. They have answered Los's call to come and help Albion, but leave most of the work to his prophetic spirit. Since they are themselves suffering from a degree of Albion's selfish sickness, they cannot do much except pray for the coming of Jesus the Healer. But one of them, Bath, summons up courage to make a direct appeal to Albion. Blake chooses Bath as spokesman because it is the 'healing city', famous for its medicinal springs. (In a previous paragraph Bristol, Bath's neighbouring city which also had its hot wells, is linked in this service.)

Bath calls for the help of Oxford's eloquence in presenting to Albion some leaves from the Tree of Life, which are for the healing of the nations. The reference here is to Oxford as the nurse of poets and divines, and possibly also to the leaves of the Bible, the words of God which are printed there.

But the joint appeal is all in vain. Albion, in dark self-will, keeps his 'Western Gate' resolutely closed. This means that he refuses to use his spiritual sense, to open his eyes to the divine vision, or his ears to the divine word. He treats his Friends as enemies; and his own house is divided against itself by internal disputes and condemnations.

Note 1. *Our mildness is nothing*

Here Blake is saying that all apparently fine qualities and achievements of a man are of no permanence or ultimate worth if he uses them to exalt or serve himself. 'If I have not charity it profiteth me nothing.'

It is unfortunate that the word 'mild', which Blake uses so often, should, like its comrade in misfortune 'meek', have such a poor ring in our modern ears. We should translate it into 'gentle', or 'tender'.

Note 2. *Reason not on both sides*

Blake is always warning us not to rely on reason alone as a guide in life. The mill of logic, he insists, can never grind out anything *new*. The persistent doubter, questioner, arguer, reasoning both yes and no, he regards as non-creative and imperfectly human. One must have definite and determinate faith and vision in order truly to live. Without them we are as dead as Albion.

Note 3. *The Plow of Jehovah*

Blake has many references to the final harvest and vintage of the nations, such as the angels with the sickles are seen carrying out in the Book of Revelation. He conceives it as preceded by the ploughing and harrowing of the nations, the disasters and wars through which mankind must go, until it sees clearly what is false and evil, and casts it out—which is the 'last judgment'.

Note that 'the Dead', throughout the whole book, refers to the spiritually dead 'in trespasses and sins'. It has been said that the theme of *Jerusalem* might be summed up as 'As in Albion all died, even so in Christ shall all be made alive'.

XVII

DESTROY NOT THESE LITTLE ONES

Albion broods, with his warped outlook, on what he regards as the sins and enmities of all his fellows. When Los reveals to him the results of the consequent spiritual warfare he is horrified to see that the 'little ones', the innocent, even his own beloved, are among the victims of his cursing, like children sacrificed in the fiery furnaces of Moloch. It is his own primal loving impulses that have been corrupted and tortured.

Los shares his deadly horror at the sight, but the reactions of the two are different. Los is strengthened by his vision of the Saviour visiting and comforting the sufferers. Albion puts all the blame on Los, and demands restitution, justice and punishment. Los retorts vigorously that it is Albion's own errors, pride and mercilessness, which threatens to destroy these little ones, and tries to explain to Albion how blind is his Selfhood, how cruel his punitive conception of 'Moral Virtue'.

Albion, thus defied, calls on his sons to seize Los, whom he sentences to death for treason and ingratitude. The Spectre-sons, their humanity forgotten, come up at their father's call, singing songs of worldly glory and victory, ready to punish Los, and also to dismiss into darkness the twenty-four Friends of Albion who have aided and abetted Los.

The Friends are shown once more as sick folk themselves, their eternal human forms laid, like Albion's, upon couches of spiritual death. But they are not, like him, prone in deadly slumber. They sit up, to endeavour to curb their Spectres, to watch over Albion and to pray for him.

Note 1. *The Furnaces*

Los's activity is most often pictured as that of a mighty smith labouring at his forge; he is the 'Lord of the Furnaces'. The word furnace conveys many allusions and shades of meaning.

Primarily Los is forging spiritual swords and spears for the fight for the soul of Albion. In his furnaces he also refines and tests what is good, and burns up the unreal. On his anvil he hammers out truth, and breaks up the rocky Spectres like potsherds. The furnaces are also, as in this passage, places of testing and of afflictions, in which the innocent are involved in suffering with the guilty. Every man who would redeem his brother must enter the furnaces of affliction—as Albion himself does in the end. Blake, as usual, also had Biblical reminiscences at the back of his mind. The phrase 'furnaces of affliction' occurs in Isaiah, and we remember the figure as of the Son of God walking with the three innocents in Nebuchadnezzar's furnace, and of how the Lord brought Israel forth 'from the iron furnaces, out of Egypt'.

Note 2. *A limit of Opakeness and a limit of Contraction*

To the eye of vision and faith everything is translucent; it is able to look through matter and time into eternity. But as man falls into blindness and sin everything becomes to him more and more opaque, until a stone is just a lump of matter one cannot see through, a tree is just a 'green thing that stands in the way', and a brother man is just a solid external enemy. But there is a limit to such blindness below which man cannot sink, thanks to his divine origin. This limit is named by Blake the state 'Satan'.

Similarly the pure, innocent Image of God, which had converse with angels and union with all creation, shrinks to littleness, as its spiritual senses contract and become self-centred, until again a providential limiting state of contraction is reached, the state which Blake labels 'Adam'.

These two linked states are to be observed everywhere in individual men. Our business in life is to recognize them as states of death, to reject them and regain the stature, the vision and the divine freedom of our essential Human Form.

A further limitation to the disaster of the fall is seen in the saving device of sexual generation—in other words the creation of Eve—which in the course of time enabled her creator himself to reveal himself in Human Form.

Note 3. *Their Human majestic forms*

'Their' refers here to the twenty-four Friends of Albion. When

187

Blake writes 'Man' or 'Human' with a capital letter he is thinking of the eternal element in man, that in him which reflects the Image of God.

XVIII

MERCY PREPARES A RETREAT FOR JERUSALEM

Albion, now in the very depths, sees his sons shedding each other's blood all over the earth. His attempts to enforce stern justice and punish offenders have bound him close together with the sinners, but in hatred and vengeance, instead of in brotherhood. He sees no hope for himself and sinks in bitter despair.

But the Saviour of man cannot leave him in this fallen, inhuman state. While the consciousness of what is Divine within himself seems to be dead in Albion (that is, in the human race as a whole), God's mercy provides for revelations of the Divine to be realized in individuals all through history, charged to reveal it to their fellows. Albion's eternal 'Human Form' is immortal, though sleeping, preserved on a 'Rock of Ages', set in the midst of the sea of time and space, awaiting regeneration. The interim revelations, such as those given in the Old and New Testaments, are as it were glorious decorations of this couch of repose, and prophecies of what is to come.

But Albion is not forgotten, nor Jerusalem, in her separation from him, left friendless. The comforting, helping powers of compassion and inspiration, whom Blake calls the Daughters of Beulah, endeavour to protect her. The Friends of Albion are her friends also and, with Los himself, are Divine agents in the task of mercy. With his familiar seeing of the One in the Many, Blake personifies the ranks of the helpers of mankind in the form of an 'aged, pensive woman', Erin, who presides over the creation of time and space necessary for redemption, and is willing to suffer the pains of death for Albion's sake. She co-operates with Los in his fiery spiritual activities. The place prepared for the shelter of the banished Emanation is in the West of the Land of Beulah, here labelled the 'Spaces of Erin'. For Blake the west was always the direction of freedom and of vision, just as the East stood for war and darkness.

In the next section Erin laments over the condition into which Albion and Jerusalem have now fallen, and in her words Blake once more endeavours to give a rousing statement of his gospel.

Note 1. *The Gospels and the Revelations*

It will be noticed that Blake omits the Epistles from his list of the Biblical treasures. He seems to have had little liking for St Paul, regarding him mainly as a reasoner and an organizer, and too little conscious of the visionary and mystic elements in his experience and outlook.

Note 2. *A place where Contrarieties are equally true*

This place is 'Beulah', in which, because of its atmosphere of love and insight, a soul can live happily in the acceptance of all the unresolved tensions and contradictions of human experience, knowing them to be but partial aspects of a unity.

But because of Albion's sinning, Jerusalem has to leave this state, and be willing to suffer in a strange land, until the day of redemption.

XIX

THE MOURNING FOR ALBION

Erin (Albion's pitying western sister-isle) calls on all the Daughters of Beulah to rescue Jerusalem, and her Little Ones, from a fallen earth that has become the seat of war and of human sacrifice. She describes how Albion's originally heavenly senses have withered and contracted, and how the great slimy 'polypus' of selfishness is covering the continents. She reminds the blind, materialistic Sons of Albion that God's omnipresent providence will eventually over-rule their utmost violence and bring peace. She calls for the removal of the 'terrible Surfaces', those imposing but insubstantial appearances which are the externalized institutions built up by Albion in his Satanic 'State of Death', and which he has even called 'Heavens' in his blindness.

Erin reminds her sisters (lest they forget to pity) that none of the murders, wars and punishments which they behold on earth are committed by the 'Eternal Human' who is the real Albion, but by the evil 'States' of errors possessing his mind and his powers while he is spiritually sleeping.

She foresees the descent of Jesus, the Lamb of God, and calls upon him to come quickly and teach men to forgive.

Note 1. *Where Giants dwelt in Intellect*

Originally Albion's 'Atlantic Mountains' were the seat of Innocence and Harmony, inhabited by spiritual Giants of intellectual vision. But now it is possessed by a Nature 'red in tooth and claw', and a humanity defiling it by murder and warfare. It is in the power of fallen, perverted humanity, which may equally well be described as 'stony Druids'—the human sacrificers; 'allegoric generation'—the life of the mortal flesh, which is only a faint 'allegory' of the life of immortal spirit; the 'twelve Gods of Asia'—typical of any false Gods; or the 'Spectres of those who sleep'—the rationalizing of blindness.

Note 2. *The Three Sins*

The eyes of love see man sinning in three ways. One sins and, repenting, tries to conceal his sinning; this is just human and, compared with the other sins, might almost be called lovable. Another sins, and glories in his sin; this is selfish cruelty. But a third judges others to punishment for their sins, and refuses to forgive. The sun sets, but he will remember and punish tomorrow. This is the sin of sins—enmity and unforgivingness, which ensures that tomorrow's sun will rise in blood.

Only Jesus can teach us to forgive each evening and start each day with an innocent sunrise.

At this point the second chapter of *Jerusalem* is closed with a full-plate picture showing that Hell which is the interior state of fallen man. In a dark rocky cavern, illuminated only by flames, are seen three despairing figures. On the left is Vala, who has assumed the crown and sceptre of Nature, but sits in a dark robe on a stone chair, sunk in gloom. In the centre is Hyle, the full materialist, his head bowed in hopelessness between his knees. And on the right is Skofield, the unforgiving accuser, a naked manacled figure, consuming in his own flames.

XX

LOS LABOURS FOR ALBION

The third chapter begins, like so many other sections, with a re-picturing of the parlous state of Mankind. Los, the creative, visionary element in Man, is seen as incarnated in Blake himself and all other faithful souls who in their daily work are building the City of God in London. Yet they do not escape the infection of mind and the internal disunity which result from the atmosphere of false thought and false worship in which they are compelled to live and work. They have to protect every 'Emanation'—every impulse to love and forgive—from the pervasive 'Spectre', here identified as the Tempter in the wilderness, who demands homage to himself as Lord of all the kingdoms of reason and power, and is a denier of vision and spiritual teaching.

Note 1. *This is Jerusalem in every Man*

Every man is a spiritual being and all have the same essentially divine 'Human Form'. This is clothed in its own characteristic light-garment, which Blake names Jerusalem. It covers him with a character of 'forgivingness', and it is this forgiving approach to all his fellow-men which constitutes man's real freedom. Without it he is in bondage to various forms of hate, selfishness and enmity. And without this light-garment a man is dark, rocky, chaotic, spiritually blind and dead.

Note 2. *Bacon, Newton and Locke*

See Commentary on Section v, page 169.

XXI

'THE GREAT VOICE OF ETERNITY'

This section consists of Blake's plate No. 55, which is in a script rather different from that of its neighbours, is without any pictorial design, and was apparently inserted here as a sort of interlude, to try to give us a view of Man and his history as it might be seen from the point of view of the Immortals who inhabit Eternity. They are pictured as a divine family, with a natural interest in the deeds and fate of Albion, once a mighty one as themselves, but now sunk and shrunk into a mortal way of life. They debate, in family council, whether they should go down to his level and share his experiences. After consulting with the Supreme Lord, they decide to undertake a spiritual warfare for the salvation of Albion and the rescue of Jerusalem, a warfare which proceeds to shake the whole of creation.

As usual, Blake is thinking and working on multiple levels, and he here puts into the mouth of his Immortals his own constant teaching of the necessity that we should train our spiritual senses, until we also are able to see eternity in a moment of time, and the whole harvest field in a clod of clay. In a combined simultaneous vision he beholds his Immortals working both within the individual consciousness and also through the whole course of history, in the form of the seven Spirits or Eyes of God, or again of the Four Living Creatures ('Zoas'), who plead with man to cast off indefinite good intentions and cloudy inexact ideas, and to discover truth in detailed definition, and reality in giving the cup of cold water to some little one. The Voice of God calls all men to such a prophetic service of truth and loving-kindness.

Note 1 *The Dead* and *The Veil*

The Dead are, as usual, the normal earth-dwellers, who are not spiritually, imaginatively, alive, who have not discovered their Divine Humanity. Since the Fall they have been blinded by Satan's 'Veil', the deceptions of materialsim and of worldly power-seeking. Their leaders and princes teach the glittering falsehoods of a selfish philosophy, the fables of a chosen race, of the divine right of kings, and the doctrine of uniform obedience. The life and death of Jesus tears asunder this veil.

Note 2. *Shiloh*

Shiloh was the place where the ark and tabernacle of the Israelites were first stationed, and is thus a holy sister-place to Jerusalem. So Blake chooses this name for the emanation of France, Albion's sister-country. He hints, in passages like this, that he could equally well have written of any land and its emanation as of his own land of Albion and its Jerusalem. His symbols are never merely national but always universal.

Note 3. *The Seven Eyes of God*

Round the throne of God stand seven mighty spirits, the Eyes, or aspects of Almightiness. Blake gives them seven Biblical names, and thinks of them as God's messengers or revealers, sent in succession to introduce a new era or dispensation in earth's history, in each of which men were thus enabled to discern some special aspect of God—his power, his justice or his holiness, for example. But their vision was always partial and they mixed much error in their attempts at religion. The sixth dispensation, that of Jehovah, covers the whole Old Testament history of the Hebrews, and then came Jesus, with his revelation of God's essential love and forgivingness. But Christianity has also been infected with error, and Blake foresees the necessity for an eighth, and perhaps a final, revelation. Who the revealer is to be remains unknown. Possibly Blake thought it might be the 'human form' itself, to be realized in everyman, but hidden at present in the unconscious depths of mankind, the 'forests of Albion'.

Note 4. *They plow'd*

The Living Spirits, who shake creation by their immortal labours for man's redemption, are shown as also carrying out their own teaching by working at humble creative tasks, minute particulars. The golden ploughs which they drive are symbolic of the arts of life, just as swords and spears symbolize the arts of war and death.

Note 5. *On circumcision and not on virginity*

The Immortals here proclaim Blake's favourite doctrine of the need for definiteness in thought and deed, and his horror of cloudy generalizations and refusals to accept the pains of the spiritual experience of suffering with and for others. Truth, he repeats, is revealed by the constant cutting away (circumcision) of errors, and never by a negative, empty rejection of the labours and risks of creative living, such a rejection as is shown by the Church's exaltation of holy 'virginity'.

XXII

THE GREAT REFUSAL OF ALBION'S DAUGHTERS

This plate 56 of *Jerusalem* is again an odd one, differing from its neighbours in handwriting and slightly in size. It was probably written and engraved earlier, and inserted without much regard to continuity. It deals with a subject which has already been treated on a previous page (see Section XII, *ante*), and a few lines are common to both passages. The theme is the subjection of men and of history to a 'female will', a 'monstrous regiment' of mothers and wives, monstrous in spite of all their tenderness and care because it tries to replace vision and knowledge of the eternal by the satisfactions of the flesh and of human affections. Woman, who nurses, feeds, consoles and inspires man, invites him to rely upon her rather than to seek for God. So religion remains earthly and sexual, avoiding the fires of experience and the cross of self-annihilation.

The argument is put in the form of a dialogue between Los–Blake and the Daughters of Albion. In the previous parallel passage they were personified, collectively, as the lovely Vala, whose 'veil', cast around men, obstructs his sight of God; and here they are shown doing the same thing.

I find the plate very difficult to interpret in detail. I give it here in full, and instead of brief notes on obscurities I have ventured, perhaps too rashly, to attempt a continuous commentary. For reasons of spacing, this will be found in an appendix on page 230.

The reader may well omit this section on his first reading.

XXIII

ALBION'S FRIENDS STILL SEEK TO SAVE HIM

Again we hear Albion's friends, his spiritual healers and advisers, here typified as Bath, Canterbury, York and Edinburgh, challenging him to vision. Cannot he see the One Man in mankind? Must he always be 'treating contraries as negations', in a hard, Pharisaic morality which labels everything black or white, evil or good, and thereby fosters cruelty and pride? Cannot he see the harlot as a woman who needs to be loved and forgiven into a new purity, and not ostracized and stoned to death? Can he not see a theatre as a place in which God may speak, as well as the Devil tempt? Can he not see that politics and religion should join hands, since both should mean brotherhood?

But Albion will not listen to such truths. He, who should be a leader of nations, a ploughman labouring for a spiritual harvest, by his refusal brings fire and confusion upon the earth. He falls under the plough instead of guiding it. While his evil Selfhood remains active, his human-divine essence has fallen as if in death; but it will be preserved by God's mercy on a 'Rock of Ages' until its day of resurrection.

Next we are shown another group 'labouring and sorrowing in the Interior Worlds'. These are the 'Daughters of Los', the feminine, more emotional elements in the forces working for man's awakening and redemption. Blake is here thinking of all the humble and self-sacrificing mothers and wives (his own good wife no doubt in the first rank), in whom this spiritual power is incarnated. Regardless of themselves, suffering servants of the divine, they weave the fibres of life and love that unite men to each other and to God. Here Blake is making his *amende honorable* to womanhood, providing a tender contrast to the many passages in which, I cannot help feeling with a certain morbidity, he details the tortures inflicted upon mankind by the unredeemed 'Daughters of Albion', in their jealousy and possessiveness.

Characteristically, Blake sees also the whole of Nature involved in the spiritual drama of Man, as the Daughters of Los here call to their aid silkworm and woolly lamb, and all little fellow-weavers and providers of material for the garment of man. They all have their share in love's purpose, their element of human meaning; the inner eye beholds them as 'men seen afar'.

XXIV

JERUSALEM COMFORTED

The lives of faith and energy lived by those who retain a clear spiritual vision constitute the 'Furnaces' of Los, and it is their activities which bring about the visitation of man's darkness and idolatry (the 'wheels and Druid temples of Albion') by the Divine Vision, identified as the Lamb of God, the Good Shepherd, Jesus. He gathers Jerusalem's little children in his arms and weeps over the city. For here we see Blake's power of speaking of many things under one image, and in this case particularly of Jerusalem as at once 'a city yet a woman', both the ideal soul of humanity, personified as a woman, and the historic city, once holy and free, but fallen into sin and captivity, yet to be restored as the New Jerusalem. When, in this passage, the Divine Voice seeks to recall the historic Jerusalem from her idolatries, so fatal in their results, Blake is thinking all the time of the idolatries of his own day and land, and the social cruelties they involve. And yet the historic Jerusalem, in its own day, had its own soul, the real spiritual Jerusalem. This immortal form was to be seen in the teachings and sufferings of the Hebrew prophets, those faithful sons who were to be found not in the temples, but in the dungeons, of Babylon. In them Blake's great mythical figure of 'Jerusalem' was incarnated, and she speaks here, scorned and despised in her sufferings by her false opposite 'Vala'. So Blake passes over very easily into a dialogue, held in the real or spiritual world, between the Saviour and the soul, the Divine Lamb and Jerusalem, culminating in an assurance of comfort and salvation, expressed in the language of the Gospels.

Note 1. *Thou hast bound me down upon the stems of vegetation*

To be 'bound down upon the stems of vegetation' is to enter the 'vegetable' world of matter, sense and mortal consciousness. Man's fall, the separation of Jerusalem from her spiritual source, makes it necessary for redeeming spirit to become incarnated and to suffer, to be crucified. See the note on the picture of the crucifixion, page 209.

Note 2. *A secluded place of rest and a peculiar tabernacle*

Jerusalem's refusal of 'liberty and life' takes her into the secluded groves and sanctuaries of heathen religions. There is also a reference to the life of exclusive selfishness, and to woman's claim to be the object of worship. The result is that she weaves for her children veils of sorrows instead of garments of beauty.

Note 3. *This is the song of the Lamb, sung by slaves in evening time*

This line is a curious interpolation. I can only guess that Blake had a sudden pitying thought of the negro slaves in America, singing their songs of their coming redemption round their evening camp-fires, and wished to record that the Divine Voice was to be heard in their singing.

Note 4. *The Satanic Holiness*

This is a common description of the false, negative, restrictive religion which Blake felt it to be his mission to oppose and expose. 'Holiness' is of course here an ironic term of abuse, as is 'chastity' also.

XXV

THE HOLY SPIRIT IS—FORGIVENESS

This is a very remarkable page of *Jerusalem*. It is inserted, somewhat abruptly, in the middle of the dialogue between the Divine Voice and the human soul, to give an illustration of the meaning of forgiveness as the basis of spiritual life. Blake was incensed by two elements common in the church teachings of his day. One was that sex and sex relations were contaminating and unspiritual. But to him the idea of a 'virgin Eve', or of a Mary kept 'virginal' by a miraculous preservation, both in her own birth and in that of her child, from this sexual contamination, was something untrue and blasphemous. Eve, he held, had been created for Adam in order that mankind might, through the experience of the union of man and woman, be given a way of entry into the experience of eternity, and also that in due time the Divine Saviour might be born as a child into the human world, to consummate its redemption. To restrain and try to kill desire, including desire for sexual union, was to refuse to live after the divine plan. It was negation, and its so-called 'purity' a blank emptiness, or a hypocrisy.

The second doctrine that aroused the ire of William Blake was that of a legalistic, punitive 'atonement', the teaching that God could not forgive until His sense of justice was satisfied, seeing that the sin had first been punished, and that his Son had volunteered to endure this necessary punishment, of suffering and execution, in place of every sinner. Such an idea was also a blasphemy to Blake, a denial of real love and mercy in God. He believed that Jesus came, not to pay a penalty to a justly angered judge, but to reveal to man that God was the Great Forgiver 'without money and without price', and that man could only discover his 'eternal' life by showing continuously a like forgiveness to his fellows.

Blake refuses to interpret the story of the birth of Jesus in conventional religious terms, and rewrites it for us here in what he thinks would have been a truer way, if Joseph and Mary had had a deep understanding of its meaning. His startling version is of course 'visionary' rather than historical. Both the man and the woman speak in Blake's own language! Mary sees beyond the 'state' of anger in her husband, and speaks directly to the 'human form' in him, to his essential love of her. Joseph recounts how he has been taught, in vision, to forgive, and so to give a welcome to God, the forgiver of sins, passing through the gates of birth to come and dwell among men, in the form of a human child. United in great joy the man and the woman recognize that she is 'with child by the Holy Ghost', the holy spirit which brings forgiveness among men.

This lesson, together with a mission to care for the holy child, Mary passes on to Jerusalem, the soul of every woman— and of every man. They all must share in the joy of the birth; as they all will have to share later in the pain of beholding the cross.

It does not much matter that we cannot be clear about what characters are speaking through the different 'voices' here. The experience of union through forgiveness is so supreme that Mary is able to sing *O felix culpa!*, and Jerusalem having come to the same discovery, is able to sing with her.

XXVI

'I AM THE RESURRECTION'

The dialogue between the Divine Vision, Jesus, and Jerusalem, the forgotten and banished soul of mundane man, is here resumed from section XXIV. Jerusalem expresses a longing, doubtful faith in the resurrection of Albion from his spiritual death, and in her own eventual union with the Christ risen in him. She wonders at the miracle of the birth of the divine saviour, the 'seed of the woman', into a physical material 'body of death', at the end of the long line of the generations of the daughters of mother Vala. Blake emphasizes this wonder by picking out of Mary's ancestry not, as in the Bible, the lawful and direct descendants of Adam and Jacob, but a whole succession of strange women from heathen tribes who had contributed to the line of descent of Jesus. But Jerusalem sees beyond the physical and, like Mary Magdalene in the garden of the tomb, beholds the spiritual risen body of the Master. (The whole of this section, like so many others, is full of allusions and phrases derived from the Bible: Job, John, Jesus, the prophets and the psalmists, all contribute consonant elements to Blake's ideas and language.)

Jesus replies that, impossible as it seems to ordinary perception, he has passed through the grave, and *is* now resurrection and life. He has left behind him in the grave the sons of man, still in the grip of selfish passions (Luvah) and the illusions of Nature (Vala); but He will yet redeem humanity, and re-create Luvah and Vala into new spiritual forms. He proceeds to comfort Jerusalem with promises of His perpetual presence and help.

Meanwhile, the world is in agony, whelmed in the confusion and cruelties which follow false beliefs, indicated briefly here by images now very familiar to us, conglomerating into one meaning—dark night, clouds and blood, giant wheels grinding out cruelty on the mountains, Druid altars fired for human sacrifice, and little weeping boys hanged at Tyburn.

But Los (Blake himself—anyone who holds fast to faith and vision) though often travelling through dark night and despair, and often on the point of falling into division and being cut off from his personal Jerusalem, 'Enitharmon', still turns to labour at his spiritual forge, 'though in terrible pains'.

Note 1. *An immense amount of written material*

Some of this is no doubt lost, but there still survives a somewhat earlier attempt to write the inner history of man and his universe in free verse, which is as long as, and even more confusing than, the *Jerusalem*, and which Blake never engraved. It was entitled at first *Vala*, and later *The Four Zoas; a Dream in Nine Nights*. A number of passages, as well as individual lines, from this store of material are used verbatim in *Jerusalem* Blake probably rejected most of the earlier work because his main theme had become clearer to him, particularly in the central importance given to the figure of Jesus, and to the necessity for the mutual forgiveness of sins as the basis of true living.

XXVII

THE DARK HERMAPHRODITE: AND HUMAN MISERIES

Here we find Los, with his visionary clairvoyance, seeing all the 'Daughters' of fallen Albion, who in their selfish loves and acquisitive lusts weave hatreds, quarrels and jealousies among mankind, personified into the gigantic figure of Vala the deceiver and destroyer. He hears her cry out her denial of the reality of the 'Human Divine'; humanity is as mortal as a worm. Woman is the goddess of all; she suffers men to be born, and nourishes them, only because they are necessary to help her to breed; they are sub-females, serving female ends. Let them play about with their semblance of power, become popes and kings; but it is woman who rules.

Los denies her claims, and tries to show her that such reasoning is murderous, leading to mutual accusations, loss of innocence and worship of gold. Her 'loves' are no real love, for they know nothing of forgiveness.

Then the Great Spectre—the 'Sons' of sleeping Albion united into one gigantic figure—appears, in the guise of a serpent clad in glittering gems and gold, yet afflicted with the agonies of 'self-contradiction' which accompany lack of faith and insight.

The two huge figures flow together into one, the final personification of error and evil, two-sexed, but united into one dark portent of destruction. Blake sees it towering over London's river.

Our eyes then turn again to the multitudes on earth, and we see what the disaster of this monstrous blindness has meant for them. First, looking back over the six thousand years of human history, we see the tortures inflicted by men on men, by Druid priests in Britain and by Roman soldiers in Judaea. Even the places of holiness and healing, Lambeth and Bath, have been desecrated by the inhumanities of false religions; incarnate Love is slain, and there is darkness over the face of the earth.

Then, coming down to his own day, Blake instances the cruelties inflicted by man's blindness and selfishness during the course of the 'industrial revolution' which was taking place in England, and of the wars she was fighting in Europe. He was far in advance of his time in recognizing the evil aspects of these events, such as the forcible rape of men into the navy by the press-gangs, which he describes here in a few vivid lines.

There follows a two-edged description of the excitements and delights of war, as seen by the Sons of Albion, the cruel miniature spectres, who invite Vala to share their pleasure. For it is her deceitful smiles and sighs that draw men into quarrels and wars.

Note 1. *A Dark Hermaphrodite*
Blake is fond of describing as 'hermaphroditic', or double-sexed, any attempt to include in one figure two incongruous and opposed ideas or qualities. The result could only be internal strife and negation. For example, to try to join as equals a spiritual reality and a material appearance, or to persecute and torture men in the name of a meciful God, is a 'hermaphroditic blasphemy'. There is a hermaphroditic element in all our human earthly experience. We are all, in different degrees, male-female creatures, and we are all prone to try to combine love and wrath into an impossible unity. The 'real and immortal self' of man is above and beyond the sexual separations we know on earth; in Heaven there is no marrying and giving in marriage.

Note 2. *The Sons of Urizen*

These may be taken to represent the intellectual and scientific powers of man, which may be applied to good or evil ends, to the arts of peace or to the arts of war. If to the latter they are identifiable with the 'spectre sons of Albion', who preside over battlefields. Urizen is light-king and lord of the stars, and like Phoebus he drives the horses of the sun. These horses should be yoked to the work of the divine plough, but in the general fall they are sent raging to draw the scythed chariot over the field of blood. It is named here the 'chariot of love', but the love is of course the selfish, cruel, possessive type of love with which Vala deceives her victims.

XXVIII

THE SELF-TORMENTED

In this section we have a typical set of phantasmagorical visions, with interpolated hints of interpretations, displaying the cruel and destructive activities of the Sons and Daughters of Albion, in their fallen, earth-bound state.

A main occupation of their blind hates, lusts, condemnations and jealousies is the torturing of Luvah, the suffering figure who represents the essential humanity, and in particular the affections of love and forgiveness which seek to bind mankind in unity.

Their victim is seen, primarily, as laid out for torture and death on the stone altar of the 'Druids', that is, of all those who are ready to make a sacrifice of human life. In the details of his sufferings there are also references to Samson of the seven locks, and to the thorn-crowned crucified one. Luvah is also, in the wars of that day, the France of the young revolution.

These Druid Sons of Albion having rejected Eden and sent Jerusalem into far-off captivity, are continually building their own unreal world, the world of 'natural religion' and punishments. It is built in the style of Stonehenge, and fills all space with its monstrous unhewn rocks—dead ideas and reasonings; a building of eternal death, a scene set to be filled with wars and destruction.

The meaning of the tortures with which man is afflicted by

the Daughters of Albion is, in effect, that they are separating him from eternity, are closing his immortal senses and so shrinking his range of experience that he can no longer catch any glimpse of the devine vison, and is being made small enough to be confined in the little fleshy tabernacle which these women provide for his false worshipping.

Man's perceptions are thus 'dissipated into the indefinite' The whole range of nature, instead of being crowded with clear-outlined 'minute particulars' of beauty, becomes a meaningless chaos of indefinite clouds and darkness, the mere shell of a world. The glorious sun disappears in the blackness, the moon becomes a leprous plague, the rivers run with the blood of wars, the mountains shrink and draw apart. 'The eye altering, alters all.'

And the torturers themselves are punished in the very act of torture. Having refused to be joined in love, they are yet linked together by hatred to one another, and by suffering to their victims. They become one with what they look upon, and find that they are torturing themselves.

The human society formed by these blind, lost Children of Albion is commonly seen by Blake as a writhing, evil, slimy 'polypus' whose tentacles embrace the whole earth, or, equivalently, as a tangle of roots in a rocky underworld, the roots of 'Albion's Tree' of false religion and morality.

XXIX

THE TORMENTS OF LOVE AND DESIRE

Here is a further descriptive elaboration of the frustrating attempts of men and women to find some satisfaction and fulfilment in living, while denying the existence of the immortal element in their being.

Woman, by nature a weaver, when she refuses to weave experience with threads of self-giving love, seeks to make a garment for humanity out of ideas of materialism and self-assertion—threads from the rocks! The result is that she produces her blood-stained 'veil', in which all mankind is enclosed. Within this deception men seek to find their fulfilment in the excitements of war, and women their satisfaction in tantalizing and ruling the men through their bodily beauties and their claims to be worshipped. The whole tormenting order of life which this involves, when all the senses are active, but earth-bound and misused, with all its false glories and excitements, is revealed as being nothing better than the breeding and nourishing of the great inhuman polypus-dragon, whose gigantic coils enclose the whole circuit of earth.

Note 1. *Rahab and Tirzah*

It is difficult to see exactly how Blake distinguished between these two incarnations of Vala, the female pretender to the role of Jerusalem. In general, Rahab seems to represent false religion, restrictive, moralistic and punitive, while Tirzah figures the false philosophy, which teaches man that he is no more than a reasoning child of matter. These two, the Goddesses of This World, and the Daughters of Albion who accept their direction, are only able to see the 'spectral' aspect of the Sons of Albion; they will consort with these assertive, fighting figures, but reject the absurd idea of loving those who show pity and mercy.

Note 2. *His Heart beat strong on Salisbury plain*

The reference is to Stonehenge, seen as the chief temple of the religion of cruelty, with its high stone altar for human sacrifices. Just as 'English Blake' held that true religion had its origin in Britain, and spread thence to Judaea and over the whole world, so also the source of Satanic religion was in our land; and spread its evil from there across the globe.

Note 3. *O double God of Generation!*

This may possibly refer to some specific fertility God, but I think that it is more general. We are here shown men and women fallen to the worship of their false gods; gods of cruelty and human sacrifices, such as Thor and Friga in Scandinavia (as Blake imagined them), and Molech and Chemosh, 'the abominations of Moab and of Ammon'; and gods of sensuality, such as Bacchus and Venus. And then Blake exclaims that this is just the double type of godhead that men are bound to worship while they are living only in 'generation', the purely earthly life.

XXX

A MIGHTY, THREATENING FORM

Here two plates are brought together, in each of which the 'Spectral' male element in man's experience is seen personified in a single gigantic figure. In the second (probably earlier-written) form he is given the name of Hand, one of the two leading Sons of Albion. The visions differ, but both figures are shown in torments of fear and jealousy. In the first picture the Giant Male is once again equated to a world-wide cancer-polypus, taking root in the females, and infecting them with the poisons of 'reasoning, doubt, despair and death'. The result is that all the free, innocent loves of the state Jerusalem disappear; woman's love is brought under bondage to ideas of chastity and possessiveness; and in turn she seeks to enslave man to herself. There follows mutual hate and jealousy.

The mission of Jesus is to tear down all this veil of falsehood and to destroy the mock-holy temple set up for the worship of 'purity' and 'chastity' in a world regarded as impure. It is a blasphemy to erect such an exclusively holy centre. Our union with the divine must be realized through all 'minute particulars', for 'everything that lives is holy'. With a touch of humour Blake makes a comparison with the union of two lovers. True embraces are of the whole body and being, and not confined to the entry of the male member into the Holy of Holies of woman's body—like the 'pompous High Priest' entering the temple's most secret shrine. (See Hebrews ix. 7.)

Note 1. *Leah and Rachel*

These sisters are named as exemplars, or 'allegories', of deceit and jealousy. They were daughters of the treacherous Laban, had learned his ways, and worshipped the 'images' they stole from him, images of gods of contentions and revenges.

Note 2. *Beulah*

Here, as elsewhere, Blake introduces almost gratuitously ('not like Beulah') a brief description of the earthly paradise of human love. I think he must sometimes have felt, as his readers so often feel, that he was painting a picture of human life in colours too uniformly dark. After all, man the brother-hater and sinner had his experiences of pure affections and fine comradeships, his honeymoons both of the flesh and of the spirit; Catherine had made a 'space', a quiet and lovely home, for William. These experiences, of times and places where jealousy and contention were unknown, constitute Beulah, a piece of joy stolen from Heaven and brought to earth by love.

But, he goes on, such times do not last; feelings of unjust punishment and jealousy creep in, and man deserts Beulah for the normal world of 'Generation'; heaven is not to be fully realized on earth; all must go through the experience of sin, mortality and death; Beulah was lovely moonlight; Eden will be the sun.

XXXI

WHAT IS ABOVE IS WITHIN

Here Blake again is looking at Albion—England as representing mankind—as on a map of human life. He sees Albion's land full of 'creaturely activity', having rejected the ways of 'eternal' living. But above the land, in vision, appears the redeemed England that is to be, the heavenly Canaan, with the new Jerusalem, waiting to be called down. And that is the real Albion; what is passing down below is but a shadow that shall vanish away. Each region of England's map has its corresponding region above; each hurrying, worrying child of Albion has his corresponding child of God, awaiting birth.

'I mean, of course,' Blake interprets, 'that this real life, this Kingdom of Heaven, is within you.' To the man of vision 'above' or 'in Heaven', always means 'within'. He remembers here, perhaps, a saying of St Augustine about the spiritual life, that its centre is everywhere, its circumference nowhere. So Blake here points out that an earthly, selfish, outward life, followed through, will lead to opaqueness and contraction, to a diminishing into meaninglessness, to a point, to the 'selfish centre'—which is nothingness! But to seek life within, looking for its spiritual sources and meaning, will lead to translucence, to expansion without limit, to a circumference that is—everywhere!

Then Blake returns to his map-man, and, in accordance with his theory of minute definiteness, proceeds to describe England's division into twelve regions, as Palestine was portioned out among twelve tribes. Each area is the domain of a particular, named, Son of Albion, and of his appropriately associated Daughter of Albion. But to say what particular aspect of human life, and of human error, is associated with each of these twelve, is beyond Blake's power of analysis or invention. We are presented with a rather formal and empty list of groups of counties, followed a little later by a similar treatment of Ireland, and a catalogue of the thirty-two nations of the world. I have omitted all this gazetteering, except for the inclusion of one specimen, the description of the region assigned to the first son, Hand.

Los, through the whole of man's tragic history, continues to labour at his creative forge, and to refine souls in the 'furnaces of affliction'—a Biblical phrase. But in spite of all his labours he sees humanity sinking to the limit of opaqueness and contraction, to the selfishness of a Satan and the materialism of an Adam. Blake sees two forms of 'creation' working against each other all through the long history. The false, spectral God of blind 'natural religion' creates, in his own image, the warriors, kings and nobles of the earth in all their seeming glories, while Los, for man's protection and redemption, continually creates the line of prophets, visionaries and saviours. The 'Spectres of the Dead'—that is, men who are acting as self-seekers and tyrants—foster feuds and strife in every town and village, destroying all spiritual life and unity; but all the while the 'Sons of Los' are nourishing the inward life of love and joy by continual mutual service and mutual forgiveness.

In man's fall his fourfold powers, the 'Zoas', have fallen also, into misuse and strife. The outcome is the attempt to impose, through the centuries, cruel laws and harsh moralities, leading to martyrdoms and wars. The evidence that this was still going On Blake saw all around him, in the social miseries of the London he walked in. Babylon had conquered and occupied Jerusalem, and 'Babylon' is the realm of Rahab, Mystery, uncleanness. He sees what John of Patmos saw, 'the Dragon red and hidden Harlot', a false 'religion hidden in war', and he calls on the spirit of Jesus for help. For he rejoices that Jesus has, essentially, already triumphed, has brought mercy to earth,

has broken through the bars of Death and Hell and opened
Eternity in Time and Space.

But Albion remains still to be saved, is still in the sleep of
death, refusing to look on the eternal.

Note 1. *Hand dwelt in Selsey*

The twelve districts presided over by the Sons and Daughters
of Albion have each a spiritual capital, usually one of the
cathedral towns—the 'Friends of Albion'. For Hand's area—
Sussex, Surrey, Kent and Middlesex, one would have expected
the choice to fall upon Canterbury. But Canterbury was a
national and not a local capital, and Blake made the unexpected
choice of Selsey, as the original spiritual centre of the South-
East. He had learned, probably while he lived near by at
Felpham, that Selsey had been the seat of a bishopric until it
was drowned by an advance of the sea in the year 1075, and
the seat transferred to Chichester. Blake is describing here the
happy innocent days of early Britain, and therefore selects the
earlier site. In an earlier passage he had thus described the
rebirth of Selsey at Chichester:

'Selsey, true friend! who afterwards submitted to be devour'd
By the waves of Despair, whose Emanation rose above
The flood, and was named Chichester, lovely, mild and
    gentle! Lo!
Her lambs bleat to the sea-fowls' cry, lamenting still for
    Albion.'

Note 2. *For all are men*

See the Note 2, page 180.

Note 3. *It became a limit*

Blake sees it as an ordinance of Providence that, though man
can and does fall, he cannot fall into extinction, or fall so low
as to be irredeemable. His fall is into the earthly conditions
of darkness and sexual division. And in this world Los is at
work, through the 'emanative' element in man; and in the
perpetual stream of new births on earth he will find opportunity
for the coming of redeemers.

Note 4. *States remain permanent for ever*

Blake's continual insistence that while men can pass through and be delivered from their 'states' of error and sin, these states remain 'permanent', is a puzzling emphasis. There is an obvious distinction between 'permanent' and 'eternal'. I can only suppose the meaning to be that when a man has seen clearly the falsehood of a 'state' and thrown it off, the possibility of living in this 'state' remains for all other men so long as they have to pass through earthly life. If we compare the 'state' to a garment, then, when one man discards it, it goes back to the permanent wardrobe, from which others will take it out.

Note 5. *Her twenty-seven Heavens*

As usual, Blake must be very definite in his visions. During the whole course of history the deceiver, Vala or Rahab, has induced men to embrace one error after another, and to found a corresponding 'Church' on each. In space these Churches are seen as twenty-seven indefinite 'Heavens', filling the hollow void of the Mundane Shell with their cloudy, or rocky, shapeless shapes. In space-time they are 'permanent', though they have no place in eternal reality.

As a matter of curiosity, here is Blake's list of the representative figures of these twenty-seven (a threefold number, not fourfold) eras of error. Before the flood: Adam, Seth, Enos, Cainan, Mahalaleel, Jared, Enoch, Methuselah, Lamech: from the flood to Abraham: Noah, Shem, Arphaxad, Cainan the second, Salah, Heber, Peleg, Reu, Serug, Nahor, Terah: and from Abraham to our own Protestant day: Abraham, Moses, Solomon, Paul, Constantine, Charlemaine, Luther.

The third chapter of *Jerusalem* closes here, and Blake adds as usual a full-page end-picture, reproduced in black and white as frontispiece to this book. It is one of the most moving of his visual inventions. Most of the pictures in *Jerusalem* illustrate distressful or terrific episodes in the long history of human error and of man's inhumanity to man, enlarging upon a text correspondingly dark and painful. But this picture shows a turning-point. It displays the Eternal Saviour in His suffering. The figure is that of Jesus, but it hangs, not upon the crossed timbers of Golgotha, but on the trunk of the Great Tree of

Generation, indicating that Jesus is identified with that divine, immortal element in humanity which has always had to suffer crucifixion during its multitudinous incarnations through the ages, 'bound down on the Stems of Generation'.

But now, at the heart of history, at what seems its darkest hour, we see the first rays of sunrise on the horizon, matching the radiance which streams from the thorn-crowned head. And now Albion is no longer in the sleep of death on his time-washed rock of Eternity. He has heard the Divine Word, the word of forgiveness spoken from a cross, and stands again erect, a wakened, redeemed man, stretching out his arms towards the Crucified, in an attitude of adoration.

We are told by this picture, as also by the immensely vigorous appeal to Christians for action in the name and spirit of Jesus, which follows immediately as introduction to Chapter Four, that Blake is now looking forward to concluding his Story of Man with his final vision of the Great Day, in which the human will be finally caught up into the divine.

But there is much yet to be endured before that day dawns.

XXXII

LOS FIGHTS ON. JERUSALEM MOURNS IN EXILE

Once more Blake sees Los, champion and guardian of the true humanity, waging his unending war against 'the self-righteous-nesses' in the heart and the history of man, the ravening, earth-born 'Sons of Albion'. Victory to them would involve the spiritual death of Albion, the permanent banishment of Jerusalem, the replacement of the God of love and forgiveness by the blind and cruel Mother-Goddess Vala, and an ultimate emptiness in human life in place of a fourfold creativeness.

Jerusalem has been driven by these rebellious Titans far from Albion's breast, out of every settled land, away into some unknown waste land, some 'Kabul' in the far East. This section consists mainly of her lamentations, as she looks back to the golden days of innocence, when she mothered all the world's little ones, and London was the seat of holiness and brother-hood. England was Palestine and both were Eden; joy and light spread out from them across all lands and seas.

But now, because man's organs of perception were shrunk, so that he could see only matter and separateness, all that original glory had faded from his world. He had forgotten Jerusalem. Druid temples, seats of human cruelty and pride, had replaced the tabernacles of forgiveness, guarded by cherubim.

Note 1. *The Forty-two Gates of Erin*

We have seen Erin described as a majestic and lovely figure of an aged woman, incorporating the Emanations of all the Friends of Albion. She is a female comrade of Los, issuing from his furnaces of suffering, and accompanied by her sisters the Daughters of Beulah. She weaves, in her embracing 'Spaces', a mighty shining Rainbow of hope, cast round about all the cruel and rebellious works of men, the 'Wheels of Albion's Sons'.

Her work may be done in a moment of time, but it also covers the whole allotted course of human history, for which Blake accepted, at various times, a span of six thousand, seven thousand, or, finally, eight thousand five hundred years. His liking for specific figures in describing elements of his history or his cosmogony is in line with his general insistence on definiteness and correspondences. The particular figures have little significance for us, yet it is interesting to ferret out their origins. These 'Forty-two Gates of Erin' puzzled me for a long time; the number does not occur elsewhere. I guessed that it might possibly be a reference to forty-two harbours round the coast of Ireland, the blessed Island of the West; Blake is quite capable of seeing a spiritual significance in such a count!

But I have found a more interesting possible explanation. In section XVIII (see page 100) we had a description of Erin and of her work for Albion and Jerusalem. 'The Emanations of the grievously afflicted Friends of Albion concenter in one Female form, an Aged pensive Woman'. This is Erin. 'With awful hands she took A Moment of Time, drawing it out, with many tears and afflictions and many sorrows . . . into a Rainbow of jewels and gold . . . eight thousand and five hundred years in its extension; every two hundred years has a door to Eden.'

To the spiritual eye a thousand years are but as a day, and we may hold eternity in an hour. Blake continually takes us diving into the spaceless and timeless, realized by experience in time and space. But there are special, critical times in history when man, personalized in the shape of some seer or prophet, receives a new revelation, breaks through afresh into an experience of Eden, of the abundant fourfold life. Blake reckoned that these openings had occurred at about the rate of one in each two hundred years. If so, then in the course of man's eight thousand five hundred years of history, how many of these 'Doors to Eden' will be opened? Why, forty-two! The 'Forty-two Gates of Erin'! And always the blind, self-righteous, raging Sons of Albion are encamped about these gates, seeking to close them, and to slay the Lamb of God who will make use of them to visit Jerusalem His Bride.

Note 2. *Heshbon, Zion, Ephraim, Shiloh, Goshen, Gilead*

Blake walks familiarly in the Holy Land, using his intimate knowledge of the Bible to endow place-names with symbolical meanings, usually those already attached to them by the Jewish writers. He had also tried to teach himself Hebrew and Greek, and sometimes makes use of his knowledge of the derivation of these names. Most of us are not such assiduous Bible readers today, and we have to search out the necessary references. Towered Heshbon, for example, was the seat of Sihon, king of the Amorites, who is often named together with Og, king of Bashan, as a typical Prince of This World, a spiritual opponent of God's chosen people. The dictionary says that Heshbon means 'counting', which may possibly account for its being found here as a place of sterile 'reasoning'.

We here see Jerusalem—woman, city, soul—wandering through her conquered and desolated homeland, vainly seeking for any place of comfort. The slopes of Mount Zion, once covered with vines and olives, have become a rocky waste. She visits Ephraim, the 'fruitful', and Shiloh, the place of 'rest', and finds only precipices of despair. Goshen, where the children of Jacob dwelt in light, while around them all Egypt was plagued with darkness; and Gilead the traditional source of healing 'balm', are shrunken, narrow and darkened—even as Albion is. Her mind recalls the earlier joyful times in her wider homeland, in England, in the whole world! But the English counties too have rejected her, like all the tribal divisions of Judaea. Turkey—Egypt—even America—have cast her out and are worshipping false gods.

VALA ALSO SUFFERS AND LAMENTS

Jerusalem and Vala again face each other. We remember that they were once innocent children together, in the golden days, when heavenly beauty and earthly beauty were one. But the fall, with loss of Eden, means that now heavenly, self-giving love has been rejected, and earthly, self-assertive love claims dominion. Luvah and Vala have fallen and usurped the places of Albion and Jerusalem. Men now seek to rule by force, of weapons or of law, and women seek to enslave the men by their physical charms and by assumed submissiveness, which hides ambitious pride. The result has been jealousies, cruelties and wars.

Jerusalem now asks Vala what is the origin of these evils and of the hard, proud types of men and women who are tormenting one another. She reminds Vala that the common Divine Humanity within them all is something above and beyond sexual differences; as is also the dream-land experience of Beulah, the place of true affections, the ante-world to Eden.

Vala, stiff in her 'pride of beauty and cruel holiness', and continuing to 'weave' forms for men and women after her own pattern, feels herself tormented and condemned. She tries to shift the responsibility to Luvah, here (unusually) referred to as her father as well as her lover. Fallen Luvah has become the essence and symbol of possessive love, whether sexual, or the proud love of family or nation. His is the love of the pebble of the Song of Experience, 'seeking only Self to please', contrasted with the love of the Clod of Clay which 'seeketh not Itself to please'. So Luvah wishes to assure his rule by slaying his rival 'Albion, the King of Men', and entrusts the task to Vala, mistress of deceits. She has qualms; she remembers how in the 'good old days' wars were intellectual combats between friends, in which there were no slain, for the defeated and wounded were revived again by the (feminine) affections. But now Albion was condemned to a death that should know no resurrection. He was to be permanently entombed in her bosom, embalmed with the ointment of repressive 'moral Laws' and the spice of jealousies. If Jesus should raise him from the tomb, she argues, Luvah would be slain, my type of Womanhood would be proved to be delusion, and my Heaven become an empty falsehood. So she appeals to Jesus to take the part of Luvah, and not seek to awake the Humanity in Albion. Fiercely she turns again to her work of weaving bodies for souls, bodies in forms of her own self-will. It is an attempt to enthrone a Dragon-form in Zion's Temple.

Her efforts are backed by those of Rahab, one of her earthly incarnations. But Rahab can have no definite form, for she has rejected the help of divine imagination. She is seen as a formless indefinite cloud, eddying over the Temple in Zion, as over the altars of Stonehenge, wailing in sentimental misery.

Note 1. *The Serpent Temples*

The worship of all the heathen gods is, in effect, worship of the serpent which tempted humanity out of Eden, promising knowledge and power. There is also a reference to a theory of early British archaeologists that the Stonehenge and Avebury Circles were but single convolutions remaining from huger temples shaped like serpents. One such is shown in the last page illustration in *Jerusalem*.

XXXV

LOS DEDICATES HIMSELF AFRESH TO THE SALVATION OF ALBION, AND CALLS ON HIS FELLOW-WORKERS FOR AID

Los, encouraged by signs of the birth of pity among the Daughters of Albion, reflects on his mission, and addresses first his brother Albion, and then his assistants in the work of redemption, the 'Daughters of Beulah'—all the elements of inspiration and affection in human experience. His pity for Albion's plight makes him resolve to continue his age-long labours in time, instead of rejoining, as he might, the Immortals in Eternity.

Albion is bidden by Los to recall Jerusalem, whom his self-hood has banished from his land, to wander in a far desert. Albion must end the lordship of Vala and Luvah, reunite his inhabitants, and rescue them from the dark and cruel rites of their 'Druid' religions.

Los and his spiritual helpers may leave the Daughters of Albion meanwhile to build up their shell-world of illusions, which veils the eternal reality; their own business is to work for the re-creation of London and of England. Los pictures the human seeds of the future, the 'emanations' or 'little ones' as being hidden in 'bowers of delight' in the upper reaches of the Parent river, 'Old Father Thames', to become eventually the founders of the new London, which shall replace the existing 'awful gloom of London City'. And he has a vision of his own emanation, his Enitharmon, weaving a web of life and love for the Jerusalem that is to be.

Note 1. *Pangs of love draw me down to my loins*

The probable meaning is that love of Albion draws Urthona down to be incarnated in the world of 'generation', as Los, from whose seed will come the saviours of mankind.

Note 2. *Determine a Form for Vala and Luvah*

That is, open your eyes to see the meaning of those errors, and the consequent results of them in the world of material 'vegetation'. Seeing them revealed in this definite form, you will reject them for ever.

Note 3. *The Saxon and the English*

The fall of Albion brought wars to England, in place of brotherhood. By the 'English' here Blake probably meant the British tribes who were driven into the western mountains by the Saxon invaders. The 'Saxons' are identified with the northern Woden-worshippers, practising human sacrifice, and the Britons, called a little lower the 'Tribes of Llewellyn', are thought of as the repositories of the primitive religion of innocence, which is secretly preserved in a mystical West ('America') until the restoration of Jerusalem in Albion.

Note 4. *Entuthon's Vales*

'Entuthon Benython' is one of the names, without known derivation, which Blake used for the 'Ulro', the lowest state of human existence, unilluminated materialism. In an earlier passage he speaks of 'The deeps of Entuthon Benython, a dark and unknown night, indefinite, unmeasurable, without end, abstract Philosophy warring in enmity against Imagination.'

LOS HEARS A CRY FROM BABYLON AND HAS A
VISION OF JERUSALEM

Los, the unsleeping, faithful guardian of spiritual life on this earth, leaves his own imaginative dwelling to come and watch over his furnaces of human creativeness and suffering. He has 'subdued his Spectre' to be his fellow-labourer, yet still always liable to plot and to rebel. In the night watches on the mountains Los hears voices of lament from the banks of Babylon's river. They come from the captive and banished Daughters of Albion, or of Israel—it is always the same story— who bewail the fall of London–Jerusalem. They look back to days of happiness in the Holy City with its Holy Temple, whose precious adornments have been melted down to make swords and spears for the armies of the oppressors. Babylon has conquered London as well as Jerusalem, and the Sons of Albion have been taught to worship false gods of violence. The Daughters realize their position and what has caused it, and call upon Los for spiritual illumination and help.

Los is ready with an answer that is a song; it is what comes from the mouths of prophets and poets through the ages; it is the vision on the mountain-tops illuminated by the sunlight of inspiration. The song here takes the form of an invocation to Jerusalem, calling on her to return from her wanderings in delusions and her seeking for an earthly kingdom. Los tries to describe his vision of her essential beauty and holiness; it is Blake's own vision of the threefold, six-winged figure of spiritual glory, such as he had tried to depict on the title-page of *Jerusalem*.

Note 1. *Lambeth*

See Note 1 on page 180.

Note 2. *You are now shrunk up to a narrow Rock in the midst of the Sea*

'You' is here Albion. The fall, into the contraction of selfish life, of mankind, of England, is symbolized by the shrinking of the whole island of Great Britain into a rocky islet. Upon it lies Albion in his sleep of death, awaiting the day of his arising.

Note 3. *I see London, blind and age-bent*

The pictorial illustration of this passage is copied from one used to illustrate the poem *London* in the *Songs of Experience*. It shows the bent old beggar London led by an innocent child out of the dark shadows of harsh, square buildings towards a sunlit church and the shining dome of St Paul's.

Note 4. *Where Beulah terminates in Albion*

Beulah is the intermediate, dream-like state of joy, restfulness and human loving, which lies between earth and heaven, and is thus accessible to the inhabitants of both. The people of Albion can cross its lower border and the shining ones its upper limit, and together they can plant, in imagination first, the seeds of the Jerusalem and of all other holy cities that are yet to be built on earth.

XXXVII

THE SPECTRE'S LAST FLING.
THE JEALOUSIES OF ENITHARMON

This is a difficult section. The main subject is another temptation of Los by his Spectre,—here coming near the end of the poem, just as a similar incident is told at length near its beginning. Los falls, though not completely, and, as usual, the fall involves both a division of personality and a division between persons.

But first of all we have seven lines of Blakean comment which are inserted disconnectedly here. He reminds us of the work of the 'Daughters of Beulah', all the sympathetic and loving spirits who minister to man, and who support and comfort Los in his labours, with 'Erin' as their comprehensive and typical figure (see page 188). Blake seems to be saying here that such spirits, to fulfil their tasks and to achieve their own proper bliss, will need to be incarnated in human lives. They can only become fellow-workers in the labours of Los by becoming as little children on earth and sharing redemptively, as mortals, in the sufferings of mankind, in Los's 'Furnaces of affliction'.

And now Los himself, listening to the lies of the tempting Spectre, deserts for a time his great task of the salvation of Albion. It is not quite clear how this comes about, but apparently he yields to selfish longings for his own female partner, his emanation Enitharmon. His 'fibres' of thoughts and affections, which should unite him in selfless love to all mankind, englobe themselves round her feminine figure as he 'reddens with desire', And so she is, as it were, born from him as a separate figure, lovely, but possessed with a life, a will and a pride of her own; for selfishness can only breed selfishness. After the separation Los's twisted fibres begin to grow round him and threaten to imprison him. He calls upon Enitharmon to save him with her love, and, together, to direct their fibres into the making of sons and daughters.

But she repels him, proclaiming her pride and self-sufficiency, and flings at his head wild jealous charges—that he has been unfaithful to her by giving his love to Jerusalem and to Vala, and that he is being duped by his friend Albion.

Los, who is now apparently restored to vision again, replies with a statement of what the true function of emanations should be—to act as links between human beings, enabling them to achieve integral union with each other. But Enitharmon clings to her aim of woman's domination over men, which she believes she can accomplish by teaching the secretive morality which holds sex to be shameful.

Here the Spectre breaks in to express his joy at the separation, jealousy and frustration which he has caused.

Note 1. *I will create secret places. A triple Female Tabernacle for Moral Law* . . .

A rich doubleness in the true, eternal human personality is seen as externalized in the sexual division of humanity into men and women. The female, when thus separated, seeks power and domination in her own way. She uses her sexual attraction, combined with a false moral teaching, to make a mystery of herself, elevating herself into the position of a goddess in a secret shrine, a forbidden yet a glorious place. So she can tantalize man until he obeys her will. Blake constantly insists on woman's use of secrecy. Here her holy secret place is compared to the holy Tabernacle which the Israelites erected in the wilderness, divided into the three sections of court, outer, and inner sanctuaries. And when he mentions triplicity Blake also has in mind the division of the human being into 'head, heart and loins'.

The 'female Moral Law' has a special reference, in this connection, to the doctrine that sexual union was something evil and dirty by nature. (The Spectre concurs in this when he says, a few lines later, that he is able to persuade his victims that 'the places of joy and love are excrementitious'.) Blake held that sexual experience could be a gateway into eternity.

When this false teaching is finally accepted, boasts Enitharmon, the deluded Christian will live in terror of female love, and man (and his imagined god!) will be in woman's power; for he cannot live without her.

XXXVIII

'THE COVERING CHERUB'—A VISION OF ANTICHRIST

On this plate Blake pictures the terrifying approach of the gigantic incarnation of world-evil presaging the final culmination of Armageddon. A summation of all mankind's indefinite, self-contradictory errors and sins now appears to the visionary in the immense form of Satan, Antichrist, the 'Covering Cherub', filling the skies and overshadowing the continents. It is the fearful climax of all the 'selfish holinesses' of individuals showing itself on the world-scale.

The poet pictures the terrifying form as an inverse of the glorious form of Jerusalem as described in Section XXXVI. Each is threefold—head, heart and loins—but in place of radiant wings of glory we now have black wings of woe. Jerusalem was an image of Eden; but the Covering Cherub is 'a reflexion of Eden all perverted'. The four rivers of Paradise become the rivers on whose banks live the nations which oppress and enslave the holy humanity and its 'minute particulars', the heathen nations, with their heathen gods, who have destroyed Jerusalem and kept captive God's Israel; Egypt, with its many-mouthed Nile (Gihon), its Pharaoh, the 'Dragon of the River', and his slave-drivers; Moab and Ammon, with their gods Molech and Chemosh calling for child sacrifices,

219

and their river Arnon (Pison) which leads from the false delights of the capital, Heshbon, down to the sea of death and the ruins of Sodom and Gomorrha. The third river, Hiddekel, is not so clearly identified, but runs an imaginary course through the rocky landscape of all the western lands which have in turn set up false gods and cruel kings, and sacrificed the divine humanity. Here Blake, as so often, runs times and places together in vision, and also uses his favourite symbol of 'Druid Temples' as a main image for such falsities. The fourth river, Euphrates, takes us eastward, adding the martyrdoms and slaveries of Israel in Babylon; and Babylon, as in the Apocalypse of St. John, is also Rome the persecutor of the Christians.

It seems as if Jerusalem, the holy city, has been devoured by this monster; or at least hidden far within its imposing 'tabernacle' of world-power.

A final horror issues from this tabernacle, the 'Dragon-and-Harlot' of the Apocalypse. Blake labels it as 'Religion hid in War', or conversely 'War hid in Religion'—unforgivingness, revenge, slaughter, and battle-colours hung in churches.

Note 1. *Hermaphroditic*
See Section XXVII, Note 1, page 201.

Note 2. *The Covering Cherub*
This curious phrase is borrowed from a description of the doom of a Prince of Tyre in the twenty-eighth chapter of Ezekiel's prophecies. He is described as being so exalted by his wealth, his wisdom and his success as to say, 'I am a God; I sit in the seat of God, in the midst of the seas'. To which the prophet answers: 'Thine heart is lifted up because of thy riches; therefore thus saith the Lord God; because thou hast set thine heart as the heart of God, therefore, behold, I will bring strangers upon thee, the terrible of the nations . . . and thou shalt die the death of them that are slain, in the midst of the seas.' In the lamentation which follows God is made to say: 'Thou wast in Eden, the garden of God . . . Thou wast the anointed cherub which covereth, and I set thee so that thou wast upon the holy mountain of God; thou hast walked up and down in the midst of the stones of fire. Thou wast perfect in thy ways from the day thou wast created, till iniquity was found in thee. By the multitude of thy traffic they filled the midst of thee

with violence, and thou hast sinned; therefore have I cast thee as profane out of the mountain of God, and I have destroyed thee, O covering cherub, from the midst of the stones of fire.'

There are obscurities here; we can only guess what it was that the cherub 'covered', and the meaning of the 'stones of fire'. But the reference is clearly to some known myth about an angelic being who fell, like Lucifer, through unfaithfulness and pride. The mention of the garden of Eden may be an allusion to one of the cherubs set to guard its gates.

Blake, however, identified the cherub with one of the two golden beings placed on guard above and 'covering' the ark of the covenant, as is plain from his references to the Tabernacle. But the fallen cherub covers no longer the divine contents of the ark; he now conceals only horror and woe.

It seems likely that Blake seized on the figure of the proud Prince of Tyre as a fitting type for the Prince of this world, the 'Great Satan' of man's selfish pride and cruelty.

XXXIX

THE DEMONSTRATIONS OF LOS

As he approaches the end of his epic myth Blake wishes to drive home his message as clearly as possible, and allows Los several plates in which to explain his visionary insights and convictions. First comes a reminder that the spiritual form of 'Man' has no sex. The division into male and female is just a characteristic of his passage through this world of 'generation'. The qualities which make men and women truly human and eternal are the same for both sexes—spiritual vision, love and forgivingness. Sexual love may be a type and foretaste of a more universal love. But sexual differences have also produced the selfish tyranny of 'strong' men, and the deceiving hypocrisy of 'gentle' women, each tormenting the other.

Los goes on to say that when a universal human trait is appropriated as 'mine' by any individual, when anyone claims 'I am good', or 'I am humble', or 'I am wise', he is a blaspheming egoist, placing his little mortal self on the throne of the immortal Goodness. 'Why callest thou me good? none is good save one, that is, God.'

What of Jesus Christ then? 'A vegetated Christ, and a virgin Eve, are the hermaphroditic blasphemy.' Jesus became a human individual, took on the 'Satanic body of Holiness', was tempted by the Devil to remain in it, to become a fellow 'Evil-one', a miracle-working saint and a ruler of nations. But the purpose of Jesus, born as a man of a human mother, was to reveal the spiritual basis of life, to cast off mortal flesh and its unreal world, and prove that time and death are conquerable. Those who would deny Christ's divine origin and treat him as a mere product of 'vegetable' life, and those on the other hand who would deny that his human birth was just like ours, of mother Eve, are both 'hermaphroditic blasphemers', blindly and irreverently confounding mortal with immortal. They will even show themselves capable of keeping slaves and captives and teaching them about a God of mercy!

Such messages of Los always arouse fear and opposition among the worldly 'giants', the sons of fallen Albion. For Blake, who is a mouthpiece of Los, these turn up in his own day as the 'Deists', who worship reason and nature, and refuse to recognize inspiration and revelation. And also as the good Christian church-men, who envy and calumniate their neighbours, and patronize the folk they help to keep poor—the modern hypocritic (or, as Blake would say, hermaphroditic) Pharisees.

Los–Blake sends his Spectre (now his obedient servant) to warn such people, and to announce the truth in words that repeat and enlarge the message which he wrote as a young man in his announcement of the 'Marriage of Heaven and Hell'. To know God, he says, begin by discovering man; honour the greatest human exemplars of love and wisdom, and you are honouring God; you cannot mean anything by saying 'God is love', unless you have had some experience of what love is— first from an individual, your mother or father or friend, then in a forgiving, sharing family or group and finally in the personal meeting with Jesus. Look into the 'minute particulars', into children, into little daily deeds of pity and kindness, in order to find the meaning of human existence, and not into cloudy philosophies, analytics, and codes of cold moral commandments.

This is a section which we can read again and again with a thankful emotion.

Note I. *Rocking-stones*

There was an archaeological theory current in Blake's day that the rocking-stones, or Logan-stones, found in various places in England, had been erected by the same 'Druids' who had built Stonehenge, and that they had some religious significance. Blake therefore uses them here as a symbol for the false religious theory and practice of the opponents of imagin-ation, in place of his more usual 'Druid Temple'. Perhaps he seized upon the symbol because it suggested something with no real security or foundation.

XL

THE SIGNAL OF THE MORNING

In reading this section we must remember that everything is still overshadowed by the approaching Satanic terror, the 'Covering Cherub'. (This Death would ride today upon a mushroom-shaped cloud.) While all the others dread anni-hilation, Los can see through the insubstantiality of the cloud, and recognizes crisis as a sign of approaching salvation—the signal of the coming morning. And Blake applies this faith to the conditions of his own day in England.

We are given here first a reminder of the completeness of Los's victory over the Spectre. That figure of earthly pride had achieved marvels, had conquered space, and built a Babel-tower to reach from its Hell into the Heavens. It had tried to constrict the senses of Los, of Mankind, so that they should see nothing beyond these physical marvels, and fall down in worship. But Los has reversed the process; with his faith and vision he has unbound his Spectre's own eyes and ears. Now he sends out the Spectre to look at his own miracles again, and behold! they are mere nothingness; Los sees the world in a grain of sand. The Spectre now sees his whole imposing world as no more than—a grain of sand. 'Though I understand all mysteries and all knowledge, and have not love, I am nothing.'

Los now proclaims the need for truth and wisdom to replace hypocritical or formal 'holiness'. Looking upon poor sleeping Albion he still sees there the 'human form divine'. The nations which, in history, have fought against each other, are essentially united in their common humanity and will prove this in the end—just as Britons, Saxons, Romans and Normans have already become united in one English nation. Albion himself is about to awake, to see and rejoice in the unity.

But Enitharmon, Los's loved emanation, and the female partner who has been labouring with him at her creative looms, has not yet attained to the same vision. If Albion is perfected, she thinks, and sexual differences transcended, then her reason for existence will be at an end and she will die. And she shows still a trace of female jealousy, for she avers that Los will create another woman for his love.

Los, in exaltation, replies: 'Yes! the sexual, and other, divisions of earthly life as we know it will vanish; and with them will go all the crimes and cruelties that have afflicted fallen, divided mankind. And, living in unity and forgivingness, we shall then know them as a mere memory, a possibility, a warning history, which will help us to avoid another fall and another judgment.'

Then follows a difficult passage. Enitharmon, still anxious, believes that Rintrah and Palamabron (two of the sons of Los and Enitharmon, who play a part in previous myths) are still in disobedience, and joined with Satan in pride, bringing woes upon the whole family of love. But Los cries, reassuringly, to these and all his sons, that the awakening of Albion will not mean their death, but a wonderful new life 'in Jesus'. They must not fear the imposing, but illusory, power of evil. The seeming triumph of the false gods today is the prophesied beginning of the day of salvation tomorrow.

Note 1. *The Smaragdine Table of Hermes*

This refers to the famous words alleged to have been found by Alexander the Great written upon an emerald (smaragdine) tablet discovered in the tomb of the occult philosopher 'Thrice-greatest Hermes'. The message begins with the words: It is the truest and most certain thing of all things; that which is above is as that which is below; and that which is below is as that which is above; to accomplish the one thing of all things most wonderful.

The document has for centuries been used as a supreme magic text by alchemists and occultists. Blake, as he shows here, rejected such mysterious indefinite statements. The spectre would like to use it to tempt him into wordy indefiniteness, but Blake was always insisting that truth lay in definite outlines and minute particulars, picking out the stars in Heaven and not seeking to find meaning in the voids between them.

Note 2. *Divided him into a separate space*

The Spectre, or reasoning power, makes continuous efforts to claim dominance in interpreting all things; but Los, by a continual discipline, confines him to his proper, limited place, in which he can serve humanity.

Note 3. *This waking Death*

That is, this Albion, now about to wake from his long death-like sleep.

XLI

THE AWAKENING

We are given here a last look at Albion before his awakening. He lies on his rocky islet (shrunken England), like a corpse in a tomb, in a world of confusion, desolation and hunger, and assailed continually by waves and thunders and storms. In space above him history takes its course; his giant sons erect their Satanic mills; Los labours at his divine task of keeping his spiritual fires aglow. And yet divine providence has built marvellous beauty into the world which is the tomb of Albion; and there are yet on earth spirits of love and tenderness ('Erin') who watch over sleepers and sufferers.

Sleeping humanity is still 'sexual'. Once or twice previously Blake has joined to the figure of Albion that of his wife, or female counterpart, whom he names England, or Britannia. He has said that Britannia may be now Jerusalem, now Vala. Here he shows her as fallen with Albion; she has no definite form and is not *within* him, but lies upon his bosom like a heavy, clinging cloud.

Vision now pierces forward to the end of time, when the sleeper will wake into eternity. We note that the first to hear the divine voice calling is not the male but the female.

And her awakening is into pity, self-accusation and repentance. It is through her voice, lamenting her past cruelty to him, that Albion is also aroused to see and hear.

Albion arose; but in power, not in pity. His resurrection is compared with the sunrise. As the morning sun sends out the arrows of his rays in all directions, directing men to their various daily occupations, so Albion, now glowing with a heavenly power, directs the elements of his full nature—brain, body, heart and imagination—to their proper tasks. The 'four Zoas' are united in a working harmony. Albion's spiritual energy also shows itself as indignation, a fierce condemnation of what his fourfold vision now sees to be blasphemous and evil.

Britannia can now 'enter into his bosom rejoicing'; the sexes have vanished—into each other, into unity.

But Albion is not yet fully saved. He needs a further, final insight and experience before he reaches the innermost secret of his divine humanity. He must know self-sacrifice and forgiveness. Now that his Britannia is within he will be able to meet with—Jesus.

Note 1. *Los as 'Urthona's Spectre'*

The use of the word Spectre in this connection is confusing. It is a reversion to an earlier use of the term and does not bear the usual condemnatory character. In another place Los is called the 'vehicular form' of Urthona, meaning a human vehicle of a spiritual power and reality. Every seer and creative artist shares in Los's labours as an instrument of 'Urthona'.

XLII

THE OFFERING OF SELF

Here Albion learns the last truth about the meaning of human life, and, acting upon it, finds that he has entered the Kingdom of Heaven; here is the Second Coming, in its simplest and quietest form, with no sound of trumpets—'Then Jesus appeared, standing by Albion as the Good Shepherd by the lost sheep'; here is the vision on the road to Damascus; here is the Last Judgment, when error and sinful pride are cast out, and man rises into his new and heavenly life.

Jesus is the revealer. He has long been speaking through
the mouth of his servant and brother Los. Now he explains what
atonement means—giving and forgiving, without limit, as the
Father gives and forgives, and thereby realizing brotherhood
and unity. This is love, and God is love; and Man, made in the
image of God, is also love. The 'Selfhood' which has hidden this
from him is now annihilated; indeed it never had any real
existence. Give yourself, completely, for others, even to death
in a fiery furnace—and the flames will become living waters.
Death 'in the Divine Image' is the gateway into resurrection
and life.

The mention of the 'Divine Image' here, and its interpretation, reminds us of the most profound of the early 'Songs
of Innocence', and shows how consistent Blake remained in his
religious thinking. The poem is called the Divine Image, and
says:

> For Mercy, Pity, Peace and Love
> Is God, our father dear;
> And Mercy, Pity, Peace and Love
> Is Man, his child and care.

XLIII

THE VISION OF ALBION REDEEMED

The awakening of Albion is the signal for the return of
Jerusalem from her banishment; in fact, as Britannia, she has
already 're-entered his bosom rejoicing'.

Blake now has the tremendous task of trying to describe
the awakened humanity, Man restored to the image of God, and
the city in which he will dwell; Jerusalem in Man, and Man in
Jerusalem. How can this be done in words, when our language
has been made but to fit the needs and outlooks of earthly life?
In the apocalypse of John the attempt to convey the final vision
is restricted to picturing a four-square, jewelled city of light,
in which evil, death and sorrow are unknown. But Blake is
concerned to describe, not the externals of such a city of light,
but the inward life and activities of its inhabitants, the psychology of the Kingdom of Heaven; and further, to do this not

merely for its individual citizen, but for its peoples and communities, for Albion's twenty-eight cities, for a Jerusalem which 'overspreads all nations', for all humanity as 'One Man'.

No man, not even a Blake, could fully succeed in this; it is far easier to describe the struggle of today than the glory of the final morrow. And Blake's effort is hampered by his habit (which is also useful to us) of interpolating statements of his favourite doctrines in the middle of his visions. Yet we share some of his exaltation and his faith as we read these visions, and accompany him more easily the more we have become familiar with his names and symbols and images.

The city of Jerusalem is fourfold. Albion, now fully *living*, knows himself also to be fourfold, and acts with the whole man—body, brain, heart and spirit; a unity of the 'Four Zoas' within him. He takes up his 'bow of burning gold', his spiritual weapon of 'mercy and loving-kindness', of love which opens men's hidden hearts, and whose arrows annihilate the Antichrist of Selfhood, the 'Druid Spectre'. The two horns of this mighty bow symbolize the male and female elements in Man, separate on earth but made one in Heaven.

And the cleansed eyes of the new Man are now able to see the innumerable 'chariots of fire', in which, drawn by the horses of spiritual energy, sit all the seers, saints, poets, prophets and martyrs who have fought the battle for humanity; and among them are not only Albion's imaginative poets, his Milton and Shakespeare and Chaucer, but the reasoners and thinkers, whom Blake had feared and denounced as misleaders, his Bacon and Newton and Locke!

And Living Man now also uses his senses, enlarged to behold reality, to clear away all the old 'husks and Coverings', and reveal the true form and lineaments of Mankind. The body of mortality, and the little sinful self that inhabited it, are annihilated, and God's new covenant is accepted, which is this:

'Throughout all Eternity
I forgive you, you forgive me.
As our dear Redeemer said,
This the wine and this the bread.'

Blake's enormous pictorial imagination seized upon, and gave deeper meaning to, the figures of the four great 'living creatures'

of Ezekiel's vision, which 'went every one straight forward';
he sees them also as 'beautiful Paradises' expanding eternally
within the immortality of Man.

Our scientists have presented us with one 'expanding
universe'. To *live*, man needs to discover the other three also;
and to know that the four are one.

XLIV

THEY WALKED IN ETERNITY

Here, in great compression, is a description of how all men,
when once spiritually awake and aware of their unity in the
'One Man', will talk and act creatively. They will see, with
the opened eye of human Imagination, the whole world of
space, and its whole history in time, transformed; and death
swallowed up in the victory of resurrection.

And then, almost as a postscript, we are told of a final and
astounding grace. God's Covenant of Forgiveness unites man
not only with fellow-man, but also with every created thing.
Every living creature, and every tree and stone, is, like every
man, in essence and meaning spiritual, not material; all in
their due fitness and order. They can all join with Man in the
hymn of praise for the overcoming of delusion and death.

One is reminded of Paul's words about the whole creation
groaning in pain until the final revelation of the Sons of God;
of how visionaries and mystics have sought to describe their
experience of a new glory and a 'new smell' in all creation; of
how saints have had speech with beasts and birds, and poets
have tried to tell us of their exchanges with trees and flowers.

Blake sums it up, in his own now familiar language, by
saying, in his final sentence, that he too, even in this planetary
life, has found that all things have their own 'Emanations', and
that all the Emanations have a common name—Jerusalem!

Analysis of Section XXII (*Plate 56 of 'Jerusalem'*)

In this passage Los makes appeal to 'The Daughters of Albion', the feminine elements in mankind. Blake held that the common 'Human Form', the divine, immortal essence of Everyman, was above and beyond sex, that division into males and females was just a feature of 'Generation', of life in our physical bodies, and would be superseded in eternity. Union between a man and a woman on earth was a symbol and a foretaste of heavenly reality.

To believe that there was something divine in a separate maleness or femaleness was a blind blasphemy. Self-will, an appropriation of universality by an ego, is always an evil (there can be no good self-will, says Blake; only the Will of God is good), and there may be male and female forms of self-will, each seeking to dominate others, though in different ways. In this passage Blake is lamenting the 'Female will' which he saw at work in his world. This might be shown in the perceptive and emotional, as distinguished from the rational, element in a male; but in general it is the woman's failing. Woman, he says, seeks to have her own way, and to exercise power, by serving the man, mothering him, attaching him to herself by various wiles, disciplines and attractions, claiming his allegiance and service—in fact, trying to take the place of God in his life, and so hiding the eternal from him by weaving a lovely but deceitful veil around him.

Let us now attempt a detailed interpretation of this page, with the warning that some lines will still remain dark, and that others are susceptible of an alternative hearing.

Los, the visionary forge-man, sings as he blows up his fires with the wind of the Spirit, for his mighty labours in the 'Valley of Middlesex', where Blake saw him—just outside London, on its western or spiritual side.

'If Man', he cries, 'is a mystery, is not Woman a greater mystery, for she takes charge of every infant in his cradle and orders his ways throughout his life-time.'

When Blake speaks of birth and cradle he is always thinking primarily of the descent of a divine and innocent soul into our world of restrictions and experience. The child is Joy, but at once meets with sorrow—rebuffs and swaddling-bands. The Saviour alone, whose cradle was a manger, knows fully the meaning, and the pains, of incarnation. The whole world continues to be a cradle for the learning and wandering soul, rocking him with the swing of time.

This thought of the meaning of time here reminds Blake of what he has written before (see *Milton*, pp. 27–28), and he slips in a word of comfort about the ministry of the 'Daughters of Beulah'. They are the spirits of inspiration who feed the eternal element in the 'vegetating' man, through messages given within 'a pulsation of the artery'. This is what Blake means by 'between every two moments', an interval which may be 'equal in its period and value to six thousand years, for in this Period the Poet's work is done, and all the great events of Time start forth and are conceived in such a Period'.

Los now calls upon human womanhood to render spiritual service also to each newly-incarnated soul. They are to weave a fitting garment and cradle for it, give it such a loving and understanding reception that it will not shrink back from the world's cruelty into non-existence again.

Blake's female characters are usually represented as weavers; if they have vision they weave garments of joy with threads or 'fibres' of self-giving love; if they are themselves 'dead' they weave entangling nets and veils and garments of woe, with threads of self-love and jealousy. Los, as the creative spirit of Time, now offers them his help in their true task. His figure is that of a burning youth and not of an old man with a scythe. He measures out the intervals of Time, which are filled with human history. His sun rose and set on scythed chariots of the armies of Boadicea, and his moon lighted the voyages of Drake and his adventurers.

But Albion is now a desolate land. The Daughters of Albion are in despair. Things have gone wrong in spite of the tears and care they have devoted to the nourishment and training of their children. (They are blind to the fact that they are rearing 'no Human Form, but only a Fibrous Vegetation, a Polypus of soft affections without Thought or Vision'. *Milton*, p. 26, l. 37.)

Los bids them to keep singing, and to cast back their minds to their experience of dark and difficult days, and to tell him where the infant, the awe-inspiring Human wonder, had come from.

But they cannot tell him. To them the child was not an incarnation of immortal spirit, but just a lost wanderer, discovered weeping at their wintry door. They recognize with horror that they have fallen into terrible depths, with their father Albion's fall. Gwendolen and Merlin are named as two leading representatives of the daughters and sons of Albion, who once lived a life of creative joy, power and mutual forgiveness, in the golden days of innocence before their father fell. But now, having lost their spiritual sight, they behold Gwendolen as no more than a lump of clay, and Merlin as no more than a low form of life that creeps upon the ground.

Los renews his appeal to them, reminding them that he is Albion's ever-wakeful watchman, whose mission it is to guard the soul's visionary power through times of darkness. The Daughters must recognize his authority; he will not submit to their wills and wiles. In the midst of his appeal he breaks off suddenly, as if overwhelmed with sorrow at the sight of the human disaster. The cradled incarnation of the 'Eternal Man', the 'Human Form Divine', even when fully revealed in Jesus the Saviour, born on earth out of the compassion of God, has not been recognized. Matter and physical life had been provided by Providence as a field of experience, to be cultivated for the sustenance and growth of spirit. But now spirit itself had been treated as mere matter and 'the Living plowed in among the Dead', the young immortal looked upon as nothing more than a lump of clay or a worm of the valley.

The women, in reply, do start singing at their looms, but only to repeat their great refusal. They express their fear of the light, and their intention to go on weaving fleshly veils for shrines in which no spirit dwells.

Los, in indignation and despair, thunders out his cry of protest. 'The Female Will, the curse of Albion! It has always been so, from the days of Jesus until now.'

The retrospect which Los here asks for, is condensed into two lines, whose full mening must be largely a matter of guesswork. (It may be that this was partly due to the fact that Blake had now only two lines left at the bottom of his expensive copper plate!) The 'Church Paul' was one of the twenty-seven churches or periods into which Blake divided human history, each partly a revelation, but also each a depositary of some particular false teaching. (See Section xv, Note 5, p. 183). I think Blake imagined that the 'three Women around the Cross' did not realize who the Crucified was, and what was the meaning of his death. They showed their human love and sorrow, they had ministered to his bodily needs, and now they wove him garments to wear in the tomb, which Jesus had to discard when he rose in his spiritual body. And similarly the women who joined Paul's churches failed to see the glory of full love and forgiveness, for they regarded Christ's death as a necessary payment for mankind's sin to a God who exacted satisfaction.

I think William was a little hard on womankind. He makes amends elsewhere, for this page does not stand alone. On other pages there are plenty of lashes, and tears, for the men and their male self-will.

APPENDIX B

Sidelights

There are very many passages in other writings of William Blake which supplement or illuminate corresponding passages in the *Jerusalem*. A whole commentary could be constructed from them, but only a few striking specimens will be given here, and the reader may himself go quarrying for others.

First, from that vast quarry named, *Vala or The Four Zoas*:

(The pair) . . . walk'd forth on the dewy Earth,
Contracting or expanding their all-flexible senses;
At will to murmur in the flowers, small as the honey bee;
At will to stretch across the heavens, and step from star to star
Night II 11. 503–506

Arise, you little glancing wings, and sing your infant joy!
Arise, and drink your bliss!
For everything that lives is holy; for the source of life
Descends to be a weeping babe:
For the Earthworm renews the moisture of the sandy plain.
Night II 11. 572–576

As the seed waits, eagerly watching for its flower and fruit;
Anxious its little soul looks out into the clear expanse,
To see if hungry winds are abroad, with their invisible array;
So Man looks out in tree and herb and fish and bird and beast,
Collecting up the scatter'd portions of his immortal body
Into the Elemental forms of every thing that grows.
Night VIII 11. 546–551

Not for ourselves, but for the Eternal family we live.
Man liveth not by Self alone; but in his brother's face
Each shall behold the Eternal Father, and love and joy abound.
Night IX 11. 638–640

The main theme of Blake's *Milton*, which was apparently begun in the same year as *Jerusalem*, namely 1804, is the story of how John Milton journeyed back from Eternity into this world of time, in order to preach a new gospel, and make good the damage he had done by a false gospel contained in *Paradise Lost* and *Paradise Regained*. Milton's spirit was now to speak through the lips of William Blake, renouncing his former doctrine of God Almighty as a reasoner and punisher, and preaching instead Jesus' doctrine of brotherhood and limitless forgiveness. The following description of his mission, given by Milton himself, shows how completely he had come to adopt all Blake's beliefs and antipathies!

'Obey thou the words of the inspired man!
All that can be annihilated must be annihilated,
That the children of Jerusalem may be saved from slavery.
There is a Negation, and there is a Contrary:
The Negation must be destroy'd, to redeem the Contraries.
The Negation is the Spectre, the Reasoning Power in Man.
This is a false Body, an Incrustation over my Immortal
Spirit, a Selfhood, which must be put off and annihilated alway.
   To cleanse the Face of my Spirit by self-examination,
To bathe in the Waters of Life, to wash off the Not-Human,
I come in Self-annihilation and the grandeur of Inspiration:
To cast off Rational Demonstration, by Faith in the Saviour:
To cast off the rotten rags of Memory by Inspiration;
To cast off Bacon, Locke and Newton from Albion's covering;
To take off his filthy garments, and clothe him with Imagination;
To cast aside from Poetry all that is not Inspiration;
That it shall no longer dare to mock with the aspersion of Madness
Cast on the Inspired by the tame high finisher of paltry Blots
Indefinite, or paltry Rhymes, or paltry Harmonies,
Who creeps into State Government, like a catterpiller, to destroy;
To cast off the idiot Questioner, who is always questioning,
But never capable of answering; who sits with a sly grin
Silent plotting when to question, like a thief in a cave;
Who published doubt and calls it knowledge; whose Science is Despair;
Whose pretence to knowledge is Envy; whose whole Science is
To destroy the wisdom of ages to gratify ravenous Envy,
That rages round him like a Wolf, day and night without rest.
He smiles with condescension; he talks of Benevolence and Virtue;
And those who act with Benevolence and Virtue they murder time on time.
These are the destroyers of Jerusalem; these are the murderers
Of Jesus, who deny the Faith, and mock at Eternal Life;
Who pretend to Poetry, that they may destroy Imagination,
By imitation of Nature's Images, drawn from Remembrance.
These are the Sexual Garments, the Abomination of Desolation,
Hiding the Human Lineaments, as with an Ark and Curtains,
Which Jesus rent, and now shall wholly purge away with Fire,
Till Generation is swallow'd up in Regeneration.'

Milton, Book II. p. 46, l. 29, to p. 48, l. 28.

234

Finally, I give two valuable extracts from Blake's elaborate description of a large fresco painting he had made, representing his own 'stupendous vision' of the Last Judgment. This picture has unfortunately not been preserved, although a drawing of the same subject exists, which has plainly many similar features. For Blake, the Last Judgment has no date; it is taking place all through history, and in your experience or mine, when an error is cast out and a truth experienced.

'The nature of Visionary Fancy, or Imagination, is very little known; and the Eternal nature and permanence of its ever-Existent Images is considered as less permanent than the things of Vegetative and Generative Nature. Yet the Oak dies, as well as the Lettuce; but its Eternal Image and Individuality never dies, but renews by its seed. Just so the Imaginative Image returns, by the seed of Contemplative Thought. The Writings of the Prophets illustrate these conceptions of the Visionary Fancy, by their various sublime and Divine Images, as seen in the Worlds of Vision.

This World of Imagination is the World of Eternity; it is the divine bosom into which we shall all go, after the death of the Vegetated body. This World of Imagination is Infinite and Eternal; whereas the World of Generation, or Vegetation, is Finite and Temporal. There Exists in that Eternal World the Permanent Realities of Every Thing which we see reflected in this Vegetable Glass of Nature. All Things are comprehended, in their Eternal Forms, in the divine body of the Saviour, the True Vine of Eternity, the Human Imagination; who appeared to me coming to Judgment among his Saints, and throwing off the Temporal that the Eternal might be established. Around him were seen the Images of Existences, according to a certain order, suited to my Imaginative Eye.'

'Around the Throne, Heaven is opened, and the nature of Eternal Things displayed, all springing from the Divine Humanity. All beams from him. He is the Bread and the Wine; he is the Water of Life. Accordingly, on each side of the opening Heaven appears an Apostle. That on the right represents Baptism; that on the left represents the Lord's Supper. All Life consists of these two,— throwing off Error and Knaves from our company continually; and receiving Truth, or Wise Men, into our company continually. He who is out of the Church, and opposes it, is no less an Agent of Religion than he who is in it; to be an Error and to be cast out is a part of God's design. No man can embrace True Art till he has explored and cast out False Art, or he will be himself cast out by those who have already embraced True Art. Thus my picture is a history of Art and Science, the Foundation of Society, which is Humanity itself. What are all the Gifts of the Spirit but Mental Gifts? Whenever any Individual rejects Error and embraces Truth, a Last Judgment passes upon that Individual.'

235